The Concept of Constituency

Political Representation, Democratic Legitimacy, and Institutional Design

In virtually every democratic nation in the world, political representation is defined by where citizens live. In the United States, for example, congressional districts are drawn every ten years as lines on a map. Why do democratic governments define political representation this way? Are territorial electoral constituencies commensurate with basic principles of democratic legitimacy? And why might our commitments to these principles, including political equality, self-rule, and deliberative diversity, lead us to endorse a radical alternative: randomly assigning citizens to permanent, single-member electoral constituencies that each looks like the nation they collectively represent? Using the case of the founding period of the United States as an illustration and drawing from classic sources in Western political theory, this book describes the conceptual, historical, and normative features of the electoral constituency. As an institution conceptually separate from the casting of votes, the electoral constituency is little studied. Its historical origins are often incorrectly described. And as a normative matter, the constituency is almost completely ignored. Raising these conceptual, historical, and normative issues, the argument culminates with a novel thought experiment of imagining how politics might change under randomized, permanent, national electoral constituencies. By focusing on how citizens are formally defined for the purpose of political representation, *The Concept of Constituency* thus offers a novel approach to the central problems of political representation, democratic legitimacy, and institutional design.

Andrew Rehfeld is Assistant Professor of Political Science at Washington University in St. Louis, where he has been teaching since 2001. He is the recipient of the University of Chicago Century Fellowship and the Mellon Foundation Dissertation-Year Fellowship. The dissertation on which this book is based was nominated for the American Political Science Association's (APSA) William Anderson Award in 2002 and the APSA Leo Strauss Award in 2001. His previous articles have appeared in *Studies in American Political Development* and the *Dictionary of American History*. He is a member of the American Political Science Association and the Association for Political Theory, among other associations.

The Concept of Constituency

Political Representation, Democratic Legitimacy, and Institutional Design

ANDREW REHFELD
Washington University in St. Louis

CAMBRIDGE
UNIVERSITY PRESS

CAMBRIDGE UNIVERSITY PRESS
Cambridge, New York, Melbourne, Madrid, Cape Town, Singapore, São Paulo

Cambridge University Press
40 West 20th Street, New York, NY 10011-4211, USA

www.cambridge.org
Information on this title: www.cambridge.org/9780521849845

First published 2005

Printed in the United States of America

A catalog record for this publication is available from the British Library.

Library of Congress Cataloging in Publication Data

Rehfeld, Andrew, 1965–
The concept of constituency : political representation, democratic legitimacy, and institutional
design / Andrew Rehfeld.
    p.   cm.
ISBN 0-521-84984-5 (hardback)
1. Representative government and representation.   2. Constituent power.   3. Representative
government and representation – United States.   4. Constituent power – United States.
I. Title.
JF1051.R44   2005
321.8–dc22   2004019645

ISBN-13   978-0-521-84984-5 hardback
ISBN-10   0-521-84984-5 hardback

To
the memory of
Ruth Wolf Rehfeld

Contents

List of Tables

Preface

Democracy is the only form of government that allows people to rule themselves. Ironically, political representation enables modern democracies to exclude virtually everyone from the institutions that govern them. The concept of constituency defines how, in any particular nation, the excluded are legitimately reconstituted prior to, or simultaneously as, they select their representatives who will rule them. The electoral constituency, then, is the quintessential institution of official exclusion, for it defines how it is the excluded get reconstituted for their only formal roles as members of a modern democracy.

Democratic government in its direct or representative form has been around for thousands of years. Yet given the thousands of sovereign cities and states that have laid proper claim to its name, there has been a remarkably small set of institutions by which democracies have actually been governed. Thomas Pogge recently put it this way:

> It cannot be said that experience and reflection have produced convergence upon this [set of institutions]. Most of the other possibilities have never been tried or discussed. Indeed, many could not have been tried or discussed because they are becoming feasible only now, in the dawning information age. It is not good reasons that keep practice and reflection within the narrow sector, but habit and entrenchment. We are deeply accustomed to the conventional forms of democracy.[1]

It is likely that our limited exposure to these "conventional forms of democracy" has dulled our imagination of what could be. Even worse, these forms have become so familiar that we risk treating them as somehow natural and therefore "obviously" preferable to those we have yet to consider.

Among these familiar institutions of democracy stands the electoral constituency, the group in which a citizen's vote is counted toward the election

[1] Pogge, Thomas, 2002, "Self-Constituting Constituencies to Enhance Freedom, Equality, and Participation in Democratic Procedures," *Theoria*, June: 26–54.

of a political representative. In most contemporary democracies, where you live defines your electoral constituency (at least in part). In the United States, for example, the fifth Congressional District of Illinois is defined by territorial boundaries found on a map. But the practice of using territory to define constituencies is widespread; almost every modern democratic government uses territory in some form to construct constituencies for their national legislature.

In this book, I trace the origins of the territorial constituency in the United States and describe how its justifications changed at the very start of the republic. I argue that justifying territorial representation because it allows "communities of interest" to receive political representation is remarkably weak, and this justification received little historical support, because territorial constituencies for national representation have always spanned multiple communities of interest. A much stronger argument thus rests on the inverse of this claim: Large territorial constituencies open the possibility of increasing the amount of diversity within an electoral constituency. This has multiple benefits, the first among them being the deliberative benefits that come from forcing representatives to justify themselves before a heterogeneous population.

The virtue of heterogeneous electoral constituencies emerges from a set of uncontroversial principles of democratic legitimacy (such as the notion that representatives should be accountable to those who elect them). Following this, I argue we should also favor constituencies in which citizens remain permanently. And, because the consequentialist formulation of political equality that supports cries to "make votes count" and avoid "wasted votes" as if they were a cancer on the body politic is a surprisingly trivial value, I argue that constituencies should be defined at the constitutional level and not voluntarily decided by citizens. To show what such a system of permanent, heterogeneous, and involuntary constituencies would look like, the book ends with a fanciful thought experiment in which citizens are randomly assigned to permanent, single-member, nonterritorial, electoral constituencies. If you are interested in a taste of the whole argument, you may skip ahead directly to the short, whimsical epilogue, which summarizes some of the main findings of the book.

I emphasize at the outset that I am arguing for a default position that, in the light of any particular case, may have to be modified because of other contingencies. Perhaps arguments in favor of group representation will be more compelling over the default position for which I argue here. The point of this book is thus not to argue *against* group and proportional representation per se. It is, however, to argue that supporters of group and proportional representation must do more than show that theirs is a good argument. If the argument here is right, they must justify the significant costs to democratic legitimacy that, I argue, a move away from this default position entails. I do not think this is an impossible task, but I do think it is much more difficult than has previously been acknowledged.

Substantively, I am sympathetic to the aims and political commitments that lead many writers to endorse group representation. Remedying historical oppression, addressing present group harms, and caring for future generations are all critically important ends, ends that appear in contemporary politics to be tragically fading into the background even as they are on the forefront of contemporary academic writing. At the same time, though, I worry that institutional fixes for these problems miss the very point of the problem and ignore the limitations of institutional changes to affect problems of justice. Indeed, institutional fixes for problems of substantive justice may amount to no more than (purportedly) enlightened despotism by another name. I will not defend this position much more in what follows. But what remains is essentially a defense of institutional design that presumes certain limits to what political representation can achieve without giving up hope that justice can be achieved by other means.

A NOTE ON "REPUBLICANISM"

Throughout this book, I refer to "republican" thought, contrasting it with pluralist political theory. By "republican" I mean a set of public regarding values toward which constituents *and* representatives should aim. At the center of these values are certain strains of deliberative democracy: Public deliberation should concern the common good, and advocacy should be introduced only to the extent that it fosters deliberation about the common good. By "pluralist," I mean a theory in which individual interests are to be promoted and advocated by constituents and representatives alike. I argue, with many others, that pluralism can be plausibly justified only by reference to the role of advocacy of individual interests in the promotion of the common good. Republicanism, sometimes called "civic republicanism," has historical linkages to Rome, the American founding, and the English Commonwealth, and has been developed in the late 1980s and through the 1990s most prominently by Cass Sunstein and later by Philip Pettit and Quentin Skinner among many others.[2]

Perhaps the most sustained book-length account of republicanism is Philip Pettit's *Republicanism: A Theory of Freedom and Government*. Owing to my late engagement with this work, the book is mentioned only in passing in what follows, and had I done so earlier, many of the underlying issues in this book would have been framed differently. I cannot present Pettit's views adequately here, nor can I flesh out in great detail the consequences of them for this book. But I can give a general sense of why I believe his account of republicanism would have changed the framing of two important parts of the following argument: first concerning my own presentation of republican institutional design, and second in terms of my presentation of why we should care about how

[2] For examples, see Philip Pettit, *Republicanism: A Theory of Freedom and Government* (London: Oxford University Press, 1997); Quentin Skinner, *Liberty before Liberalism* (Cambridge, UK: Cambridge University Press, 1998); Cass Sunstein, *The Partial Constitution* (Cambridge, MA: Harvard University Press, 1993).

electoral constituencies are defined at all. In doing so, I hope to give a clearer sense of my own motivations for this project.[3]

Pettit's theory of republican freedom as nondomination emerges as a third way between Isaiah Berlin's negative and positive liberties, between liberty as noninterference and liberty as self-mastery. Freedom as nondomination means valuing increases in nondominated choices, not simply increases in noninterference, where domination is distinguished by real or potential arbitrary interference. Thus, although laws represent a reduction of freedom for someone (and will thus always be viewed with suspicion by negative libertarians no matter how much overall freedom the laws wind up allowing), when properly constructed, they are not arbitrary interference. Law and government are essential to the achievement of a maximally free society (in Pettit's republican sense of the word "free") because government stands as the most effective eliminator of social and economic domination. The society that emerges is at once more activist than the libertarian view would allow but also far less instructive and programmatic than the communitarian position would hold, using these terms somewhat simplistically (as Pettit argues, some liberals such as Charles Larmore would qualify as this kind of a republican).

The random constituency that I describe in what follows would promote these republican values because, I argue, it is more likely to create the kinds of institutional incentives that would allow representatives to so deliberate and seek the good of all without giving up their roles as protectors and advocates of their constituents' interests. Since each constituency looks like the nation the constituencies together collectively represent, constituents and representatives both have self-regarding incentives to act *as if* they cared about the common good. Of course, such a plan of representation also works well with individuals who actually do care about the common good, as should any such arrangement.

When individual voters and representatives *are* motivated by deliberating and seeking the common good, it conforms very well with the spirit of Pettit's argument because it reduces the arbitrary power of individual representatives (their skills and talents, their seniority, their interests in pursuing their own constituents' interests, and so on) that emerges from the pluralist system or advocacy representation. To frame it in terms used by Pettit, the random constituency is intended to promote "debate-based" rather than "bargain-based" deliberation within the legislature.[4] In doing so, the random constituency would enhance the "psychological feasibility" of republicanism as Pettit has outlined it, because it structures the institutional incentives of representatives and constituents to encourage such "debate-based" behaviors.[5] Moving to a system of electoral constituencies that looked like the nation they collectively represent would increase the level of nondomination that is built into the electoral system.

[3] I thank Frank Lovett for a discussion of this section.
[4] Pettit, *Republicanism*, pp. 187–8.
[5] Ibid., pp. 206–9.

Second, part of the argument against territorial constituencies presented here, and part of the rationale for offering an historical account of their origins, is that the use of territory for representation has never been explained or justified to (let alone by) the individuals whom it helps govern. In having never been contested, and remaining uncontestable in any meaningful sense, territorial constituencies qualify as an arbitrary institution by which the nation is governed. Given the limit of freedom that this entails (I cannot, for example, be represented as an academic, a citizen of the United States, or simply as a bald white guy), the arbitrary preference this gives to territorial interests over other kinds, and the relative importance of representative institutions in democratic governments, the project that follows might be considered a project of republican reconstruction (not that different from a project of Hegelian reconciliation that I describe in the introduction, although with very different purposes). Finally, and related to this second point, the preference I express in Chapter 8 for placing the decision about constituency formation at the constitutional level (rather than, for example, allowing citizens to choose regularly from a limited set of parties as they would under proportional representation) is, I believe, consistent with Pettit's argument.

Whether the argument that follows is in fact consistent with this theory of government, particularly given that I endorse greater majoritarianism within a nation's legislature, is again beyond what I can defend in any detail here. Nor does a judgment about its consistency with this republican view alter any of the conclusions that follow. But I do believe these brief remarks outline the general path that such a reformulation would take and importantly indicate to readers the intentions, if not necessarily the success, that lie behind the account that follows.

Some scholars work in the isolation of their closets, others with friends in a coffee shop. Although parts of this work were written quite literally in an apartment closet on the south side of Chicago, much of it emerged from conversations that I had with an extraordinary community of scholars. I am obliged to acknowledge the many debts I have accrued in writing this book.

This book is a substantive revision of my doctoral dissertation completed in the Department of Political Science at the University of Chicago under the supervision of Charles Larmore, Susan Stokes, and Cass Sunstein. I owe them each a tremendous debt for the foundation upon which this book was built.

Cass Sunstein oversaw the project from its beginnings as a short research paper and the dissertation benefited from his insight and substantive attention to the founding period. As any reader of his work knows, Cass has a knack for creative and unexpected approaches to social science and the law, and I owe him a great debt for keeping this work focused and relevant. Indeed, it is not unlikely I would still be in James Harrington's *Oceana* but for his acute observation about the contributions of other scholars to that work. I am indebted to him for his quick response time, honest enthusiasm, and skepticism that occasioned the best kind of support a student could receive from a supervisor. In short, Cass made the project possible and kept the argument fresh in ways that probably were not always obvious to him.

Charles Larmore helped me clearly frame the problems with which this book deals, and particularly how the normative and conceptual arguments are presented throughout. Substantively, Charles introduced me to the work of Searle and helped me see the relationship between the structure of language and the structure of political representation, a project that is only hinted at in what follows but critical to what I think is necessary in a proper account of the concept of political representation. Charles' concern with precision also kept my writing as clear as possible; as you will see, I have much still to learn.

Sue Stokes was of extraordinary help to me at every phase of this project. She was an extremely close and critical reader and I am grateful for her availability even during a sabbatical year. She had a particularly strong hand in the structure and substance of the final section of the dissertation and this book. In the end, I doubt I have persuaded her of my positive argument, though she has convinced me of the importance of trying. The book would simply look and sound much different had she not been involved.

The University of Chicago provided a rare intellectual community in which to work and develop as a student. I owe the institution a tremendous debt. I am particularly grateful to a University Fellowship to study public policy, for the Century Fellowship program that sponsored my graduate education in political science, and to the Mellon Foundation, which provided a dissertation year fellowship in 1999–2000.

Among the faculty at Chicago, John Mark Hansen unknowingly gave rise to this project during a graduate course on American politics almost a decade ago. Along with him, Daniel Brudney, Michael Dawson, Ralph Lerner, and Gerry Rosenberg formed a "shadow" committee of sorts, for which I am grateful. Jim Fearon, Martha Nussbaum, Marion Smiley, and Nathan Tarcov also offered extremely helpful comments on an early proposal. I am also grateful to informal discussions with my graduate school cohort and in particular thank Fonna Forman Barzili, Michael Neblo, Eric MacGilvray, Chris Rohrbacher, Dante Scala, and Christina Tarnopolsky for conversations along the way.

In 2000–2001 I began turning the dissertation into a book manuscript. Charlie Glaser and Bob Michael at the Irving B. Harris School of Public Policy, and John Lucy at the college, arranged a teaching position and office at Chicago where I undertook my first revisions. I thank them for their efforts on my behalf and to Rachel Bindman, Howard Margolis, Patchen Markell, Jeff Milyo, Duncan Snidal, and Iris Marion Young for discussions during that year.

I arrived in St. Louis in 2001, where my colleagues at Washington University have provided a nurturing and supportive environment in which to teach and do my work. After receiving a contract for this book, I spent an extra year working through the arguments, displeased about some, overly content with others. During this time I am particularly grateful to Jack Knight for ongoing conversations about this project. Joel Anderson, Lisa Baldez, John Bowen,

Randy Calvert, John Carey, Gary Miller, Andy Sobel, and Norman Schofield have similarly provided insights. Eric MacGilvray and Larry May commented on an earlier draft of the entire manuscript, and I have tried to respond to as much of their very helpful commentary in what follows.

Since each of the chapters of the book has been presented separately, I here acknowledge, in addition to Larmore, Stokes, and Sunstein, those who helped shape each one; I apologize to those who I have inadvertently left out. For Chapter 1, I thank Ethan Bueno de Mesquita, Jack Knight, Bill Lowry, Andrew Martin, Yordanka Nedyalkova, and Lester Spence. Early versions of Chapter 2 were presented to the Department of Political Science at Western Michigan University and at the Political Theory Workshop at the University of Chicago. I am grateful to the audiences for their responses and particularly to Jeff Hayes, Emily Hauptmann, Mike Neblo, William Ritchie, Frank Sposito, and Joel Westra. Chapters 3, 4, and 5 are revised versions of papers presented at American Political Science Association (APSA) annual meeting panels in 1997. I thank Anthony Peacock and Mark Rush, who commented on parts of these. Ralph Lerner, Steve Pincus, Ed Rehfeld, and Dante Scala provided other comments on this material. And I thank Stephen Skorownek and Karen Orren of *Studies in American Political Development* (and two anonymous reviewers for that journal) for their comments on material in Chapters 4 and 5 that first appeared there in 2001.

During the 2000–2001 academic year, I was invited to present Chapter 7 before a number of audiences. I acknowledge the faculties and students in the departments of political science at George Washington University, Middlebury College, University of Pittsburgh, University of Texas at Austin, and Washington University in St. Louis. I am particularly grateful to John Bowen, David Braybrooke, Howard Brick, Ingrid Creppell, Randy Calvert, Murray Dry, Jim Fishkin, Benjamin Gregg, Bob Luskin, Sunita Parikh, Lee Siegelman, Jeff Tullis, and Allison Wylie for their probing questions and helpful remarks on these occasions, and to Suzanne Dovi, Noah Schwartz, and Zach Sufrin for written comments on later versions of the chapter. Chapter 8 was presented at the 2003 meetings of the APSA, and at the Workshop on Politics, Ethics, and Society at Washington University in St. Louis. I thank Joel Anderson, Keith Topper, and those present for their comments. Suzanne Dovi, Bill Lowry, and Gary Miller were helpful in working out the details of Chapter 9. And for Chapter 10 I thank Ethan Bueno de Mesquita, Joe Lowenstein, Bill Lowry, Andrew Martin, and Gary Miller for their help.

Finally, I am grateful to Stephen Macedo and two anonymous reviewers for Cambridge University Press. Although I was eager to see it published quickly, they provided the impetus for sharpening the arguments and restructuring the original manuscript in unexpected ways. Lew Bateman has served as a terrific editor, shepherding the process along judiciously and providing a terrific sounding board. Andy Saff copyedited the manuscript, clearing up a number of striking infelicities. Finally, Yordanka Nedyalkova compiled an initial draft of the index, a daunting process for which I am grateful.

The book would have been a better work had I followed all the suggestions of the preceding; they should of course be held blameless for what remains.

Parts of Chapters 1, 2, and 3 are reprinted with permission of Cambridge University Press. Previous versions of Chapters 4 and 5 are reprinted with slight changes with permission of Cambridge University Press.

I close with a number of personal debts that need to be acknowledged. First among these is to my mother Beverly Rehfeld for taking care of her grandchildren during critical moments when deadlines approached. Far beyond this, she laid the foundation that sustained me in long periods of silent writing; for this I am grateful beyond words. This book was also written with the often unexpressed patience of my children. Emma and Hoben learned the word "dissertation" at an age liable to corrupt their youth, but by forcing their father to confront bodily functions at the dinner table, they kept me sane in moments of despair. Miggie Greenberg has been an unfailing source of strength and support for more than a decade. She understood the deepest significance of this work, and why, despite appearances to the contrary, its completion was never simply foreordained. The dissertation on which this book was based was dedicated to her with love; this book is a tangible result of that relationship.

In 1927, Ruth Wolf Rehfeld was born in Aachen, Germany ("home to Charlemange," she would remind her stepson). At the age of twelve, Ruth was unexpectedly uprooted from her local town. Morning border crossings into Belgium to buy a dozen eggs (that were inexplicably cheaper to buy by the half dozen) were replaced many years later by morning walks around her neighborhood in Baltimore (where, inexplicably, a used car lot was violating clear zoning regulations that she had written). She spent her life as an advocate for African American, Jewish, and urban neighborhoods and understood the importance and possibilities of local community involvement. For these reasons, Ruth was skeptical of the arguments in this book and never hesitated to let me know. Yet without her commitment (and that of my father Rex) at a critical point in time, it is impossible to imagine I could be writing this now. Ruth died as I was completing the revisions on this manuscript, and indeed, knowing her, I suspect she hoped this would prevent its publication. Alas, it only delayed the result; but at least she is now saved from having to suffer through what follows. The book is dedicated to her memory.

PART I

CONCEPTUAL FOUNDATIONS

On Constituency and Political Representation

I

Introduction

[P]olitical philosophy may try to calm our frustration and rage against our society and its history by showing us the way in which its institutions, when properly understood from a philosophical point of view, are rational and developed over time as they did to attain their present, rational form.

– John Rawls[1]

Man is very much a creature of habit. A thing that rarely strikes his senses will generally have but little influence upon his mind.

– Alexander Hamilton[2]

All politics is local.

– Tip O'Neill[3]

I.I GENERAL INTRODUCTION

In almost every democracy in the world, citizens are represented by where they live.[4] In Canada, India, and France, political representatives are elected by groups of voters who live in the same place, whether that location is a province, state, district, or municipality. In Germany, India, and Russia, too, territorial representation is a central feature of legislative design. And every

[1] John Rawls, *Justice as Fairness*, ed. Erin Kelley (Cambridge, MA: Belknap Press, 2001), p. x.

[2] Alexander Hamilton, The Federalist, ed. Jacob E. Cooke, Essay 27 (hereafter *Federalist 27*) (Middletown, CT: Wesleyan University Press, 1961 [1787]).

[3] Thomas P. "Tip" O'Neill is reported to be the author of this maxim, though I have not been able to find that definitive source. The quip became the title of a book that he wrote that was published just before his death. Thomas P. O'Neill with Gary Hymel, *All Politics Is Local* (New York: Times Books, 1994).

[4] Israel and the Netherlands are two exceptions. In Israel, political representatives are elected by party lists nationally. The Netherlands is a slightly more complicated case in which some seats in parliament are linked to the geographical distribution of their votes, but constituencies are not formally territorial. I thank Eric Schliesser for clarification of this point.

ten years in the United States, congressional districts are redrawn, physically
constituting political representation in the House of Representatives by where
its citizens live. Why *do* democratic governments define political representation
by where people live? Are territorial electoral districts commensurate with basic principles of democratic legitimacy? And why might our commitments to
these principles lead us to endorse a radical alternative to territorial or group
representation: randomly assigning citizens to single-member, national electoral
constituencies in which they remain for life? These are the basic questions of this
book.

The answers to these questions are conceptual, historical, and normative,
thus reflecting the organization of what follows. The answers are conceptual
because they depend on divorcing the concept of constituency from other features of electoral systems, features such as voting rules and election procedures;
the definition of constituency is independent of, and prior to, how votes get
cast and counted. The answers are historical or explanatory because we are
interested in knowing why territorial constituencies came to be used; in the
particular case of the United States House of Representatives, the justification
for territorial representation dramatically changed, not, as some have argued,
with the emergence of modern technologies in the twentieth century, but two
centuries earlier at the founding of the United States, when the size of electoral
districts increased by an order of magnitude. And the answers are normative,
because we want to know how any government's legitimacy – here understood
as a government's *right* to make and enforce law – is affected by the institutional
design of electoral constituencies. To give but one example, if representatives
facing reelection should be held accountable to the people who elected them, we
should have a strong preference for electoral constituencies whose membership
does not change over time.

I will define what I mean by "constituency" in much greater detail later in
Chapter 2, but at this point we can say that an electoral constituency is the
group in which a citizen's vote is counted for the purpose of electing a political
representative. Electoral constituencies do not need to be defined by territory.
Historically, the state has defined them according to race,[5] class,[6] and political
party.[7] But as an institution conceptually separate from the election of representatives, the electoral constituency is little studied. Its historical origins, at least
in the United States, are incorrectly described. And as a normative subject of
inquiry, the constituency is almost completely ignored. It is neither as symbolic
as "the right to vote" nor as determinate as a "voting system." Yet its exclusion
from the central principles of normative and analytical democratic theory is

---

[5] In the United States, electoral constituencies defined by race have been permitted to varying
degrees since the Voting Rights Act of 1965.

[6] The Estates-General of France was defined in part according to social class.

[7] Gerrymandered districts in the United States are often drawn to create districts defined by political
party. For reasons I discuss in Chapter 2, most forms of proportional representation effectively
define electoral constituencies by political party.

a considerable oversight that, for reasons I will explain, has undermined the normative legitimacy of democratic governments.

The Concept of Constituency thus offers an approach to the central paradox of modern democratic government: Political representation excludes almost all of a nation from the institutions that "democratically" govern it. In any two-year period, the average U.S. citizen has a 25 percent greater chance of being struck by lightning than serving in either the U.S. Senate or the House of Representatives. Of course, lightning strikes some parts of the country more frequently than others, and office holding depends on, among other things, wealth, race, and gender. So if you are a poor, black woman living in rural Missouri, you are about a million times more likely to be struck by lightning than ever serving in either branch of your national legislature.[8]

The exclusion of political representation is a structural feature of democratic governments worldwide. In 2003, for example, .0000183 of the adult population of France served in either branch of its national legislature. The same year in India and Russia, the proportion of lawmakers to adult citizens was .000001117 and .000004349 respectively. Very small nations such as Iceland and Belize (with populations of less than three hundred thousand) emerge only slightly better with proportions of .000257 and .000262, respectively.[9]

To be sure, one can participate in politics without writing and voting on legislation. Citizens can give money to campaigns, if they have money to give. They can spend time advocating for legislation, if they have the time to give. They can attend deliberative sessions, voice their opinions, and participate in letter writing campaigns, if they have the skills, patience, and fortitude that such endeavors usually demand. But in terms of taking an official role in deliberating about and voting on the laws that bind us all, the nature of political representation necessarily leaves most (I am tempted to say all) of us out of the loop.

The fact that political representation excludes so many has long been viewed with ambivalence. On the one hand, representation weakens traditional, ancient notions of democracy that emphasize the close connection between people and the laws that govern them. Representation increases the distance between citizens and the concerns of their representatives and it also limits the number of

---

[8] The "million times" is a guess based on the fact that parts of Missouri are struck much more frequently by lightning than elsewhere, and there has yet to be a poor black woman serving in Congress. On average, the odds of being struck by lightning in a two-year period are about .000003334, roughly 25 percent greater than .000002725, the proportion of the adult U.S. population that serves in Congress. Lightning data come from "Interesting Facts, Myths, Trivia and General Information about Lightning," 13 January 2004, http://www.srh.noaa.gov/mlb/ltgcenter/ltg.facts.html (accessed 13 January 2004). Population data come from Mary M. Kent and Mark Mather, "What Drives U.S. Population Growth?" *Population Bulletin* 57(4), December 2002: p. 27, http://www.prb.org/Content/NavigationMenu/ PRB/AboutPRB/Population.Bulletin2/57. 4_USPopulationFINAL.pdf (accessed 12 January 2004).

[9] World Factbook: France 2003; World Factbook: Russia 2003; World Factbook: Iceland 2003; World Factbook: Belize 2003, all at http://www.cia.gov/cia/publications/factbook. By "adult population" I mean all people over fifteen or sixteen years old based on the population figures.

perspectives and interests that can be represented in the legislature. This line of thought, began by Jean-Jacques Rousseau, can be traced through the U.S. Anti-Federalists down to many democratic theorists today such as Ben Barber, John Burnheim, and Iris Marion Young.[10]

On the other hand, political representation may temper democratic excesses because better than average individuals may be voted into the legislature, or because a small legislature is more conducive to deliberation, reflection, and compromise than is a large group. This second line of thought can be traced from James Harrington and James Madison, through Francois Guizot and John Stuart Mill, down to supporters of group representation who see representation as a means by which group rights are secured against the will of the majority.[11] More recently, Bernard Manin has argued that the exclusion of representative government – whether beneficial or not – makes it an elective aristocracy rather than a purely democratic form, a claim with which the aforementioned impoverished, black Missourian might well agree.[12]

If political representation is necessarily about exclusion, electoral constituencies define how the excluded are re-formed, how they are grouped, and how they are districted for the purpose of political representation. The concept of constituency, then, is part of a theory of democratic exclusion because electoral constituencies define the way that the excluded are legitimately constituted for the purposes of political representation. Working this out means turning our view from what goes on within the legislature, and asking instead what happens to those who remain outside of it. And we proceed by delineating the conceptual, historical, and normative components of this project.

Conceptual Foundations. The right of a government to make and enforce its laws depends in part on whether its political institutions and practices are justifiable to those who are governed by them. This in turn depends on the substantive

---

[10] Benjamin Barber, *Strong Democracy: Participatory Politics for a New Age* (Berkeley, CA: University of California Press, 1984), pp. 145–6. John Burnheim, *Is Democracy Possible?* (Los Angeles, CA: University of California Press, 1985); Jean-Jacques Rousseau, *On the Social Contract*, trans. Judith R. Masters, ed. Roger D. Masters (New York: St. Mary's, 1978 [1762]); Iris Marion Young, *Justice and the Politics of Difference* (Princeton, NJ: Princeton University Press, 1990), pp. 184–6.

[11] Francois Guizot, *The History of the Origins of Representative Government in Europe*, trans. Andrew R. Scoble, ed. Aurelian Craiutu (Indianapolis, IN: Liberty Fund, 2002); James Harrington, "The Commonwealth of Oceana," in *The Commonwealth of Oceana and a System of Politics*, ed. J. G. A. Pocock, Cambridge Texts in the History of Political Thought (New York: Cambridge University Press, 1992 [1656]); David Hume, "Idea of a Perfect Commonwealth," in *David Hume, Essays: Moral Political and Literary*, ed. Eugene F. Miller (Indianapolis, IN: Liberty Fund, 1987), pp. 512–29; James Madison, *The Federalist*, 10; John Stuart Mill, *Considerations on Representative Government* (Amherst, NY: Prometheus, 1991 [1861]); Iris Marion Young, *Inclusion and Democracy* (Oxford, UK: Oxford University Press, 2000).

[12] Bernard Manin, *The Principles of Representative Government* (New York: Cambridge University Press, 1997).

virtue of the proposed institution or practice, that it be publicly known, and that its justifications are at least accessible if not in fact known to all citizens.[13] When we ignore the dynamics and justifications for electoral constituencies, we ignore an institution that should be included among those more familiar institutions and practices that purportedly legitimize a government's rule – institutions such as "fair and free elections," and practices such as deliberation, transparency, and accountability.

Why should electoral constituencies be counted among these other well-studied institutions and practices? As Melissa Williams has put it, constituency definitions "mediate" the relationship between voters and their representatives.[14] The definition of electoral constituencies shapes how citizens qua citizens interact with one another. And, they structure the incentives representatives face when they deliberate on and make law. For reasons I explore throughout this book, the definition of electoral constituencies helps a nation determine the way it comes to understand itself.

Electoral constituencies define how voters are grouped for the election of their representative and are conceptually different from the particular selection rule that they use to select their representatives. For example, if voters were grouped by professions – doctors forming one electoral constituency, janitors another, and so on – they would still need other rules to decide how each of these groups would select its representative or representatives. Maybe they would use majority rule or plurality rule. Maybe they would select a representative by lottery. Our concern here is not, then, with voting rules or the questions of single-member or multimember representation. It concerns the prior question of how constituent groupings themselves affect the legitimacy of a political regime.

Conceptually, electoral constituencies can vary on many dimensions. They may be more or less voluntary in the sense of allowing individuals (rather than the state) to choose how they are defined. They may be more or less stable, describing the extent to which their membership changes between elections. And they may be more or less heterogeneous, describing the extent to which the members of an electoral constituency share a certain feature, such as the same race or profession, territorial location, or political party membership. Each of these features will affect how citizens relate to each other as constituents, the choices they make as voters, and the incentives that representatives therefore face when campaigning and serving in office. Finally, a particular definition of an electoral constituency – more or less stable, more or less voluntary, and more or less homogeneous – may be justified for a host of reasons, including "to protect a group's rights," "to represent local interests," or "to foster citizenship skills among citizens." We can only appreciate the normative implications of

---

[13] I will defend these claims in section 1.2

[14] Melissa S. Williams, *Voice, Trust, and Memory* (Princeton, NJ: Princeton University Press, 1998), pp. 23–56. Williams' argument referred to political representation more broadly, including, but not limited to electoral constituencies. On Williams, see also section 2.1.

electoral constituencies when we treat them as conceptually independent of other democratic institutions.

Historical Origins: The Silence of the Land. Why should we care about these particular features of democratic institutions? The conceptual argument helps us map the historical origins and normative justifications of our contemporary institutions and their alternatives. It thus provides a set of tools by which we can justify the institutions by which we govern ourselves (a role of political philosophy emphasized by Rawls's summary of Hegelian reconciliation quoted at the start of this chapter).

When we ignore the dynamics of and justifications for our shared political practices and institutions, we let them lie silently in our midst, and risk making them appear natural or necessary for that apparent silence. In this way we may think of territorial constituencies as "the silence of the land": Territorial constituencies have become such a habit of mind that it may seem "natural" for political representation to be defined by where people live. If, by nature, all politics *were* local, this naturalness might be a good justification for territorial representation. But the truth of Tip O'Neill's aphorism, that all politics is local, depends not on the nature of politics per se but on the institutional incentives that lead politicians to serve *local* interests over *nonlocal* interests, incentives that arise only because electoral constituencies are defined territorially. The localness of politics is thus epiphenomenal, nothing more than a byproduct of territorial electoral constituencies. If electoral constituencies were defined by profession (and not by residency at all), all politics would be "vocational." If constituencies were defined by political party (again, without regard to where members lived), all politics would be "ideological." These facts are obscured by the silence of the land.

So why are territorial constituencies used for political representation? I take up the answer to this question in Chapters 3–6. Perhaps the most apparently obvious reason is that the communities in which we live seem to form "communities of interest" that should matter to national political representation. Indeed, territorial constituencies arose for this reason in medieval England.[15] But in the case of the United States – the case on which this book focuses – this justification was not a foundational one, having fallen away by the time the U.S. Congress was being created. This justification no longer could apply to national electoral constituencies because their size extended far beyond what anyone at the time thought was a coherent "community of interest."

Territorial congressional districts would have been much too large to map onto existing towns, boroughs, and counties, and this fact generated the now familiar positions for and against political representation. For supporters of the proposed U.S. Constitution, the large size of the district was a virtue of the system – political representatives would be more independent within Congress, free from the factionalism that supporters thought controlled representatives in

[15] See Chapter 4.

the smaller state legislatures. For opponents of the proposed federal plan, the fact that local communities could not be represented in the national councils of government illustrated one of the fundamental flaws of the system and political representation more generally. But all sides shared the expectation that the electoral district for Congress would be too large to represent coherently local communities of interest.[16]

Territorial constituencies, however, enabled other democratic aims to be achieved, such as "between-citizen" deliberation, and they made it possible for citizens to hold their representatives to account.[17] This is not to say that the "territoriality" of the electoral constituency itself was much noticed. But the American experience illustrates how deeply seated "territorial districts" were even for people who self-consciously created and re-created their institutional design. Even when the territorial district became too large to represent a "community of interest" coherently, no alternatives were offered for it.[18] The use of territory to define electoral constituencies persisted as a habit of mind, a historical remnant no longer serving its original purpose of representing communities of interest, but so ingrained that it was never seriously challenged.

Normative Justifications. The choice of the United States as the historical case should not obscure the broader theoretical implications of this study. Virtually all nations, no matter what voting systems they use, utilize some form of territorial districting without giving much thought to its alternatives. Half of the lower house of Russia's legislature is defined by territorial districts, as is the lower house of India.[19] Even those who have called for group representation through proportional representation often rely on territorial boundaries to subdivide groups to select candidates, as is the case in Chile. In other cases, territorial lines are used to achieve group representation, as in the case of the U.S. gerrymanders of the last four decades in which district lines were drawn to facilitate minority representation. Thus, while the historical questions are of particular importance to citizens of the United States, they do not address the pressing contemporary ones. Are there good reasons to favor territorial representation in large nations today? In Chapters 7 through 9, I take up these issues.

There are many reasons we might think that where we live matters and should matter for national political representation today. Perhaps, as Nancy Schwartz has argued, territorial proximity helps foster citizenship because it allows individuals to deliberate face to face and otherwise act as citizens with each

---

[16] See Chapter 5.

[17] See Chapter 6.

[18] In Chapter 3, I address the concern that the question itself is anachronistic because there were no alternatives available in the eighteenth century. See section 3.1.

[19] Like the U.S. Senate, the upper houses of Russia and India are also territorially defined, but in both cases, territory is only incidental to a functioning subnational administrative unit. Thus it is more appropriate to call this constituency defined by "political community" than by territory per se. For more, see the discussion in Chapters 2 and 3.

other, rather than from a distance.[20] The large size of territorial constituencies – in the United States, each constituency for the U.S. House of Representatives contains on average more than six hundred thousand individuals – also allows them to encompass many different interests, so that representatives may have to appeal to a wide range of interests in order to be reelected. This underlying diversity may help moderate a representative's deliberations and votes, and may make it more likely that a policy commensurate with the national good emerges from the national legislature.[21] Other kinds of constituency definition in which voters are concentrated more homogeneously (by race, political party, nationality, ethnicity, and so on) may create bad incentives for particularistic legislation that are unlikely to encourage a representative to think about the welfare of the greater whole. If legitimate political institutions ought to pursue the interests of the collective they govern, then its institutions ought to be structured to provide incentives to act on behalf of the public good.[22] So, assuming nonbiased districting and residential integration of all kinds, territorial districts may have the potential to do that.

Because the allocation of territorially specific goods such as highways, medical centers, and schools is important for the good of any nation, it may even be possible to justify territorial constituencies because they create what would purportedly be the right kind of incentives for representatives to secure territorially defined goods for their constituents. In this account, the process of logrolling – "if you vote for my project, I'll vote for yours" – purportedly produces the national good through a series of trade-offs between representatives within the legislature. The problem, though, is that the incentives to allocate goods territorially must be justified against the other kinds of incentives that would be created if constituencies were defined along nonterritorially based dimensions such as race, gender, or profession. So we need a prior argument that logrolling between advocates of *this* particularity – whether territory, race, profession, or so on – is what will most likely produce good outcomes that aim at the national interest. We cannot simply say that logrolling ensures the national good without considering what kinds of logs are being rolled.

Territorial constituencies are more justifiable than some people might suppose, because they can potentially capture a good deal of heterogeneity among constituents. But territorial constituencies may be less justifiable because they introduce a set of incentives that arguably skew legislative decision making away from the public good. All of which raises the evaluative questions: What makes greater heterogeneity among constituencies better than less; and how should we structure the incentives of legislators if not by locally deliverable goods? In sum, if not territory, what else?

[20] Nancy L. Schwartz, *The Blue Guitar: Political Representation and Community* (Chicago: University of Chicago Press, 1988). See section 2.1 for a discussion of Schwartz's argument.

[21] This is, arguably, the central logic behind James Madison's *Federalist 10*. For more, see the discussion in Chapter 5.

[22] This claim is defended in Chapters 7 and 8.

The answer to these questions will vary depending on the particular case – a nation that has historically oppressed groups, systematically denying its members "voice" in the legislature, for example, might have a stronger case for group representation than in other cases.[23] Or will it? Following the work of David Lublin, sometimes the best way to achieve good legislative outcomes for groups is to spread their voice – and thus their influence – throughout many different electoral constituencies, denying them the ability to elect "one of their own" in exchange for having their voices as constituents heard.[24] Still, the point here is that we need to be sensitive to the particular context in deciding how to draw electoral constituencies or the structure of most political institutions.

Sensitivity to "context" may sometimes provide an easy excuse for not following through the implications of a theory, especially when these implications cut against the grain of popular (or academically popular) opinion. I think we can say much more about how constituencies should be defined for *any* nation that purports to have a legitimate government, given *any* plausible account of normative legitimacy, an argument I develop in Chapter 8.[25] I simply assume that citizens ought to authorize and hold to account their own representatives; that diversity of perspectives is important to political deliberation; and that representatives should not act in "improper" ways. Such a minimalist account (in which we do not even say what it means to act in "proper" let alone improper ways) leads me to the default position that electoral constituencies should look like the nation they collectively represent and be permanently assigned.

Controversially, the argument here depends on rejecting a familiar consequentialist formulation of political equality, the call to avoid wasted votes and "make votes count." Put differently, it rejects as trivial the claim that each citizen should have an equal chance to affect the outcome of an election. Despite its democratic-sounding framing, this "equal chance" claim in fact reflects one of the least democratic values we could imagine, as if everyone should have an equal chance of individually deciding an election, each of us standing an equal chance of being our own petty tyrant for a day. The concern with wasted votes is a surprisingly trivial one because we properly should not worry about unequal distributions of inconsequential goods, and an individual vote in a large election is as inconsequential a good as any. The fact that an individual vote is (and ought to be) inconsequential to the outcome of an election does not mean

---

[23] For a particularly thoughtful argument about how to determine when groups should be given rights or representation, see Williams, *Voice, Trust, and Memory*. For a persuasive account, see Jane J. Mansbridge, "Should Blacks Represent Blacks and Women Represent Women? A Contingent 'Yes,'" *Journal of Politics*, 61, no. 3, August 1999: 628–57.

[24] David Lublin, *The Paradox of Representation* (Princeton, NJ: Princeton University Press, 1997).

[25] I thus concur with the arguments of Charles Beitz about the practical application of theory to institutional design, though I think that normative theory – whether of justice or legitimacy – is more determinate when forming a default position than Beitz allows. See Charles R. Beitz, *Political Equality: An Essay in Democratic Theory* (Princeton, NJ: Princeton University Press, 1989), p. xiv and passim. See also Chapter 8.

nonconsequentialist versions of political equality are trivial ones; nor does it follow that the state should use biased rules in distributing votes to individuals (bias being a different concern from equality). In the analysis of Chapter 8, the triviality of equal vote shares will mean that in a conflict with other values, "making votes count" must yield to other more important ends.

How, then, can electoral constituencies be defined so that they look like the nation they collectively represent? One way is to assign voters randomly into single-member electoral constituencies in which they would remain for life.[26] The "random constituency" is a default position, one that we should assume when designing or altering democratic institutions, much as we assume "one person, one vote" when assigning political shares. But as I said, context is always important to institutional design. The case for the random constituency may be trumped in a particular case by other, more compelling arguments for group representation. If so, however, these arguments for group representation must be framed not simply in terms of how well they achieve their important normative aims (such as group advocacy or rights protections). Rather, they must explain why we should favor these group aims given what I argue are the costs to legitimacy of moving from the democratic default position I develop here.

Plan of the Book. Considering a default position as novel as the random constituency allows our own familiar practices to come into clearer relief.[27] This book is thus not about advocacy but legitimacy, and that requires coming to terms with the history and contemporary justifications for the institutions under which we are presently governed. This book seeks to explain why the random constituency is at least worth our sustained attention.

The book is structured in three parts to address the conceptual, historical, and normative threads that I have touched on previously. In Part I (Chapter 2), I develop the conceptual structure of an electoral constituency. I emphasize its three analytical dimensions of heterogeneity, stability, and voluntariness and illustrate ten different kinds of normative justifications that have been given for a host of different arrangements. In Part II (Chapters 3–6), I utilize the analytic framework historically by asking why electoral constituencies in the United States are based on where its citizens live. Rejecting the familiar justifications that local communities of interests mattered for political representation, I argue that territorial representation was merely justified for logistical reasons. And in Part III (Chapters 7–9) I take up three normative issues, arguing that 1) territorial constituencies are not particularly well justified for large nations today (Chapter 7); 2) that any plausible account of political legitimacy will endorse a default position of electoral constituencies that are permanent, look like the nation they collectively represent, and not decided by individual citizens (Chapter 8); and 3) that large nations should randomly assign

[26] See Chapter 9.
[27] I thank Cass Sunstein for repeatedly emphasizing this point.

every citizen to single-member (nonterritorial) electoral constituencies for life (Chapter 9).

The book ends in Chapter 10 with a short, fanciful epilogue that describes what an observer might report were she to view the United States fifty years after the adoption of this proposed random constituency. You may find it helpful to read this brief epilogue first to see where the argument of this book is heading. The epilogue, however, should not be mistaken for the substantive arguments of the book.

In the remainder of this introduction, I take up a set of preliminary issues that provide the background for the book. In section 1.2, I explain what I mean by normative legitimacy and why the concept of constituency matters for anyone who is concerned about a government's right to make and enforce the laws that it passes. In section 1.3, I set out certain conceptual, normative, and historical errors that this book seeks to correct. And in section 1.4, I raise a problem concerning the fundamental exclusion of political representation that deliberative democrats have not sufficiently addressed: The cost of securing diversity of voice within a legislature is the exclusion of voice from within an electoral constituency. Solving that problem illustrates the theoretical value of thinking about the concept of constituency in its own right.

1.2 LEGITIMACY AND POLITICAL REPRESENTATION

In this book, I argue that constituency definition should be placed among other more familiar institutions that increase or lessen a government's legitimacy.[28] Before embarking, though, I want to offer a brief discussion of the concept of legitimacy as it relates to political representation and institutional design. I will not offer a comprehensive account of the topic nor a detailed defense of the position I take – tasks that are well beyond the scope of this book. I do, however, want to make clear what stands in the balance of this account. In section 1.2.1, I will briefly explain how this account differs from other sociological and normative accounts. And in section 1.2.2, I explain how this treatment helps to legitimize contemporary political institutions by making them more transparent and justifiable.

1.2.1 Normative versus Sociological Legitimacy

I care about the conditions under which a government has the right to make and enforce laws for a particular population – a government, that is, which

---

[28] To clarify this sentence, I assume legitimacy is a continuous variable such that one system may be more or less legitimate than another. If legitimacy is a discontinuous variable, then systems either are or are not legitimate, a description that I think obscures too much complexity and nuance. I cannot argue this point here, nor does anything in the present argument hinge on whether legitimacy is or is not a continuous variable. I thank Charles Larmore and Michael Neblo for raising this point.

is normatively legitimate. A comprehensive account of normative legitimacy would specify what these conditions are. The account might include particulars familiar from recent deliberative theory: that the content of the law be just[29]; that the deliberation and publicity surrounding the law be fair and open[30]; and that the form of government under which those laws were passed be open to the consent of the people.[31]

In what follows, I will not propose any comprehensive or "systemwide" account of legitimacy. I begin instead with one assumption: It is a necessary condition of any legitimate representative government that its political representatives themselves be legitimate. If this is so, then any comprehensive account of legitimacy will include an account that specifies why *these* individuals, but not those, have the right to constitute the representative legisture.[32] The legitimacy of political representatives thus forms a precondition for the enactment of legitimate law. Because the definition of electoral constituencies dynamically changes the way citizens relate to one another qua constituents, the incentives of representatives, and thus the deliberation and output of a legislature, it must rank among the other features that a comprehensive account of normative legitimacy would specify.

In Chapter 8, I will develop this position in more depth, and explain how the definition of electoral constituencies fits into a normative theory of legitimate representative government. Here I want to differentiate this account of normative legitimacy from two other kinds of accounts: a more expansive normative account in which a government's legitimacy generates obligations of citizens to obey the laws of a rightful government, and a sociological account in which legitimacy is equated with public approval.

The first very brief distinction I want to make concerns what kinds of moral rights or obligations the term *legitimacy* generates. Here, with Allen Buchanan, I treat the concept as applying only to a state's right.[33] This is all that is necessary for the account here to be intelligible. I thus leave as an open question

---

[29] Ronald Dworkin, *Taking Rights Seriously* (Cambridge, MA: Harvard University Press, 1977); David M. Estlund, "Who's Afraid of Deliberative Democracy?: On the Strategic/Deliberative Dichotomy in Recent Constitutional Jurisprudence," *Texas Law Review*, 71, no. 7, June 1993: 1437–7.

[30] James Bohman and William Rehg, eds., *Deliberative Democracy: Essays on Reason and Politics* (Cambridge, MA: MIT Press, 1997); Amy Gutmann and Dennis Thompson, *Democracy and Disagreement* (Cambridge, MA: Belknap Press, 1996); John Rawls, *Political Liberalism*, John Dewey Essays in Philosophy, vol. 4 (New York: Columbia University Press, 1993); Bernard Manin, "On Legitimacy and Political Deliberation," trans. Elly Stein and Jane Mansbridge, *Political Theory* (London), 15, no. 3, August 1987: 338–68.

[31] John Locke, "Second Treatise of Government," in *Two Treatises of Government*, ed. Peter Laslett, Cambridge Texts in the History of Political Thought (Cambridge, UK: Cambridge University Press 1988 [1690]); Rawls, *Political Liberalism*.

[32] Or, as Locke put it, "a Man can never be oblig'd in Conscience to submit to any Power, unless he can be satisfied who is the Person, who has a Right to Exercise that Power over him." John Locke, "First Treatise of Government," in *Two Treatises of Government*, Section 81.25, p. 203.

[33] Allen Buchanan, "Political Legitimacy and Democracy," *Ethics*, 112, no. 4, July 2002: 689–719.

whether the laws of a legitimate government generate a corresponding political obligation for its citizens.[34]

Second, I want to distinguish the normative position from a "sociological" or empirical position in which *legitimacy* merely describes whether a population approves of a particular government or particular government institutions without assessing the correctness of this approval. In this treatment, *legitimacy* has become virtually synonymous with "public approval" and is studied through public opinion research. The contemporary origins of this position lie with Max Weber, who used the term *legitimacy* descriptively to describe three ways that governments lay claim to their authority. In the mid-twentieth century, Seymour Martin Lipset furthered the sociological view, arguing that "Legitimacy involves the capacity of the system to engender and maintain the belief that the existing political institutions are the most appropriate ones for the society."[35] By this account, a legitimate government is one that has and maintains its people's approval without reference to how it gained that approval – a government is still legitimate by Lipset's account if it coerces its citizens to approve of it – nor whether the institutions that are approved are in fact fit objects of choice.

Equating "legitimacy" with "public approval" is endemic to contemporary empirical research on legitimacy. It may give the field of public opinion research an artificial gravitas – artificial because the literature never actually speaks to the question of legitimacy. Consider this excerpt from an article entitled "On the Legitimacy of National High Courts": ". . . our goal is to broaden the study of the relationships between courts and their publics by examining mass attitudes toward the legitimacy of national high courts. . . ."[36] As the authors explicitly say, they are interested only in whether people *view* the high courts as legitimate, not, as one might think given the title of their article, *whether* the high courts are *in fact* legitimate.[37] Even if a government's legitimacy required that most people approved of them as legitimate, it leaves open the following question: What are individuals judging when they judge a government (or institution) to be legitimate?

The sociological equivalence of "the people's approval for the government to use force" with "the right of the government to use force" is overly broad,

---

[34] For the defense of separating the rights that legitimacy generates to the state from possible corresponding citizen obligations see ibid; David Schmidtz, "Justifying the State," *Ethics*, 101, no. 1, October 1990: 89–102. For the claim that legitimacy implies both rights and obligations, see A. John Simmons, *Justification and Legitimacy* (New York: Cambridge University Press, 2001). My own feeling is that if a state has a right to coerce that might give me a reason to obey, or, with Simmons, perhaps give me some nonfinal obligation to obey. But it is enough to differentiate these two threads, and I will not argue for either position here.

[35] Seymour Martin Lipset, *Political Man: The Social Bases of Politics* (Baltimore, MD: Johns Hopkins University Press, 1988), p. 64.

[36] James L. Gibson, Gregory A. Caldeira, and Vanessa A. Baird, "On the Legitimacy of National High Courts," *American Political Science Review*, 92, no. 2, June 1998: pp. 343–58.

[37] I thank Jim Gibson for an extended e-mail discussion about this subject.

for it appears that individuals could never be wrong. What happens, for example, if a people approves of a government because it has been tricked into thinking the elections are fair? If attitudes about the government are *all* that matters for legitimacy to accrue, then such trickery would not in and of itself be problematic. Instead, I am in agreement with a long history dating back to Locke (if not Plato) that there are limits on what kinds of governments may rightly make and enforce laws no matter what the people think.

None of this comprises a particularly original set of observations, but merely serves to delineate the meaning of *legitimacy* I am using here.[38] I am concerned foremost with the kinds of institutions that individuals *ought to* judge as legitimate, rather than merely whether they actually do judge them to be so. And by this I mean that, I care about the conditions by which the government, in fact, has the right to make and enforce laws over its people.

1.2.2 Transparency and the Legitimacy of Political Institutions

The sociological view of legitimacy is a familiar one, because of its close relation to the social contract tradition of Hobbes, Locke, and Rousseau. Under various social contract formulations, public approval is a necessary but insufficient condition for normative legitimacy. In fact, the normative view of legitimacy that I am using here treats public approval in exactly this way, necessary at some level, but insufficient for legitimacy. I also assume that any comprehensive account of legitimacy will include some provision of justification: Citizens must have good reasons to endorse the particular institutions that govern them, whether or not they actually do justify them to one another.[39]

Justification implies that three conditions be met. An institution must be: (i) substantively justifiable; (ii) it must be transparently known to all it governs; and (iii) the reasons it is justifiable should be publicly available. Fleshing this out will clarify how the argument of this book helps legitimize the actual institutions under which we live.

The first condition of justification is a substantive one: Before a population can justify an institution, it must be endorsed by a comprehensive account of legitimacy. So, for example, an account of political legitimacy might endorse the extension of universal suffrage to its citizens because this is the only way to institutionalize equal respect for each individual. Or an account of political legitimacy might endorse *this set* of voting rules but not *that set*.[40] Before any institution of government can be justified, it must be an institution that *can* be substantively justified.

---

[38] See, for example, Buchanan, "Political Legitimacy and Democracy"; Robert Grafstein, "The Failure of Weber's Conception of Legitimacy: Its Causes and Implications," *Journal of Politics*, 43, no. 2, May 2002: 456–72.

[39] See, for example, John Rawls, *Justice as Fairness: A Restatement* (Cambridge, MA: Harvard University Press, 2001), p. 27.

[40] Beitz's endorsement of complex proceduralism is an example of how this may be worked out. Beitz, *Political Equality*.

The second condition of justification concerns transparency: To be justified, the institution must be known by those it governs. This transparency of fact stipulates that the institutions of a political system should be public and known to its citizens by reasonable means.[41] Transparency of fact can be as important for the legitimacy of a polity as are the institutions that are made transparent by it. For example, the knowledge that suffrage is universal is as important as the right to vote itself: Imagine every citizen had the legal right to vote, but no one knew she did (the law was secretly passed). In this case, the first, substantive condition – universal suffrage – would by assertion have been met, but it would not have been known to those whom it governs. A government that concealed the fact that its citizens were permitted to vote would be illegitimate only because it violated transparency of fact and not because people were forbidden to vote – by stipulation, they could vote. This is why transparency of fact, in addition to the substantive condition itself, is a necessary condition for any government to be justified as legitimate.

The third condition for justification also concerns transparency of a different kind: To justify their government, citizens need to have good reasons to endorse the institutions that govern them. This transparency of reasons stipulates that the reasons to endorse these institutions ought to be available (or at least not withheld) from citizens; in the case of universal suffrage, it is important for citizens to know why the state guarantees political equality for its citizens. In fact, justification rests on giving reasons, and thus this third condition is necessary for a government to be justified as legitimate. A polity, for example, in which all citizens have the right to vote, know they possess this right, and can give to each other good reasons why they all have the right to vote is presumptively more legitimate than a polity in which no one can say *why* they have that right, even as they all know they do.[42]

As a normative matter, the obligation to ensure transparency shifts from the state to its citizens as we move from establishing institutions, to making them known, to justifying them. That is, it is the state's responsibility to maintain legitimate institutions.[43] But the state shares with its citizens the obligation of publicizing them: The state's obligation is to make them known in some "reasonable" way, while the citizen's obligation is to exert enough effort to find out about them. Thus, the state need not hire messengers to tell every citizen that, for example, they can register to vote at this polling place or that.

---

[41] Acknowledging it is a term of much debate, the meaning of "reasonable" here can be defined in whatever reasonable terms the reader wishes.

[42] A fourth condition corresponding to Hegelian reconciliation might be argued for. Call it a "transparency of history" whereby the accurate history of an institution is publicly available. I think this is less persuasive as a necessary condition of legitimacy except insofar as it becomes practical to the transparency of fact. Further, these transparency conditions could continue to infinite regress (transparency of reasons for reasons, for example) that I do not think is necessary or helpful to pursue.

[43] I assume there will be some moral regress to citizens to ensure that the state establishes and maintains these institutions, but I am less concerned with those issues here.

But the state has a responsibility to publish the information in a public place, easily accessible to all citizens who must make the effort to stay informed. Thus partnerships between government and nongovernmental organizations (NGOs) supporting "get out the vote" campaigns seem likely to be an appropriate mix of government and citizen involvement in making the right of suffrage known. Finally, the state has a negative obligation in terms of justifying its institutions to its citizens: It must not get in the way of citizens justifying them to each other, even as it can facilitate and support this justificatory activity through funding public service programs. These three stages are not necessarily sequential or simultaneous: Justifications for an institution will often precede its adoption by government[44] and the knowledge that a law has been adopted is in most cases delayed by the time it takes a citizen to read about it in a newspaper or otherwise discover its provisions when they apply.

A government's legitimacy is undermined when its power is used either to unmake a legitimate institution or to obscure transparency of fact about that institution. Because citizens are central to the maintenance of the justifications of their political institutions, however, transparency of reasons can be obscured for less venal reasons: When institutions become overly familiar and uncontested, justifications atrophy from desuetude.[45] And it may be more or less dangerous given the institution. For example, democracy and representative government have so forcefully emerged throughout the world that arguments in their favor appear to be out of practice and thus potentially threatened by strong nondemocratic arguments. Compare, for example, the sophistication with which pamphleteers during the American Revolution argued for democratic forms with even the best contemporary arguments in favor of democratic rule in China. These contemporary arguments are ones of tactics (for example, will free trade or sanctions bring about democracy) and not whether or not democracy itself is good. Now, consider the much more sophisticated arguments waging around the issue of global free trade – an institution not yet as fully accepted as democracy is. In this case, we see justifications being worked out in more sophisticated ways. When a system becomes so well accepted, the reasons it is accepted often fade into the background.

Desuetude is often evidence of progress. For example, the absence of justifications for democratic forms is certainly related to their acceptance among debaters and the lack of any serious threats to democracy. Most people would judge the dominance of democracy as a good thing. Perhaps no one rehearses the arguments for democracy because everyone *knows* they are derived from some norm of equal respect for persons. But when justifications atrophy, they

---

[44] These three conditions may be temporal in a strict sense: Prior to an institution's adoption, it is not a formal institution of government. Thus the justifications that lead to its adoption did not justify an actual institution, but served as a justification for a proposed institution.

[45] Or in Mill's words, "Both teachers and learners go to sleep at their post, as soon as there is no enemy in the field." John Stuart Mill, *On Liberty and Other Writings*, ed. Stefan Collini, Cambridge Texts in the History of Political Thought (New York: Cambridge University Press, 1989 [1859]), p. 44.

lie dormant for attack because their reasons, as John Stuart Mill argued, are "unrehearsed."

By focusing on the concept of constituency, we implicitly draw attention to a substantive feature of representative government in need of justification. By focusing on the history of the territorial district in the United States, we explicitly make transparent that territory is used as well as the reasons that it was used. And by questioning the use of territory in any large nation and proposing an alternative institution, we make transparent the reasons that territory may or may not be consistent with our considered judgments of what constitutes legitimate rule. The argument of this book is thus not only an abstract analysis of institutional arrangements but one that aids in the justification and legitimation of government itself.[46]

1.3 CONCEPTUAL, NORMATIVE, AND HISTORICAL CORRECTIVES

The arguments of this book are also important to correct three errors or imprecisions about electoral constituencies. The first is conceptual, in which the concept of constituency is inextricably linked to the particular selection rules that are used to select candidates. This failure to disentangle "constituency" from "voting rules" has led to a second, normative error: that the only way to solve the problems with territorial constituencies is to use a different voting rule, one that usually involves greater proportionality. Finally, in the United States, critics of single-member districts have made an historical error, asserting that territorial constituencies were originally justified because they represented "communities of interest," a claim I reject. I will treat each of these in turn.

1.3.1 Conceptual and Normative Errors

The first conceptual and normative errors arise from failing to distinguish the dynamics of the electoral constituency from the voting rules that determine the election of a representative. In particular, collapsing constituency definition with voting rules allows the norm of "one person, one vote" to dominate institutional design because once constituencies are defined, it may well be the most important norm in governing fair voting rules. In the empirical and positive theoretic literature on voting systems, and among advocates of proportional representation, the only value that seems to be worth maximizing is that every vote should count. The "wasted vote" – votes cast that do not contribute to a candidate's winning – has thus become a pox on the house of democracy.[47]

---

[46] I thank Yordanka Nedyalkova for this formulation.

[47] For the most prominent of recent accounts, see Gary W. Cox, *Making Votes Count* (New York: Cambridge University Press, 1997); Michael L. Balinski and H. Peyton Young, *Fair Representation: Meeting the Ideal of One Man, One Vote* (Washington, DC: Brookings Institution Press, 2001); Douglass Amy, *Real Voices New Choices* (New York: Columbia University Press, 1993). The titles of these books alone make the point well enough. Normative theorists

The literature on voting systems goes back at least to Condorcet in the eighteenth century describing how voting rules and multimember systems affect electoral outcomes.[48] Empirical, formal, and normative theorists of elections and electoral reforms have followed, raising the concept of constituency only insofar as it addresses the normative and empirical problems of voting, whether to "make votes count" or because groups purportedly deserve to elect candidates responsive to their interests. For example, in Andrew Reeve and Alan Ware's excellent analysis, they take up the concept of constituency, noting that ". . . it is important to separate, at least initially, this issue from the debate over how to aggregate votes." Their case being England, they note that territory and "universities" have been used to define constituencies. But they too quickly collapse their discussion of constituency definition into their discussion of voting systems, ". . . this analytic separation of constituency structure from electoral formulae cannot be sustained completely." There may be practical and historical justifications for looking simultaneously at voting and constituency definition, just as there are practical and historical justifications for looking at the methods of vote aggregation and conceptions of political equality.[49] But these are not only analytically separable; sustaining the separation is the only way to treat the concept at hand adequately, a point I will develop in Chapter 2 and throughout the remainder of this book.

In part the emphasis on voting rules stems from the strategic importance of voting in determining the outcome of an election and the normative importance of individual votes and voting. A democracy, after all, is premised on the idea that each individual counts equally. Anyone concerned with the legitimacy, justice, or the efficiency of a democratic system ought to be concerned with how voting rules affect outcomes. So formal theorists, empirical social scientists, normative political theorists, and advocates have all taken up questions of electoral reform in terms of the effects on government formation, policies produced, party responsiveness, and the legitimacy and justice of the corresponding institution.[50] With a few important exceptions,[51] the electoral

have been more sensitive to the many different normative values that might contrast and conflict, the best of the recent treatments being Beitz, *Political Equality*; Richard S. Katz, *Democracy and Elections* (New York: Oxford University Press, 1997); Williams, *Voice, Trust, and Memory*.

[48] The best recent treatment is Cox, *Making Votes Count*. See also Arend Lijphart and Bernard Groffman, *Choosing an Electoral System: Issues and Alternatives* (New York: Praeger, 1984); Andrew Reeve and Alan Ware, *Electoral Systems: A Comparative and Theoretical Introduction* (New York: Routledge, 1992); among many other treatments.

[49] For Reeve and Ware, the reason was contextual: "[I]t is now important to recognize that in the British context the two issues [constituency definition and vote aggregation] are intertwined." Reeve and Ware, *Electoral Systems*, p. 121.

[50] For a sample see Amy, *Real Voices New Choices*; Beitz, *Political Equality*; Cox, *Making Votes Count*; Anthony Downs, *An Economic Theory of Democracy* (New York: HarperCollins, 1957). Michael Rabinder James' new book is an important addition to this literature. See *Deliberative Democracy and the Plural Polity*, (Lawrence, KS: University Press of Kansas, 2004).

[51] I will take up the arguments of Nancy Schwartz and Melissa Williams in Chapter 2. Schwartz, *The Blue Guitar*; Williams, *Voice, Trust, and Memory*. See also James, *Deliberative Democracy*, 2004; Thomas Pogge, "Self-Constituting Constituencies to Enhance Freedom, Equality, and Participation in Democratic Procedures," *Theoria*, June 2002: 26–54.

constituency as such has not been seen as a location for legitimacy or strategic interaction apart from the voting rules used once constituencies have been defined.

Once constituency definition is fully conceptualized, however, voting rules may themselves come into clearer relief. Conceptually, proportional systems should be understood as cases in which an electoral constituency is defined simultaneously at the moment one votes.[52] By contrast, in territorial systems the electoral constituency is defined prior to an election. And strategically, voting rules underdetermine the outcome of an election and underspecify the incentives that representatives have when in office or running for election. For example, the fact that representatives regularly vote for spending projects that will benefit their home districts is explained not simply by their desire for reelection, but by the territoriality of electoral constituencies. As I repeat in various forms throughout this book, territorial districts explain why representatives care about "local" pork rather than some other kind.

Analyses of the redistricting controversies in the United States have been slightly more cognizant of the analytics of the electoral constituency, but again, never in much of a sustained way. Robert Dixon's early opus on the redistricting cases of the United States in the 1960s focused on the effects of the Supreme Court's call for population equality between districts, but never seriously questioned the use of territorial districts themselves.[53] Lublin's more recent work on the dynamics of minority-majority districts emphasizes legislative outcomes based on the racial homogeneity within a district.[54] And advocates of proportional representation focus on the purported irrelevance of the territorial district in contemporary life but, again, do not pursue the underlying dynamics of constituency definition itself.[55]

Failing to distinguish constituency definition from voting systems allows normative critiques of territorial constituencies to be solved with a change of voting rules. Changes in voting rules would solve voting problems, but they can only indirectly get at the problems of how a constituency is defined. We can see this by focusing on the problems of consent that attend to territorial districts through the practice of gerrymandering, and second by looking at why proportional representation appears to solve the problems of territorial constituencies.

Territorial districts are said to violate notions of consent because representatives, rather than constituents, determine the district lines. This has been a powerful argument against *partisan* districting, as illustrated by a staff aide of

---

[52] For the same point see Beitz, *Political Equality*, p. 150.

[53] Robert G. Dixon, Jr., *Democratic Representation: Reapportionment in Law and Politics* (New York: Oxford University Press, 1968).

[54] Lublin, *The Paradox of Representation.*

[55] Amy, *Real Voices New Choices*; Lani Guinier, *The Tyranny of the Majority: Fundamental Fairness in Representative Democracy* (New York: Free Press, 1994); Robert Richie and Steven Hill, *The Case for Proportional Representation*, eds. Joshua Cohen and Joel Rogers (Boston: Beacon Press, 1999).

one member of Congress describing to Richard Fenno the process of drawing lines with a "neighboring congressman":

Dave Sullivan and I redrew the lines of our two districts. I remember once we were down on our hands and knees on the floor of Henry's Washington office with the map in front of us dividing the districts block by block, bargaining and compromising. Dave would say "I don't want that son of a bitch in my district, you take that block." Or I'd say, "We won by 70 percent in that block, no way you're going to get that one." Henry just sat in his chair and laughed at us. Things like that bore him. He thinks it's an aberration that Dave and I should be interested in such things as census tracts and demographic reports of all sorts.[56]

The unfairness of partisan redistricting is a conflict that may undermine the plausible degree to which a population can claim it consents to the representation it receives. Yet this familiar critique does not argue against territorial districts per se, it only critiques the unreflective way that partisanship interferes. As has been argued for at least forty years, random districting procedures could be instituted to avoid this problem, or non-partisan districting commissions might be established.[57] Thus, the value of territorial districts itself is not threatened by the problems of improper districting. Rather, the manner in which the boundaries are drawn is, in this regard, the central problem.

A second kind of critique focuses on the unfairness of territorial districts by focusing again on the voting rules by which representatives are elected: First-past-the-post, plurality elections can "waste" over half their constituency's vote because a candidate needs only to win the most votes to be elected. In a three-person race, a winner can emerge with less than 40 percent of the vote. Even in a typical two-person race, it is common that a third or more of a district's votes are cast for a losing candidate.[58] So a proportional system, in which voters face more choice of candidates and "voluntarily" choose a constituency as they vote, appears to solve both problems, even though most proportional representation (PR) systems continue to group voters by where they live.

In Chapter 8 I will argue that the concern for wasted votes, votes that do not contribute to the winner of an election, is remarkably trivial and misguided, for two reasons. First, we do not usually care about the unequal distributions

[56] Richard Fenno, *Home Style: House Members and Their Districts* (Boston: Little, Brown, 1978). The redistricting drama that unfolded in Texas in 2003 is yet another illustration.

[57] Rawls endorses such a plan in John Rawls, *A Theory of Justice* (Cambridge, MA: Harvard University Press, 1971), p. 223. Citing W. S. Vickrey, "On the Prevention of Gerrymandering," *Political Science Quarterly* 76, March 1961: 105–10. See also Dixon, *Democratic Representation*. And Micha Altman has offered an important discussion of the difficulty of drawing "unbiased" districts even through computer programs. See Micha Altman, "Districting Principles and Democratic Representation," Ph.D. Dissertation, California Institute of Technology, Chapter 5. The point is that biased line drawing is an argument against territorial constituencies only if there are no *unbiased* ways to draw lines.

[58] In 1996, losers in well over half of all U.S. congressional races (249 seats, or 57 percent of the total) received at least 33 percent of the district's vote. *Statistical Abstract of the United States: 1998* (Washington, DC: U.S. Bureau of the Census, 1998), Table 465.

of inconsequential goods, and an individual vote in a large election is an inconsequential good.[59] Second, structuring a voting system to maximize close elections emphasizes and overvalues tyranny: Why should we endorse a system in which any *one* individual could actually decide the outcome of an election? Rather, we should design systems that aim at consensus and broad political support. Of course, politics will not achieve consensus, and if true consensus were achieved on many issues of the day, other worries might arise.[60] But the point is that aiming at consensus should form a default position.

In any case, the focus on wasted votes has led to repeated calls for group representation – representation that presumes some underlying (and often nonexisting) consensus of the group. Proportional voting schemes are the most familiar of these forms of group representation. Such calls are valued because they maximize the value of every vote. Yet the violation of partisan districting is not that voters lack freedom of choice at election but that someone else decided to aggregate their vote by where they lived prior to election day. The alternative to gerrymandering that solves its consent problems is the voluntary constituency, a constituency in which individuals decide for themselves how to be grouped for political representation.[61]

Beyond this, the problem of any kind of electoral constituency is deeper than "who draws the line": Why should territory or any other particularity be used to group citizens? By not distinguishing the concept of constituency from voting rules, critics of the territorial system improperly answer the districting problem with a solution for voting. Habits of mind hide problems as much as they do solutions: Critics are fitting a square block into a round whole.

1.3.2 Historical Errors

In Part II (Chapters 3–6), I present evidence that territorial districts at the founding of the United States were not expected to map onto small communities

---

[59] The fact that a vote is *inconsequential* does not mean equal votes and political equality more generally are trivial concerns. But it does mean that *consequentialist* framings of political equality such that voters should have an "equal *power* to effect the outcome of an election" are trivial. See Chapter 8.

[60] If broad consensus were achieved, we should be worried that we are mistaken with no easy corrective, and that dissent will suffer. Rousseau's praise of consensus in *On the Social Contract* is conditioned on a properly constituted polity, which is the only reason that split decisions are troublesome. Thus we should understand a unanimous decision as evidence of either a completely perfect state or a completely imperfect state. For a recent development of the dual virtue and vice of consensus in epistemic terms, see Robert E. Goodin, and David Estlund, "The Persuasiveness of Democratic Majorities," *Politics, Philosophy and Economics*, 3, no. 2, June 2004: 131–42. For the classic development of the value of diverse opinion see Mill, *On Liberty and Other Writings*. For a recent treatment that incorporates empirical evidence, see Cass R. Sunstein, *Why Societies Need Dissent* (Cambridge, MA: Harvard University Press, 2003).

[61] For a particularly well-developed plan for self-defined constituencies, see Pogge, "Self-Constituting Constituencies to Enhance Freedom, Equality, and Participation in Democratic Procedure."

of interest, such as the town, county, or boroughs of the individual states. Rather right from the start, electoral constituencies for the House of Representatives were expected to be large and heterogeneous. This claim challenges some contemporary treatments of the founding. These treatments misrepresent the normative justification for its institutions so that it appears that moving to proportional systems today is somehow consistent with founding intent and expectations. In these accounts, territorial districting is understood to have been expressive of the founders' desire to represent territorial "communities of interest" that existed within states. As Pamela Karlan has argued:

> In the nineteenth century, geographic districting made tremendous sense. People's interests – especially to the extent that those interests were relevant to the very limited government of the era – often were primarily defined by where they lived. Transportation and communication were sufficiently rudimentary that political campaigns and voting itself were necessarily based on geography. Today, of course, many citizens' most pressing interests, particularly at the federal level, are not primarily defined by where they live, and we probably would pick a different system if we were starting from scratch.[62]

Here, Karlan rightly emphasizes the importance of logistics in the use of territorial districts. But the last line of the preceding passage contains the force of her point. Some form of *interest* representation made possible by today's technological advances would purportedly be consistent with founding intent. Critics of territorial districts thus claim their system is simply a contemporary adaptation of representational theory extant at the founding of the nation.[63]

Despite the expectations of the founders that territorial constituencies would likely be used, the founding system of representation was intended to represent only those interests of the nation as a whole. This undermines the claim that the founders would have favored districts that corresponded with partial interests within the nation. In the American case, constituencies for the House of Representatives were meant to obscure and defeat communities of interest.

---

[62] Pamala Karlan, "A Bigger Picture," in *Reflecting All of Us: The Case for Proportional Representation*, eds. Joshua Cohen and Joel Rogers (Boston: Beacon Press, 1999), p. 76.

[63] For examples of advocacy, see "Testimony of Roger Clegg...before the House Judiciary Committee Subcommittee on the Constitution regarding H.R. 1173" (taken from http://www.house.gov/judiciary/clego923.htm); "Testimony of Theodore S. Arrington...before the House Judiciary Committee Subcommittee on the Constitution regarding H.R. 1173" (taken from http://www.house.gov/judiciary/arrio923.htm); Center for Voting and Democracy, "What Is Proportional Representation" (taken from http://www.fairvote.org/pr/q_and_a.htm). For examples in the academic literature, see Williams, *Voice Trust and Memory*, pp. 25–6, 39, 173; Rosemarie Zagarri, *The Politics of Size: Representation in the United States 1776–1850* (Ithaca, NY, and London: Cornell University Press, 1987), p. 108. See also Guinier, *The Tyranny of the Majority*, p. 121, passim. Guinier never explicitly makes the argument concerning the founders' intent. But the implication of her argument, building from Madisonian representation and "turn taking" to arrangements today, leaves the connection implied. Hovering over her discussion is thus this point: Madison thought the territorial district captured the right kinds of interests; they may have in his day but they do not now. It is the historical part of the implication that I reject.

Madison's own hope was that by obliterating communities of interest within the electoral district, representative government in an extended republic stood a chance of being successful. Properly understood, the first question of constituency definition is not *which* interests ought to be represented; it is, rather, whether interests should be represented at all.

If the congressional district was always too large to define a coherent set of local interests, what justified territory as the way to organize political representation?[64] Perhaps territorial districts were expected to facilitate attachment to the new, national system. Maybe the founders expected them to better protect property rights in land. Perhaps territorial constituencies were preferable because they enabled voters to consent to their own constituencies: If you did not like how you were being represented, territorial districts allowed the possibility for exit. As I argue throughout Part II, the evidence fails to support any of these reasons.

In Chapter 6, I offer evidence that territorial districts were justified for national political representation because they enabled certain democratic practices, including citizen deliberation, personal communal accountability *between constituents*, and the expectation that voting days would continue to be tangible moments of consent. This then forms an extended version of what Karlan suggested: that territorial districts were logistically useful.

Emphasizing the founders' institutional approach to the collective good that attempts to minimize particularity within a legislature is not a theory of representation that sits well with advocates for PR. Indeed, contemporary districting arguments in the United States assume exactly the opposite than had the founding generation: Electoral districts advocates argue that districts should be drawn around interests that are homogeneous in certain ways so that those interests may be replicated in Congress. The familiar case over the last four decades in the United States involves creating black and Hispanic majority districts.[65] But proponents of proportional or group representation do not have to use original intent as their interpretive filter; indeed, I suspect many reformers explicitly reject original intent as the proper view of constitutional interpretation. And I agree: What the founding generation thought of territorial constituencies is not a particularly good reason for our endorsing their use today. Advocates should thus abandon historical reasoning to bolster their position because their

---

[64] I consider the possibility that this is an anachronistic question, and lay out the method of my analysis in Chapter 3.

[65] Importantly, many arguments for creating "minority-majority" districts hinge on electoral outcomes, and not, strictly speaking, on the representation of interests. Thus, the concern is to increase minority *representatives* within a legislative body whether or not there are neatly defined "black" issues. For some examples see, Mansbridge, "Should Blacks Represent Blacks . . . "; Anne Phillips, *The Politics of Presence* (New York: Oxford University Press, 1995); Young, *Justice and the Politics of Difference*. The descriptive makeup of a legislative body is an analytically separate issue from creating districts around homogenous interests, and there are other ways to achieve descriptive diversity within the legislature without homogenizing interests within a constituency. *Parité* in France is an excellent example of this.

proposals would, in fact, be at odds with the historical foundation of the United States.

1.4 EXCLUSION AND DELIBERATIVE DIVERSITY

In section 1.1, I argued that political theorists have been ambivalent about the exclusion of political representation. One way to deal with this exclusion has been to increase the descriptive similarity between the legislature and the people it excludes. Descriptive representation has been justified for two rather different reasons. First, increasing the descriptive similarity of the legislature ensures that the legislature has the relevant "hard knowledge" it needs to operate well. By "hard knowledge," I mean anything that could be written down on paper. In this case, descriptive representation is useful because it ensures that the legislature has relevant information it needs for making good decisions about the nation's welfare. Second, increasing descriptive representation can ensure the legislature has the "soft knowledge" it needs to operate well. By "soft knowledge," I mean something more akin to "ways of processing information," often described as a particular group's "perspective." In this case, descriptive representation is purportedly useful because it ensures that the legislature has the relevant set of perspectives and hears the right kinds of voices it needs for making good decisions about the nation's welfare.

The interest in descriptive representation is particularly strong among deliberative democrats, because of the effects of descriptive representation on deliberation within the legislature. Unlike an interest-based account of representation, descriptive representation for either "hard-knowledge" or "soft-knowledge" reasons is premised on the influence that this increased information, perspective, and voice will have on deliberation within the legislature. There remains, of course, the critical question, which information, voice, and perspective should be descriptively mirrored in the legislature? But the notion that there should be diversity or heterogeneity of views is broadly endorsed as a condition of good deliberation.[66]

Although I am sympathetic to this position, I offer no defense of it here, nor will I even offer an argument for why I think some groups ought to have voice within the legislature. I want to focus instead on a more immediate paradox that arises in implementing deliberative diversity in the legislature: A more inclusive or heterogeneous legislature is often achieved at the cost of greater homogeneity within the electoral constituency. For example, securing the election of African Americans to the U.S. Congress has meant forming "majority-minority" districts – that is, districts that are homogeneous enough to secure a representative who purportedly shares a particular homogeneous characteristic. The

---

[66] See James, *Deliberative Democracy*, for the best analysis to date of the relationship between the ideals of democratic deliberation and electoral institutions. For other important treatments of the role of diversity as a deliberative aim, see Gutmann and Thompson, *Democracy and Disagreement*; Mansbridge "Should Blacks Represent Blacks . . ."; Phillips, *The Politics of Presence*.

point applies with equal force to proportional plans: To ensure that political parties have a voice in their legislatures, proportional representation effectively creates perfectly homogeneous electoral constituencies by pooling votes for a particular candidate or party.[67]

Consider the paradox this creates for those who support deliberative diversity. If constituencies are defined by their members' similarity of voice (if African American representatives, for example, come from predominantly African American districts), then we promote diversity of voice within a representative body by denying it within the constituency. The demand that representative bodies should be diverse thus subordinates the deliberative diversity *within* a constituency to that of the legislature. Yet, if good or proper deliberation requires that all voices are heard, then it would appear that we have to choose between diversity within the legislature and diversity among their electoral constituents. Or, in terms of exclusion, the question becomes, do we exclude "voice" from the representative body itself, or from the constituent groups who select their representatives?

The problem illustrates how attending to constituency definition may permit more innovative institutional designs. The makeup of legislatures is determined only in part by the definition of constituency, but also by the set of rules that govern who can run for election and who can serve as a candidate. These rules are, and always have been, conceptually distinct from the underlying constituency. They could specify how the legislature should look without changing any feature of the underlying definitions of "constituency."

The American system has *always* stipulated what its legislature would look like in certain ways that have little to do with the underlying constituency. Candidates for the House of Representatives must be at least twenty-five years old and citizens of the United States for at least seven years. Indeed, the Constitution only requires members of the House be members of the state from which they were elected; the provision that requires candidates to be a resident of their home district is a matter of state law. There is no reason that such requirements might not stipulate a far more diverse set of representatives simply through attention to qualifications for office. So there are then, two ways of ensuring a diverse legislature: We can homogenize electoral constituencies (black districts elect black representatives), or we could alter qualifications for certain seats (40 percent may be held by blacks, no matter what their underlying constituency looks like).

I will explore some of these possibilities in more detail in Chapter 9. I discount the problem that an individual who represents a group that looks more diverse than he is (such as a black man representing a multiracial constituency) may be limited in what views he can subsequently express once in the legislature.[68] Instead, this is an important limitation both to the views that can be

---

[67] "Closed Roll" systems like that used to secure Maori representation in New Zealand have a similar dynamic. See James, *Deliberative Democracy*, p. 162.

[68] See James, *Deliberative Democracy*, pp. 162–4, for a similar discussion.

legitimately expressed and to the votes that can be justified, and also limits the marginalization of any particular representative. As I will discuss, the fear that a loss of minority districts will decrease minority influence in the legislature because minority representatives will not be able to vote as they talk ignores the emerging data that legislatures with highly homogeneous districts are paradoxically far more likely to pass legislation at odds with the purported interests of those minorities for whom those districts were created.

These ideas essentially show how the arguments of Anne Phillips might be institutionalized in a way that does not depend on further homogenization of the electoral constituency.[69] And they are currently being employed in Europe and Latin America in the form of gender quota laws that require parties to field women as a significant percentage of their candidates for office.[70] The principle of restricting candidates to look like or be like a particular kind is not new. But the ability to use that, rather than increasing the homogeneity of the underlying constituency, offers an alternative to achieve diversity within the legislature while maintaining it within the electoral constituency, a possibility not fully recognizable until the concept of constituency itself emerges as a separate institution for analysis.

[69] See Phillips, *The Politics of Presence.*
[70] Lisa Baldez, "Elected Bodies: The Gender Quota Law for Legislative Candidates in Mexico," *Legislative Studies Quarterly*, 29, May 2004: 231–58.

2

The Concept of Constituency

> The second section of the Estates encompasses the *changing* element in *civil* society, which can play its part only by means of *deputies*; the external reason for this is the sheer number of its members, but the essential reason lies in the nature of its determination and activity. In so far as these deputies are elected by civil society, it is immediately evident that, in electing them, society acts *as what it is*. That is, it is not split up into individual atomic units which are merely assembled for a moment to perform a single temporary act and have no further cohesion; on the contrary, it is articulated into its associations, communities and corporations which, although they are already in being, acquire in this way a political connotation.
>
> G. W. F. Hegel[1]

Imagine that Alex, a French citizen, came to observe an election in the United States. Upon her return home, she wrote the following description of what she saw:

> Democracy in America is a system in which its adult members step into booths or other private rooms to register their opinions of who should lead them. This is the meaning of democracy: Individuals can punch chads, pull levers, and darken ovals to select their leadership.

Alex is not exactly mistaken, but she has missed the point. Voting is not the *meaning* of democracy, it is its central mechanism. Political theorists would want Alex to talk about political equality and look deeper at the fact that every vote is of equal value (in theory if not in practice). Formal theorists would want Alex to describe how votes are counted because elections will produce very different results depending upon which kind of rule is used to aggregate votes. Even the proverbial "man on the street" might appeal to fundamental rights or freedoms if asked what the meaning of a liberal democracy is. In any

[1] G. W. F. Hegel, *Philosophy of Right*, Section 308, ed. Allen Wood (New York: Cambridge University Press, 1991), pp. 346–7.

case, no one seriously thinks that voting booths and chads are the *meaning* of democracy; as I said, they are its mechanisms.

The concept of constituency has been conceived of virtually at the level of the voting booth, a necessary but not very interesting mechanism of democracy. Voting rights, political representation, checks and balances, freedoms of speech and association – these are the familiar timbers from which liberal democracy is built. Built on a foundation of political equality, the structure seems to have no place for the concept of constituency. At the American founding, constituency was treated as a tool for other purposes of deliberation and participation. Theoretical and empirical accounts of democracy relegate the concept to a similar status, if it is noticed at all. But the concept of constituency is not a tool; it is not even a group of tools. More accurately, the concept of constituency is part of the blueprint from which the structure is built. Take those same timbers but use a different blueprint and the structure will look radically different and produce different outcomes. More importantly, it stands to reflect and promote a litany of normative values that may or may not be commensurate with each other: from citizen development and rights protections, to the promotion or neutralization of group interests. This chapter is about that blueprint and its resulting importance in constructing legitimate forms of government.

This chapter offers a more rigorous and sustained account of the concept of constituency that separates it from the act of voting and develops its conceptual and normative contours. These contours will enable more formal and sustained comparisons between different kinds of plans, showing how they could be compared and, again, emphasizing the centrality of constituency to democratic theory. The analysis also provides an additional tool for normative and comparative study of democracy, political representation, and electoral systems in particular. After a brief review and discussion of the concept as it has been treated by political theorists in section 2.1, I define the term in section 2.2, limiting its scope to electoral politics. In section 2.3, I illustrate variations of electoral constituencies and develop its analytic structure in section 2.4. I conclude the chapter in section 2.5 by considering ten normative arguments that have been made for various constituency definitions. In all, this chapter prepares us for the historical and normative analysis with which the rest of the book deals.

2.1 THE CONCEPT OF CONSTITUENCY IN POLITICAL THEORY

The concept of constituency has been discussed previously, but always wedded – welded really – to other normative and analytical considerations. Hegel's argument that "association communities and corporations" should form electoral constituencies is an argument about the proper definition of constituencies.[2] John Stuart Mill's advocacy of Thomas Hare's proposal for

---

[2] In a good illustration of how an argument of constituency is collapsed with an argument about voting, John Rawls classifies Hegel's argument as consistent with a decent hierarchical society: John Rawls, *The Law of Peoples* (Cambridge, MA: Harvard University Press, 1999), p. 73, ibid., n. 13.

proportional representation was, to use Anne Phillips' phrase, a politics of ideas and justified the claim that constituencies should be properly defined by ideas, interests, and the likelihood of electing the best and the brightest.[3] And Walter Bagehot's derision of Hare's plan as "voluntary constituencies" only hinted at the multidimensionality of constituencies: If constituencies could be voluntarily (or involuntarily) defined, they could also be sustained for longer or shorter periods and be more or less heterogeneous around a certain feature.[4] While parts of "constituency" have been noticed before, they have not been developed with the same complexity as other democratic institutions have.[5]

The concept of constituency as a subject of analysis has received only passing treatment by political theorists. John Locke, John C. Calhoun, and Mill, for example, take up particular dynamics of the electoral constituency without developing them in any great detail. Locke supported the King's prerogative power to redraw territorial districts in order to maintain rough population equality between them. Calhoun claimed that because states were sovereign political communities, they should form electoral constituencies for the national legislature with veto power over legislation that affected them (a logic that other supporters of group rights endorse to varying degrees). And Mill endorsed Thomas Hare's proposals for "voluntary constituencies," electoral constituencies in which voters would join at the moment they cast their vote for a candidate (or party). It was a proposal eloquently rejected by Bagehot.[6]

Among the more insightful theoretical analyses of the electoral constituency is James Madison's *Federalist 10*. No matter how one interprets the argument in that essay, the electoral constituency plays a central role. Under the "republican reading," Madison had hoped that the largeness of the electoral constituency would, among other things, prevent particular local interests from being represented within the legislature. The size of the constituency and the difficulty of any one particular interest dominating *within* the constituency

---

[3] Anne Phillips, *The Politics of Presence* (New York: Oxford University Press, 1995).

[4] Walter Bagehot, *The English Constitution* (Ithaca, NY: Cornell University Press, 1966 [1867]).

[5] Most of the literature on voting systems and electoral designs often ignores questions of how constituencies are defined, or treats them quickly in passing. Michael Balinsky and H. Peyton Young, for example, do not mention them, and Richard S. Katz's terrific treatment of elections gives them two pages of discussion (although it is a very good discussion). Michael L. Balinski and H. Peyton Young, *Fair Representation: Meeting the Ideal of One Man, One Vote* (Washington, DC: Brookings Institution Press, 2001); Richard S. Katz, *Democracy and Elections* (New York: Oxford University Press, 1997), pp. 110–11. For other recent examples see Gary W. Cox, *Making Votes Count* (New York: Cambridge University Press, 1997); Arend Lijphart and Bernard Groffman, *Choosing an Electoral System: Issues and Alternatives* (New York: Praeger, 1994); Andrew Reeve and Alan Ware, *Electoral Systems: A Comparative and Theoretical Introduction* (New York: Routledge, 1992).

[6] Bagehot, *The English Constitution*; John C. Calhoun, "A Disquisition on Government," in *Union and Liberty: The Political Philosophy of John C. Calhoun*, ed. Ross M. Lence (Indianapolis, IN: Liberty Press, 1992), pp. 3–78; John Locke, "Second Treatise of Government," in *Two Treatises of Government*, ed. Peter Laslett, Cambridge Texts in the History of Political Thought (Cambridge, UK: Cambridge University Press); John Stuart Mill, *Considerations on Representative Government* (Amherst, NY: Prometheus, 1991 [1861]).

also would increase the probability of representatives acting *as if* they cared about the public good. Even using the "pluralist reading" of *Federalist 10* – a reading that sees Madison as a protopluralist, solving the problem of factions through representatives as advocates for the particular interests of their constituents – the electoral constituency forms an important if different role, defining the relevant community of interest.[7]

Among contemporary political theorists, Nancy Schwartz and Melissa Williams have taken up the most comprehensive discussion of constituency definition thus far.[8] Both have advanced the discussion considerably, albeit for different reasons than our present purposes here. I will take each in turn to illustrate the work that has so far been done, and then offer my own account in the remainder of this chapter.

In *The Blue Guitar*, Schwartz argues that territorial constituencies are beneficial because they promote face-to-face citizen contact necessary for citizen development. Consider her description of the benefits of territorial districts:

It will be the argument of this book that political representation structured on local geographic districts provides suitable arenas in which the ideal of the citizen might be approximated. Under conditions where the modern citizen is also a person who labors and works, political representation provides a multi-tiered system that makes public action possible. In the local district, people interact at meetings as individual citizens seeing each other face-to-face as unique characters. Through their local meetings, of assemblies or political parties or single-issue groups, the same people come to know each other over time, and then the media help spread that local knowledge to interested onlookers. People's characters develop from personhood to citizenship as individuals enact, enrich, and understand the rules of the political game.... In competing among friends and neighbors to choose one candidate, and then one representative, the people as citizens develop standards of judgment about public character as much as explicit

---

[7] I take up some of these issues in more dept in Chapter 5. The tradition of reading Madison as a "pluralist" has its origins with Charles Beard at the turn of the twentieth century, and it was amplified and developed by Robert Dahl in the 1950s. Charles A. Beard, *An Economic Interpretation of the Constitution of the United States* (New York: Macmillan, 1944 [1913]); Robert A. Dahl, *A Preface to Democratic Theory* (Chicago: University of Chicago Press, 1956). The position appears to be a misreading of Madison's writing and is unsupported by the historical record more generally. Despite this, many political scientists appear to favor, or perhaps simply report, the pluralist reading of Dahl, without much textual support. For two examples, see Hanna Fenichel Pitkin, *The Concept of Representation* (Berkeley, CA: University of California Press, 1967), p. 195; Melissa S. Williams, *Voice, Trust, and Memory* (Princeton, NJ: Princeton University Press, 1998), p. 39. For an excellent history of the interpretation of *Federalist 10* through midcentury, see Douglass Adair, "The Tenth Federalist Revisited," in *Fame and the Founding Fathers*, ed. Trevor Colbourn (Indianapolis, IN: Liberty Fund, 1974); Douglass Adair, "'That Politics May Be Reduced to a Science': David Hume, James Madison and the Tenth Federalist," in *Fame and the Founding Fathers*, pp. 132–51. For a balanced contemporary view, see Alan Gibson, "Impartial Representation and the Extended Republic: Towards a Comprehensive and Balanced Reading of the Tenth Federalist Paper," *History of Political Thought*, Vol. 12, no. 2, Summer 1991: 263–304.

[8] Nancy L. Schwartz, *The Blue Guitar: Political Representation and Community* (Chicago: University of Chicago Press); Williams, *Voice, Trust, and Memory*.

criteria of policy. Then, at the next tier of the system, the representatives talk about justice.[9]

Emphasizing the effects of electoral constituencies on constituents, Schwartz's analysis is an innovative departure from the broader political science literature on voting systems that emphasizes the electoral consequences of different voting systems.

The substantive problem with Schwartz's argument is that electoral constituencies in any large nation are much too big to achieve the kinds of citizen benefits she extols. To recall the exclusion of modern democracy, in the United States, for example, electoral constituencies include roughly six hundred thousand individuals. If territorial constituencies are to be defended because they allow people in *close* physical proximity to deliberate, debate, negotiate, and tolerate their fellow citizens as citizens, this defense only goes as far as such deliberation and negotiation is actually possible. Indeed, Schwartz's argument is strongest in support of territorial representation at the city or local level in which a district of a few thousand may over time constitute a real community. But at the national level, the argument that being grouped with six hundred thousand other people facilitates my participation is only true symbolically. I will develop this argument in more detail in Chapter 7. But even if size defeats the purported goals, the benefit of Schwartz's analysis remains in seeing that electoral constituencies may be justified for reasons quite apart from their electoral consequences.

By contrast, Williams offers a more familiar approach to constituency design, arguing for a principle of group representation that first proposes "a set of defensible standards by which to distinguish those attributes of citizens that deserve representation from those that do not," and, second, to argue that constituencies "mediate" the relationship between the represented and their constituents.[10] In doing so, Williams rightly brings into focus the importance of justifying the way that electoral constituencies are defined at a general, theoretical level and in ways that are nuanced and nonessentialist.

Williams however does not fully develop the analytical dimensions of a concept of constituency and this leads to a few important mistakes. Consider her claims that "Individual citizens can only be represented insofar as they have identifiable interests," and that "By identifying a basis for aggregating citizens, however, a system of representation identifies, at least implicitly, communities of interest whose recognition is relevant within the political arena."[11] But a system of representation need not identify any "community of interest" beyond the nation as a whole not even implicitly, even though historically most have. As I argue in Chapter 8, some very basic presumptions of legitimacy lead to a default position against defining electoral constituencies by any kind of "community of interest" other than the nation as a whole. And by focusing on

[9] Schwartz, *The Blue Guitar:* pp. 12–13. See also at 10, 96–8, 102, passim.
[10] Williams, *Voice, Trust, and Memory*, p. 29.
[11] Ibid, p. 25.

communities of interest for representation, the account appears to ignore the other ends for which we might define an electoral constituency, such as, with Schwartz, to foster citizenship development.

Although the substantive disagreements with Schwartz and Williams stand, the broader fact that they did not develop the concept of constituency in a complete way is hardly a fair critique of their work, since it was not their purpose to offer such a comprehensive discussion. Rather, they treated constituencies only as the means by which to understand and achieve their overall arguments – for territorial constituencies in the case of Schwartz, and for group representation of a certain kind for Williams.

The more general point may explain why past theorists have not treated constituency definition conceptually: Institutions are often developed in order to implement and advocate, and advocacy seldom admits fine distinctions.[12] However one reads Madison, his goal was to defeat faction, and the electoral constituency was a mechanism by which this goal might be achieved. Hare and Mill wanted to increase the diversity and quality of the views discussed within the legislature; their "voluntary constituencies" were simply a means to that end. And for contemporary theorists who support some form of group representation, such as Lani Guinier, Will Kymlicka, Jane Mansbridge, Williams, and Iris Young (all for different reasons), the electoral constituency is a *means* of redressing past harms, protecting rights, or advancing interests. The fact that these theorists have not fully conceptualized constituency is not a critique of their projects; however, it does mean that the work is yet to be done.

2.2 CONSTITUENCY DEFINED

The etymology of the term *constituency* reflects the enmeshment in ordinary language of *constituency* with voting. The word comes from the late fifteenth century *constituent*, derived from its Latin root, *stare* (stand): A constituent is someone who "appoints another as agent," presumably "to stand for" the original constituent.[13] In the early eighteenth century, the word became more closely associated with voting per se, and by the middle eighteenth century, *constituent* took on its broader meaning of "an element of a complex whole." *Constituent*, meaning an individual person represented, was well known and used by Anglo-American political theorists of these times, appearing, for example, in *The Federalist* no fewer than fifty-three times. But the word *constituency* denoting a *collection* of individual constituents does not appear in English until the middle nineteenth century.

---

12 A similar point is made throughout Charles R. Beitz, *Political Equality: An Essay in Democratic Theory* (Princeton, NJ: Princeton University Press, 1989) in terms of electoral systems more generally.

13 The definitions in this paragraph are from the Oxford English Dictionary (OED), as is the etymology with additional material from Eric Partridge, *A Short Etymological Dictionary of Modern English* (USA: Greenwich House, 1983). For a similar account see Schwartz, *The Blue Guitar*, pp. 127–8.

The Oxford English Dictionary (OED) defines *constituency* with two different senses:

1) A body of constituents, the body of voters who elect a representative member of a legislative or other public body; in looser use, the whole body of residents in the district or place represented by such a member, or the place or district itself considered in reference to its representation.
2) A body of supporters, customers, subscribers, etc.; = clientele.

These two senses capture the electoral and non-electoral uses of the term. In the context of formal representative institutions, a constituency denotes a group of voters who elect one or more representatives. The first OED definition captures this electoral sense of *constituency*. The second definition captures the looser sense of *constituency*. Here, *constituency* denotes a group of people whose interests are "looked after" by a representative whether or not they could vote for him, as in "that representative's *real* constituents are the oil industry because they give money to her campaign."[14] Similarly, "children are the most important constituents of that representative because he likes to represent those in need."

Maintaining the conceptual distinctions of the OED definition, we can formally conceive of "constituency" in these ways:

Electoral Constituency 1 (EC1):

The group of people who voted for a particular representative (or party).

Electoral Constituency 2 (EC2):

The group of people who are eligible to vote for a particular representative (or party).

Non-electoral Constituency (NEC):

The group of people whose interests a representative (or party) looks after and pursues.

These distinctions are useful for making sense of ordinary language. They define different groups of people, although the first is usually a subset of the second, and both of these can overlap with the third. Consider some examples:

- Mustard votes for White, and White wins. Once elected, however, White ignores the interests of Mustard. Mustard is a constituent of White only in the first two senses (EC1 and EC2) of the term.
- Peacock votes for Plum, who loses to White. Ignoring the interests of his supporters, White pursues the interests of Peacock. Thus, Peacock is a constituent of White in the second and third sense (EC2 and NEC), but not in the first.
- Heston cares only about the protection of gun ownership but is ineligible to vote for White. White consistently votes to uphold the right to gun

---

[14] See Pitkin, *The Concept of Representation*, p. 115, for a similar point.

ownership. Heston is White's constituent only in the third sense (NEC) of the term.

I leave other permutations to the reader.

The nature and structure of electoral constituencies (both kinds) and non-electoral constituencies are important to considerations of political theory and democracy. Non-electoral constituencies often take the form of interest groups or emerge from voluntary associations. They have been developed by many democratic theorists, from Tocqueville through Dahl, to say nothing of the expansive empirical literature on interest group politics.[15] But, to repeat the previous point, when political theorists treat electoral constituencies, they generally treat them as a means through which voters elect representatives.

In what follows, I describe the theoretical complexity of the *electoral* constituency, the formal, institutionalized organization of citizens for political representation, and the many different dimensions in which it can serve as both an instrumental end for politics, as well as capturing independent normative goals. For the remainder of this book, the term *constituency* thus refers only to electoral constituencies – that is, the group of people who are eligible to vote for a particular representative, representatives, or political party. I focus only on electoral constituencies because of their formal institutional role to structure political representation.[16]

By "constituency definition," I mean:

> Constituency definition $=_{df}$ *the manner by which the state defines groups of citizens for the purpose of electing a political representative(s).*

Because we can define a constituency without selecting a representative, but we cannot elect representatives without somehow defining an electoral constituency, constituency is conceptually prior to voting. However, some voting systems define constituencies at the same moment a person votes, a matter I will develop in the following section.

2.3 EXAMPLES OF CONSTITUENCY VARIATIONS

In the American context, electoral constituencies have almost always been territorially defined. In most nations, electoral constituencies are defined by multiple features, though most of them are defined in part by territory. Territory and

---

[15] Dahl, *A Preface to Democratic Theory*; Robert Dahl, *Polyarchy: Participation and Opposition* (Chelsea, MI: Yale University Press, 1971).

[16] It is the formality of these structures that I care about, rather than their effects. It is thus possible, even likely, that the "oil interests" constitute a nonformal constituency with far more effective *power* over legislative outcomes than any electoral constituency. The relationship between electoral and non-electoral constituencies is important for considerations of legitimacy and justice in the structure of institutions. For example, when free association and full equality of participation allow non-electoral constituencies their full potency as an institution, there may be important consequences for how we ought to arrange electoral constituencies. This important interaction between electoral and non-electoral constituencies is beyond the scope of this work.

residency need not define electoral constituencies. One alternative, pursued in the United States in the early part of the twentieth century, is a corporatist scheme by which citizens are divided into professional groups. "District 5" might refer to "lawyers or "mechanics" or some other group. Constituencies might be defined simply as a *consequence* of voting: In systems of proportional representation, a constituency is usually taken to be that group of voters who voted for the party or candidate. So the constituents of the Labor Party in Israel are just those who voted for the party.[17] As I will describe in Chapter 5, electoral constituencies for the United States Senate are only incidentally "territorially" defined. More importantly, they represent "political communities" (that is, the states) that *happen* to be territorially defined.

Let me describe a sample of nonterritorial ways that we might define a constituency[18]:

- *Votes cast.* In proportional representation, voters choose the constituency to which they belong based on the party (or candidate) for which they voted. The voting system for the Knesset, Israel's legislature, is an example of this. Each voter gets one vote for a party, and each party gets the same proportion of seats as the proportion of votes they receive as long as they receive votes over a minimal threshold. Thus, if the Labor Party receives 50 percent of the vote, it receives 50 percent of seats in the Knesset. In other systems, PR operates in large territorial districts within the state. In Ireland, for example, voters use a single transferable vote to elect up to five candidates from each district. In such districts, constituencies are first defined by territory and then by the votes cast.
- *Class.* Income or social class can define electoral constituencies. The estate system in France between the thirteenth and eighteenth centuries used such a scheme. The Estates-General system divided the nation into three classes: the nobility, the clergy, and the bourgeois or commons. The system ended when the commons wished to change the axis of representation from these classes to equal population groups within each class. Such a move would have substantially reduced the power of the clergy and nobility that had retained the majority in parliament. The clamor for change to a different method of constituency definition contributed to the outbreak of the French

---

[17] More accurately, the constituency consists of those who voted for the party or who are likely to vote for the party in the next election. I develop this with greater precision later in this section. See also, Richard F. Fenno, Jr., *Home Style: House Members in Their Districts* (USA: HarperCollins, 1978), pp. 1–30.

[18] The comparative data are from Arend Lijphart, *Electoral Systems and Party Systems: A Study of Twenty-Seven Democracies, 1945–1990* (New York: Oxford University Press, 1994); Andrew Reynolds, Ben Reilly, et al., *The International IDEA Handbook of Electoral System Design* (Stockholm: International Institute for Democracy and Electoral Assistance, 1997). The list is meant to be illustrative of some other ways we could define electoral constituencies. See also a related discussion in Thomas Pogge, "Self-Constituting Constituencies to Enhance Freedom, Equality, and Participation in Democratic Procedures," *Theoria*, June 2002: 26–54; Reeve and Ware, *Electoral Systems*, pp. 114–22.

Revolution. Functional representation, in which constituencies are defined by the "social-vocational purpose which each individual fulfills" is a more modern version.[19]

- *Religion or ethnicity*. Constituencies may be defined by the religious or ethnic identity of their members. A contemporary example of this can be found in Bosnia-Herzegovina. Local (non-electoral) representative bodies often use this kind of constituency definition. For example, the Hyde Park–Kenwood interfaith council in Chicago divides its constituents by their faith organization, securing one seat for a representative from each local religious organization.[20]

- *Descriptive traits*. Groups into which individuals have some reasonable control in gaining membership can define constituencies. This includes but is not limited to profession and avocation, and may include economic class. Faculty committees in academic departments are often structured this way. The committee is made up of one representative of each subdiscipline, for example, a comparativist, a theorist, a methodologist, and an internationalist, each receiving equal votes on the committee.

- *Involuntary class*. Representative units are determined by membership in a class into which individuals have little reasonable control in gaining membership. This includes, but is not limited to, race, gender, and arguably sexual orientation. It may also include economic and social class. Examples include some affirmative action programs formed to maximize racial and gender diversity.

These represent some of the dimensions by which nations (and organizations) define electoral constituencies. They are not exclusive categories and may be used in tandem with each other. Imagine, for example, that a corporatist framework is used and lawyers, mechanics, and teachers elect their own representatives. Imagine also that we want to create constituencies of equal population. Since these groups are of very different sizes, second-order definitions will be needed to achieve population equality. We could subdivide these professional groups territorially, so all teachers who lived or worked "west of the Mississippi" would elect one representative and all those who lived or worked "east of the Mississippi" would cast a vote for a second. In this case, the electoral constituency would be defined along two dimensions: profession and residency. The U.S. House of Representatives in fact uses two dimensions, although each is territorially bound. Because of the compromise at the Constitutional Convention of 1787, constituencies for representation in the House are first defined by states – that is, by political community.

---

[19] Fritz Nova, *Functional Representation: An Appeal to Supplement Political Representation* (Dubuque, IA: W. C. Brown, 1950), p. 1.

[20] This last example may constitute a third kind of constituency – neither electoral, but still formal, since there is a representative of a constituency even though no election has taken place.

Secondarily, states are subdivided (by the state legislatures) into residential districts.[21]

With the exception of the United States Senate and the Israeli Knesset, few polities define constituencies on only one dimension (political community and votes, respectively). Rather, it is through the combination of these forms that more complex and common electoral constituencies are formed. The U.S. House of Representatives and the local proportional representation districts of Germany and South Africa define constituencies along two dimensions, as do many other countries. Sometimes two single-tiered systems are used side by side rather than being nested. Germany, for example, defines constituencies for half of its parliament from single-member, territorial districts, and the other half by votes in a national proportional system. South Africa, as a final example of a mixed system, defines half of its constituencies by votes in a local proportional system and the other half by votes in a national proportional system.

Electoral constituencies can vary along many dimensions. The reasons a polity might want to choose one method over another similarly differ widely, often for reasons that are very context specific. The following sections take up some of the analytical (section 2.4) and normative (section 2.5) distinctions that can contribute to institutional design.

2.4 THREE DIMENSIONS OF CONSTITUENCY: HOMOGENEITY, STABILITY, AND VOLUNTARINESS

Returning to our original definition, electoral constituencies are minimally groups of citizens who select representative(s) according to particular electoral rules (such as "majority rule," or "proportional vote," or something else entirely). The definition as it stands collapses three analytical distinctions of homogeneity, stability, and voluntariness that will figure significantly in our normative assessment of electoral constituencies later in this book.[22]

---

[21] In the early American republic many states sent multimember, statewide delegations, and did not divide their citizens into districts for representation in Congress. See Chapters 3 through 6.

[22] See Chapter 8. These three dimensions are familiar from some social choice literature, but have not been applied directly to the concept of electoral constituencies. There is some similarity worth noting in the work of Richard Fenno, Melissa Williams, and Thomas Pogge. Fenno's interest focused on the perceptions of Congressional representatives toward their constituencies. See Fenno, *Home Style*, pp. 1–30. By contrast, I am interested in developing an analytical apparatus that will work regardless of the particular electoral system, and independent of the perceptions of a candidate. There is also some similarity to Williams' account of social groupings in which she develops the dimensions of "voluntary," "dichotomous," and "shifting." Williams, *Voice, Trust, and Memory*, pp. 54–5. In Williams' case these non-electoral structures influence a normative argument about fair political representation and thus have different purposes and implications than our present concerns. Finally, Pogge's three substantive dimensions of an electoral constituency are predictive of the kinds of variation that might arise were voters freely able to define their own constituencies. His dimensions are less useful to the present account both because they describe substantive rather than analytical dimensions (such as "topics/agenda") and because they seem to me implausible. For example, though it is possible, it does not seem likely that a group of voters will voluntarily associate along a "topic" line and still have "diverse

Homogeneity

First, we can distinguish constituency definitions by how homogeneous (or heterogeneous) their resulting constituencies are. By "homogeneity," I mean the degree to which members of an electoral constituency share some similar feature. Electoral constituencies under proportional representation (PR) systems are usually perfectly homogeneous around political ideology or point of view because the constituency is defined at the moment a vote is cast, and votes are a rough proxy for a political point of view.[23] A more heterogeneous (that is, nonhomogeneous) constituency is one in which its members are more diverse along a particular dimension. A territorial constituency that contains equal numbers of liberal democrats, conservative republicans, and independent libertarians would be an example of a constituency heterogeneous around political party.

Homogeneity is a matter of tendency and degree. To the extent that a vote is in fact a reasonable proxy for a political point of view, defining constituencies by votes tends to create homogeneous constituencies. If voters vote strategically or insincerely, the level of homogeneity will probably decline.[24] By contrast, national territorial constituencies will tend to be more politically heterogeneous because within a very large territorial district, there can be a good deal of political diversity. When residency patterns *are* indicators of political points of view, territorial districts will tend to be more homogeneous than under other circumstances. This can occur when economic and social factors determine where groups of citizens live, or when authorities define district lines around smaller neighborhoods that are reliable proxies of political points of view (also known as gerrymandering). Homogeneity will be important in normative arguments about deliberative diversity of the legislature, an argument I began in section 1.4 and will continue in Chapter 8.

Stability

A second dimension we should consider is the stability or permanence of constituency membership. Stability describes the frequency with which membership in a constituency changes between elections. A completely stable or permanent constituency is one in which its membership does not change between elections. A completely unstable constituency is one whose membership completely

---

and perhaps conflicting views." To use his example, it seems almost certain to me that a voter who chooses to be defined by "foreign policy" as a topic will have some political agenda, caring greatly if his fellow constituents are or are not hawks or doves, nation builders or isolationists.

[23] Or, as Dennis Thompson has put it, "Voters in effect form their own districts, and each representative has a unanimous constituency." Dennis Thompson, *Restoring Responsibility: Ethics in Government, Business and Healthcare* (New York: Cambridge University Press, 2005), p. 176. Thompson's discussion there also illustrates the predominant thought that alternatives to territorial districts will increase constituent homogeneity.

[24] If *everyone* votes insincerely, then the voters for any party may be perfectly homogeneous around the point of view that they do not agree with the particular party for whom they cast their vote.

changes between elections. Like homogeneity, stability is a matter of degree: Any particular constituency will fall somewhere between the extremes of completely stable and completely unstable. Territorial constituencies for the U.S. House of Representatives, for example, are somewhat stable: Membership changes because people move, die, become citizens, and come of age, and because every ten years its lines change.[25] By contrast, proportional representation can be more unstable since voters can, for example, vote for Labour this election and the Greens in the next. In practice, though, voters have consistent political preferences and party positions tend not to change that much between elections, so we should expect proportional electoral constituencies to be even more stable than territorial ones.

Because of its importance to authorization and accountability, stability plays a central role in legitimating political representation. For a political representative to be accountable to those whom they represent, they must stand for reelection before the same group of individuals who elected them at the start of their term. In other words, voters who authorize a representative at one elections, should be identical to those who hold the representative accountable for her actions at some future election. We should thus as a default position strongly favor constituencies that are as stable as possible, an argument I will develop in Chapter 8. Stability allows us to distinguish between constituencies in which voters remain the same over time and those in which its members are frequently changing.

Voluntariness

Finally, given the importance of consent to theories of normative legitimacy, I consider the degree to which each kind of constituency definition permits individual choice. "Voluntariness" describes the extent to which a constituency allows entry or exit. In a *completely* voluntary system, constituencies are self-defined – individuals decide how to define themselves for the purpose of electing political representatives. If they want to be represented as plumbers, Haitians, or residents of a city, they can choose to self-define in this way.[26] By contrast, *completely involuntary* constituencies are ones in which citizens are assigned to a constituency without any option of entry or exit. If the state defined

---

[25] See also Thompson, *Restoring Responsibility*, p. 180.

[26] For a very good development of how the voluntary constituency would work, see Pogge, "Self-Constituting Constituencies" Pogge's better term is "self-constituting" rather than "voluntary." I use "voluntary" reluctantly here for two reasons. First, it focuses our attention more clearly on the issue of consent. Second, it is more consistent with the nineteenth century usage in the debate between John Stuart Mill, Thomas Hare, and Walter Bagehot about proportional representation, a debate that focused on the value of individuals defining how they wanted to be represented in politics. On "voluntary constituencies" see Bagehot, *The English Constitution*, pp. 161–70. For an excellent historical treatment of the development of proportional representation in Britain, see Jenifer Hart, *Proportional Representation: Critics of the British Electoral System 1820–1945* (Oxford, UK: Clarendon Press, 1992), Chapter 2, passim. For an accessible description of Hare's plan of single transferable votes, see Mill, *Considerations on Representative Government*, Chapters 7 and 10.

constituencies based on DNA characteristics, for example, this would be perhaps an example of a completely involuntary constituency.

Again, voluntariness will usually be a matter of degree. For example, territorial representation is more involuntary than voluntary because a third party determines district lines. But it is *somewhat* voluntary because people *can* move their residence and thus voluntarily enter or exit a constituency. Similarly, proportional representation is more voluntary than nonproportional systems because it allows voters to choose among various political party options, but it is involuntary to the extent that the range of candidates and parties that voters can choose from are usually well beyond their control. Again, a purely voluntary system would allow voters to group themselves in any manner they wanted and then vote for candidates after grouping themselves.[27]

Two important senses of "voluntary" should be distinguished from one another. First, the way in which I mean it here, is voluntariness with respect to the choice of how to define the electoral constituency itself: To what extent do individuals have the ability to define their own constituencies? Second is a broader sense of voluntariness that reflects whether the mode of constituency definition was properly consensual or not: Did the nation collectively agree to whatever definitions are being used, for example, by placing them in a publicly ratified constitution? In systems with exclusively territorial constituencies, voters can voluntarily (in the first sense) choose to live in a particular constituency. But the choice to be represented by where they live is voluntary in the second sense only to the extent territorial constituencies per se have been publicly endorsed through the legislature. It is only the first sense of voluntariness, an individual's ability to define for herself how she is represented, that I am considering now.

In Chapter 8, I will argue that voluntariness in this first sense is relatively unimportant, and far more important is the second sense of voluntariness: that whatever constituency definition is used should be publicly endorsed. But as an analytical matter, voluntariness of the constituency applies only to the first case: Are electoral constituencies voluntarily defined or not, whether or not a particular level of voluntariness itself is publicly endorsed?

It should now be clear that despite the wide variety of systems of proportional representation, they all share two characteristics: First, they create electoral constituencies at the moment of voting that are perfectly homogeneous around the feature of the party or support for the candidate selected; second, they

[27] The problem of creating equally sized constituencies might appear to get in the way of such voluntary schemes. The more narrowly I want to define myself for constituency definition, the less likely it is that other voters will do the same, and thus that my constituency does not form a full-sized constituency. If "one person, one vote" just means that each constituency is the same *size*, then this does pose a formidable problem. But if instead representatives themselves had weighted votes within the legislature, such that a person representing N constituents had one vote in the legislature, and a person representing $p*N$ constituents had p votes in the legislature, equality of influence would be maintained. For a detailed treatment of this, see Pogge, "Self-Constituting Constituencies."

TABLE 2.1. *Three Dimensions of Constituency*

Dimension	Scale	Explanation and Example
Homogeneity: the degree to which members of an electoral constituency share some relevant feature.	More homogeneous	High percentage of constituency votes for representative: e.g., a proportional system in which every vote defines an electoral constituency.
	Less homogeneous	Lower percentage of constituency votes for representative: e.g., single-member territorial constituencies in which 45% of the constituency is Republican, 43% is Democratic, and 12% is Independent.
Voluntariness: the degree to which citizens can choose for themselves how to be represented.	More voluntary	Entry and exit costs are low: e.g., constituencies formed under PR systems in which votes cast define one's electoral constituency.
	Less voluntary	Entry and exit costs are higher: e.g., constituencies defined by race, religion, or gender.
Stability: the frequency with which membership in a constituency changes between elections	More stable	Membership is fixed from election to election: e.g., territorial systems, and proportional systems in which parties are themselves stable and highly differentiated.
	Less stable	Membership changes from election to election: e.g., a proportional system in which parties are unstable and alter positions between elections.

are more voluntary in that they give voters a wider choice over which parties or candidates to vote for and what electoral constituency they wish to be in. Because of this, I will refer to PR without distinguishing between its many different forms. We should not forget that PR does take these many different forms. But neither should such variation obscure the fact that that all plans of PR lead to homogeneous and more voluntary constituencies by definition.

These three dimensions of homogeneity, stability, and voluntariness specify a range on which any particular constituency plan will fall. We can describe a constituency definition by its tendencies to promote or inhibit these features. A constituency's membership will be more or less homogeneous, more or less stable, and more or less voluntary, as summarized in Table 2.1.

We can now describe in greater clarity how the concept of constituency differs between different electoral systems by specifying its position on each of

TABLE 2.2. *Examples of Constituencies Defined by Their Three Dimensions*

	Membership More Stable		Membership Less Stable	
	High Homogeneity	Low Homogeneity	High Homogeneity	Low Homogeneity
Membership more voluntary.	1. Proportional representation systems with longstanding, highly differentiated, stable parties.	2. Unlikely: highly stable constituencies with low costs of exit are likely to be highly homogeneous.	3. Proportional representation in which candidates or parties do not regularly run for reelection, or in which candidates and parties regularly reconfigure.	4. Proportional representation systems with parties or candidates that are not highly differentiated.
Membership less voluntary.	5. Single-member territorial districts with a high proportion of one party (i.e., 70% Democratic).	6. Single-member territorial districts with an even balance of voters (i.e., 50% Republican).	7. Single-member constituencies defined for this election by residency, the next election by race, the following by party membership, etc.	8. Randomly selected groups whose membership holds a wide range of political views.

these ranges. In Table 2.2, I outline examples of these combinations. Although eight are analytically possible (2^3), one combination is unlikely: a constituency that is more heterogeneous, more voluntarily defined, *and* more stable. Such a combination is unlikely because if membership were stable *and* voluntary, then we would expect it to be more homogeneous. So while there are eight possible variations, in fact only seven will produce outcomes we are likely to see.

2.5 NORMATIVE UNDERPINNINGS OF CONSTITUENCIES

When a state designs its electoral institutions, it does not, of course, argue for or against electoral constituencies on the basis of how close the constituency falls to a particular cell in Table 2.2. Instead, the debate over electoral constituency definitions has arisen out of the greatest political struggles of the modern era, from the French Revolution to more recent struggles for group-based representation in modern democratic governments. These political struggles have focused on normative debates about the nature of political life within a particular context. Furthermore, political theorists have defended particular kinds of electoral constituencies in normative terms for over two hundred years.

James Madison and John Calhoun justified actual institutions (even if their justifications conflicted with each other). James Harrington, John Stuart Mill, and Lani Guinier offered justifications for constituencies that were either utopian,[28] practical policy changes,[29] or some place in between.[30]

In the following section, I will list ten different kinds of normative justifications that representative governments have used to form electoral constituencies in one way or another (see Table 2.3 for a summary). The purpose here is to map constituency definition onto more familiar arguments about politics and legitimate political representation, including those that emerge from group-rights claims, electoral outcomes, and social contract arguments. Importantly, while electoral constituencies help define how representatives are elected, they are seldom justified explicitly for those purposes, as the following is intended to demonstrate.

The ten justifications fall into two separate categories: those that justify constituencies for rights-based reasons, and those that justify constituencies instrumentally, for the ends they intend to bring about. *Rights-based justifications* provide moral arguments in favor of defining constituencies in certain ways without necessarily considering other electoral implications. Examples include districting by racial groups and political subunits because those groups make a principled claim to representation qua groups or because of various rights claims. By contrast, *consequentialist justifications* justify constituency formation as a *means* to some broader or functional end of politics – for example, as a means to elect a representative of a certain race or political party. These two kinds of justifications are not mutually exclusive.

These justifications form essential components of familiar debates about group representation, inclusion, and difference. Kymlicka, for example, describes three distinct kinds of group claims based on "national minorities," "ethnic groups," and "new social movements."[31] These arguments are, among other things, arguments that a particular group has a right to form an electoral constituency. Each of Kymlicka's groups may rest its claim to form a separate constituency on a different combination of the following justifications. For example, a national minority may make a claim to separate constituent status based on "involuntary assimilation," "group protection," and "reparations." An ethnic group might base its claim only on the "group protection" and "community of interest" distinction. And a new social movement (gays, women, the poor, and the disabled) may justify representation on both of these

---

[28] James Harrington, "The Commonwealth of Oceana," in *The Commonwealth of Oceana and A System of Politics*, ed. J. G. A. Pocock, Cambridge Texts in the History of Political Thought (New York: Cambridge University Press, 1992 [1656]).

[29] Lani Guinier, *The Tyranny of the Majority: Fundamental Fairness in Representative Democracy* (New York: Free Press, 1994).

[30] Mill, *Considerations on Representative Government.*

[31] Will Kymlicka, *Multicultural Citizenship* (New York: Oxford University Press, 1996), p. 19. See also Jacob Levy, "Classifying Cultural Rights," in *Nomos XXXIX*, eds. Ian Shapiro and Will Kymlicka (New York: New York University Press, 1997), pp. 43–6.

TABLE 2.3. *Justifications for Constituency Definition*

Justification	Analytical Dimension	Theoretical Development	Historical Cases[a]
1. Social contract between groups	Presumes high homogeneity around the group; all other analytical features possible.	John C. Calhoun	Continental Congress, United States Senate, United Nations.
2. Assimilation into a nation	Presumes high homogeneity around the assimilated group; all other analytical features possible.	Will Kymlicka	Canada.
3. Communities of interest	Presumes high homogeneity around the community of interest; all other analytical features possible.	G. F. Hegel, Anti-Federalists, Robert Dahl, J. S. Mill, Anne Phillips, Abigail Thernstrom, Melissa Williams, Iris Marion Young.	United States, Israel, or any system of robust proportional representation.
4. Reparations	Presumes high homogeneity around the previously harmed group; all other analytical features possible.	Williams	Affirmative-action programs; racial gerrymanders in the United States, 1965-93.
5. Group protection	Presumes high homogeneity and stability around the protected group; all other analytical features possible.	Lani Guinier, Kymlicka, Williams, Young	French Estate system; interfaith councils.
6. Citizen development	Possible under all analytical dimensions.	Federalists, Mill, Nancy Schwartz, Thomas Pogge	American founders' expectations for constituent deliberation.
7. Community development	Presumes more permanent (stable) constituencies to foster development; all other analytical features possible.	Schwartz, Federalists, Pogge	American founders' expectations for constituent deliberation.
8. Increased constituent deliberation	Presumes more permanent (stable) constituencies to foster deliberation; all other analytical features possible.	James Harrington, David Hume, Mill	Publicly held corporations.
9. Electoral effects	Possible under all analytical dimensions.	Guinier, James Madison, Phillips, Williams, Young	Political and racial gerrymandering in the United States; Voting Rights Acts of 1965 and 1982.
10. Incentive effects	Possible under all analytical dimensions.	Madison	The large U.S. Congressional district (in Madison's view).

[a] By "historical cases," I mean that these are cases where this justification reasonably describes the constituency arrangement. I do not mean to imply that the justification was ever articulated, although it often was.

plus "reparations."[32] But the point here is that other groups may appeal to similar or entirely different kinds of normative justification for defining an electoral constituency.[33]

Finally, I note that even though political representation necessitates that the state aggregate citizens into groups, contra Williams, it does not follow that all justifications for electoral constituencies need involve a "community of interest" or have a "correlative theory of groups" in mind, although admittedly most will.[34] But arguments such as those of Schwartz and Madison saw the potential for electoral constituencies to promote citizen capabilities (Schwartz) or defeat the *problems* of homogeneity (Madison), rather than promoting them, at the level of the constituency. As I argue in Chapter 9, there may be good reasons for the state to give up on trying to frame representation in terms of any coherent group at all.

2.5.1 Rights-Based Justifications for Constituencies

When a group claims a right to political representation as a separate group, it may offer a rights-based justification for becoming an electoral constituency. Rights-based justifications answer the question, what moral principles purportedly give groups the right to form a separate electoral constituency within a nation? Although there are a large number of possible rights-based arguments, four have been prevalent in the roughly four centuries of representative government: 1) social contract between preexisting groups; 2) assimilation into a nation; 3) the existence of distinct communities of interest; and 4) reparations for past harms. I will take each in turn.

1. **Social contract between groups.** Groups may claim a right to form an electoral constituency (or multiple constituencies) when a nation is created through a joining of many groups.[35] Here, the fact of this contract purportedly justifies group representation. This argument grounded the

---

[32] In the end, Kymlicka reduces the possible justification for representation for all three groups to communities of interest. Kymlicka, *Multicultural Citizenship*, p. 137.

[33] My primary concern is with the definition of constituencies for national representation. Thus, other questions concerning self-government may be related, and some of the justifications may also serve to justify representation in a national (or multinational) body. As Kymlicka puts it:

A minority's right to self-government would be severely weakened if some external body could unilaterally revise or revoke its powers, without consulting the minority or securing its consent. Hence it would seem to be a corollary of self-government that the national minority be guaranteed representation on any body which can interpret or modify its powers of self government... (Kymlicka, *Multicultural Citizenship*, pp. 32–3).

In this sense, we have to be careful how we characterize "nation" itself, though this is now well beyond the scope of this inquiry.

[34] Williams, *Voice, Trust, and Memory*, pp. 25, 27.

[35] Iris Marion Young has recently rejected this possibility, arguing "there is no constituency prior to the process of representation, no people who form an original unity they then delegate onto the derivative representative." Iris Marion Young, "Deferring Group Representation," in *Ethnicity and Group Rights: Nomos XXXIX*, eds. Ian Shapiro and Will Kymlicka (New York: New

formation of the U.S. Senate and *state* delegations for the House of Representatives (but not individual territorial constituencies within the states). Historically, Calhoun provided the strongest articulation for this kind of constituency,[36] and it continues to form the principled grounds of the states' rights platform in the United States and federalist systems throughout the world. We will see in Chapter 4 that in colonial America and early modern England, territorial constituencies were justified for similar, if not exactly the same, kinds of reasons. This social contract view is also the primary normative justification for nation-state constituency definition within multinational representative organizations such as the United Nations. Thus, this justification applies equally to sovereign and nonsovereign groups within a representative body.[37] Constituencies formed under this justification are likely to be highly homogeneous around preexisting groups – the ones forming the social contract – with other analytical features unspecified.[38]

2. **Assimilation into a nation.** Groups may claim a right to representation on the basis of their preexistence as an indigenous population, where that population comprises "a historical community, more or less institutionally complete, occupying a given territory or homeland, sharing a distinct language and culture."[39] The argument for constituency under this label is limited only to the fact of the distinctiveness of the group; it is not based on the presumed group protections or reparations that might be owed to the group because of an injustice. (See justifications 4 and 5.) Constituencies formed under this justification are likely to be highly

---

York University Press, 1997), p. 359. This may conform to a teleological sense of "priority" (as in Aristotle's comment "the state is by nature clearly prior to the family and to the individual." Aristotle, *The Politics*, ed. Stephen Everson, Cambridge Texts in the History of Political Thought (Cambridge, UK: Cambridge University Press, 1988), p. 4. But it is conceptually and historically imprecise. Conceptually a constituency may be defined "prior" (as in "coming before") representatives are even selected – the nation may be annihilated before elections are held, or it may disband for other reasons before any representation "gets going." Historically, groups have often formed an "original unity they then delegate," as is arguably the case of the European Union Parliament and the United Nations Security Council. As I argue in Chapter 4, the origin of territorial representation in England and the American colonies presupposed the existence of unified local communities. Some of the states of the United States, which form the electoral constituencies of representatives in the US Senate, are another case in point.

36 John C. Calhoun, "A Disquisition on Government," in *Union and Liberty: The Political Philosophy of John C. Calhoun*, ed. Ross M. Lence (Indianapolis, IN: Liberty Press, 1992), pp. 3–77; see also John C. Calhoun, "A Discourse on the Constitution and Government of the United States," in *Union and Liberty*, pp. 79–284. Calhoun's justifications for the constituency were not limited to contract theory but based also on the rights of the groups themselves to be protected. See, e.g., Calhoun, "A Disquisition on Government," p. 23.

37 See also Alan Hamlin and Philip Pettit, "The Normative Analysis of the State: Some Preliminaries," in *The Good Polity: Normative Analysis of the State*, eds. Alan Hamlin and Philip Pettit (Cambridge, MA: Basil Blackwell, 1991), p. 4.

38 Why wouldn't this feature presume voluntariness as well as homogeneity? The social contract is a presumed voluntary choice between groups, but membership in the group itself need not be left up to individuals to decide.

39 Kymlicka, *Multicultural Citizenship*, p. 11.

homogeneous around preexisting groups – the group so assimilated – with other analytical features unspecified.

3. **Communities of interest.** When separate communities of interest are present within a larger body, they may claim a right of defining themselves as an electoral constituency because they believe they form a distinct political interest as a group. This is based on a particular normative view of political representation in which communities of interest should, by right, receive political representation. In early America, the principles of property ownership and population formed the most frequent justifications for constituency definition. Similarly, systems of proportional representation justified the constituency by voluntary association (through elections) into separate interest groups. The French Estates-General system, caste representation in India, and corporatist schemes of representation advocated in the United States during the first part of the twentieth century were all grounded – at least in part – on these systems. To the extent that territorial constituencies are justified, their appeal is often linked to the claim that communities of interest are normally based on residency patterns. Constituencies formed under this justification are likely to be highly homogeneous around preexisting groups – the community of interest – with other analytical features unspecified.

4. **Reparations.** If a subgroup of the polity has been excluded from the political process (or the nation has exacted some other harm upon them), they may claim a right to form a separate electoral constituency as reparation for that harm. Although similar to justification 5 (rights protection) in the next section, the right of group representation is based on compensation for past harms and analytically distinct from the protection from future harms. Some cases of affirmative action exhibit this quality, where harmed groups become the constituency in part (or mostly) as reparations for the past harm.[40] Constituencies formed under this justification are likely to be highly homogeneous around preexisting groups – the group that had been harmed – with other analytical features unspecified.

2.5.2 Consequentialist Justifications

Consequentialist justifications for constituency definition justify defining a constituency in a particular way because of the consequences that definition is designed to promote. The most familiar of these consequentialist justifications is electoral outcomes: When an electoral constituency is defined in a particular

---

[40] Affirmative action shares many similar dimensions to these questions. In any case, affirmative action has been promoted for essentially three related but different reasons: to promote diversity, to compensate for past harms, and to guard against current discrimination. Although guarding against future discrimination was one of the original justifications for the program, reparations are currently the only legally justified reason for adopting affirmative action programs. Increasingly, though, advocates are appealing to the diversity justification. For the temporary nature of the reparations and discrimination justifications, see Kymlicka, *Multicultural Citizenship*, p. 32.

way, it may secure the election of a member of the group around which it is defined. This familiar case is seen in race conscious districting, where territorial districts are drawn around, for example, African American communities for the stated (normative) goal of having more black representatives in Congress. But there are a number of other instrumental reasons to define constituencies in particular ways.

5. **Group protection.** When the nation as a whole contains distinct groups, group representation is sometimes justified by the consequentialist aim of providing protection to that group. Familiar cases in the United States concern blacks, Hispanics, and Jews. Similar justifications underlie self-governing groups within the nation.[41] In these cases, group representation is not the end in itself, but rather is justified based on the expectation that such representation will have the consequence of protecting the group. Constituencies formed under this justification are likely to be highly homogeneous around preexisting groups – the ones needing protection – with other analytical features unspecified.

6. **Citizen development.** It has been argued since Aristotle that politics requires good citizens. Political institutions, from schools to representative bodies, can be arranged to maximize the development of this virtue. Electoral constituencies may also be defined in ways that promote or retard the achievement of this goal. Citizen development forms one of the two main bases for Schwartz's sustained defense of the territorial constituency.[42] Pogge's recent argument in favor of self-constituting constituencies rests in part on their purported value of fostering citizen participation.[43] The purported effects vary from increasing patriotism, increased legitimacy in the system, or the development of good political skills. In eighteenth century America, the process of voting and gathering a group together on a single day in a grand fete was an important instantiation of consent (see Chapter 6). Symbolic effects of constituency formation that accrue from recognition of a particular group's value in society would also be classified as that of citizen development because the symbolic effect is on individuals in the group. Constituencies formed under this justification may take on any analytical type.

7. **Community development.** A corollary to citizen development (and the second part of Schwartz's analysis) is that national political life in general might be strengthened if electoral constituencies are defined in certain ways. This justification is similar to citizen development (justification 6) but differs in that its goal concerns the effect of the electoral constituency on the broader community. Community development is also different from communities of interests (justification 3), because here the concern

---

41 Kymlicka, *Multicultural Citizenship*, pp. 32–3.
42 Schwartz, *The Blue Guitar*.
43 Pogge, "Self-Constituting Constituencies to Enhance Freedom, Equality, and Participation in Democratic Procedures."

is with the effects that constituency definition has upon groups, whereas the communities of interest justification depends on a purported right of groups to receive representation because they have already formed a community of interest. Constituencies justified by their effects on community development usually presume highly stable constituencies, and may vary along the other dimensions.

8. **Increased constituent deliberation.** Recent (and not-so-recent) theorists of deliberative democracy have argued that government should be more participatory and deliberative at all levels of functioning.[44] Under this justification, constituencies would be defined because they tend to promote better deliberation *among* constituents; one value of territorially defined constituencies is that your neighbor is more likely to be a fellow constituent, thus increasing the opportunities for deliberation.[45] Constituencies justified by their ability to increase deliberation usually presume highly stable constituencies and may vary along the other dimensions.

9. **Electoral effects.** Particular constituency definitions are often justified because of their likely electoral effects. For example, African American districts in the United States have been justified in part by the desire to have more black representatives in Congress. Or, as Harrington, Madison, and Mill had hoped, defining constituencies in certain ways might promote the selection of better political representatives. Madison, also hoped that the definition of constituencies might defeat the problems associated with group representation. Constituencies defined for their electoral effects take on any of the analytical types.

10. **Incentive effects.** The definition of constituencies will shape the electoral incentives representatives face at reelection time, and thus will likely shape their behavior in office. This behavior includes but is not limited to the *kinds* of issues for which representatives advocate, deliberate,

---

[44] For a very small sample of the vast literature on deliberative democracy, see Joseph Bessette, *The Mild Voice of Reason: Deliberative Democracy and American National Government* (Chicago: University of Chicago Press, 1994); James Bohman and William Rehg, eds. *Deliberative Democracy: Essays on Reason and Politics* (Cambridge, MA: MIT Press, 1997); Joshua Cohen, "Deliberation and Democratic Legitimacy," in *The Good Polity*, pp. 17–34; John S. Dryzek, *Discursive Democracy* (Cambridge, UK: Cambridge University Press, 1990); James S. Fishkin, *Democracy and Deliberation: New Directions for Democratic Reform* (New Haven, CT: Yale University Press, 1991); Amy Gutmann and Dennis Thompson, *Democracy and Disagreement* (Cambridge, MA: Belknap Press). For a rather innovative decentralized plan of encouraging citizen participation, see John Burnheim, *Is Democracy Possible?* (Los Angeles, CA: University of California Press, 1985).

[45] The goal of fostering good deliberation within a representative assembly should be distinguished from this justification. To the extent that good deliberation within an assembly requires representatives to have certain characteristics (be members of a certain group, be advocates for certain things), this falls under justification 9 – defining constituents with an eye toward electoral outcomes. To the extent that good deliberation requires that representatives have the right kind of incentives, it will fall under justification 10. Justification 8, increased *constituent* deliberation, applies only to deliberation *between constituents*. I am grateful to Joel Westra for clarifying this point.

and support. As I have said, a significant reason a representative supports *local* issues but not, for example, professional ones is because their electoral constituents are territorially defined. Thus, constituencies may be justified based on how they structure these incentives. Although these kinds of effects are most noticeable in homogeneous constituencies where the *kinds* of issues are clear (territory, race, party ideology, and so on), incentive effects can also emerge out of highly heterogeneous constituencies. Arguably, this was Madison's hope in *Federalist 10*: If the electoral constituency contains enough heterogeneity, representatives would be freer to deliberate about the good of all precisely because of the underlying electoral incentives created by highly heterogeneous constituencies. Incentive effects for national deliberation factor into the argument in Chapters 8 and 9. These effects presume that once in office, representatives are responsive to their constituents' needs. Electoral constituencies justified by their incentive effects may take on any of the analytical types.

These ten justifications (see Table 2.3) are not mutually exclusive; perhaps African Americans in the United States *should* form their own electoral constituencies because they form a distinct community of interest (justification 3), to protect that community from harm (justification 5) *and* to guarantee the electoral success of black candidates (justification 9). Each of these justifications, however, remains analytically distinct.

As stated, these ten justifications are merely descriptions of plausible and historical justifications for electoral constituencies; I have offered no arguments yet for or against them. Are any of these normative justifications compelling for a polity? The answer, of course, depends on the nation, its history, and underlying social facts. A nation such as India, for example, might have a compelling argument to structure electoral constituencies on the basis of group protections (specifically religious groups), whereas in Iceland this argument might be less persuasive. The analysis of this was meant only to clear the ground, to delineate the concept of constituency, and to demonstrate the complexity of justifications found in familiar arguments from political theory onto the concept's contours.

How should a nation define its electoral constituency? In the end, the answer to that question depends greatly on the context. But whatever the context, minimal considerations of legitimacy create a strong default position in favor of heterogeneous, stable, and nonvoluntary constituencies, from which deviations must be justified. I will take up that argument in the third part of this book. But before we get there, I take up the historical case of the United States. Over the next four chapters, I illustrate how context mattered, and in particular how the very longstanding practice of territorial constituencies got started in the place of their longest continual use: for representation in the U.S. House of Representatives.

PART II

HISTORICAL JUSTIFICATIONS

*On the Origins of Territorial Constituencies
in the United States*

3

Justifications and the Use of History

3.1 SILENCE OF THE LAND

On March 17, 1999, Representative Melvin Watt (D-NC) introduced House bill 1173.[1] "The States' Choice of Voting Systems Act (VSA)" stipulated that:

1) there may be established by law a number of districts equal to the number of the representatives into which such State is so entitled and representatives may be elected only from single member districts so established, or

2) such State may establish a number of districts for election of Representatives that is less than the number of Representatives to which the state is entitled and Representatives may be elected from single member districts, multi member districts, or a combination of single-member and multi-member districts if that state uses a system that meets the constitutional standard that each voter should have equal voting power and does not violate the Voting Rights Act of 1965 (42 U.S.C. 1973 et seq.).[2]

In plain language, the bill would have allowed states to use a wide variety of electoral systems to elect representatives to the House.[3] The VSA would have returned to the states their authority over elections where it had been in the period just after the founding of the United States. Article 1, Section 4 of the U.S. Constitution establishes that each state has the right to choose its own electoral system provided that "Congress may at any time by Law make or alter such Regulations...." Congress *has* acted a number of times, most recently in reestablishing single-member, territorial districts in 1967.[4]

---

[1] HR 1173, 106th Congress, 1st Session.

[2] Ibid.

[3] HR 1173 failed to pass the 106th Congress. In March 2001, Representative Cynthia McKinney (D-GA) introduced a similar bill (HR 1189, 107th Congress, 1st Session) entitled the Voters' Choice Act. It also failed to pass.

[4] Public Law (PL) 90–196. It was not the first law of its kind, but made uniform the practice of single-member districts that has been the norm for House elections since the middle nineteenth century. The most important exceptions to single-member districts came during the fifty

In hearings on the bill before the House Judiciary Committee in September 1999, supporters decried the irrelevance of territory to representation in contemporary society, implying or asserting that the original function of the territorial district was to represent distinctive communities of interest. As Theodore S. Arrington testified, "Single-member district systems may be less reliable [than in an earlier period] in [translating votes to seats] because of the increase in diversity within this country and the decrease in geographically defined communities of interest."[5] Arrington's assumption was that, at the founding, territorial districts were originally less diverse ("more homogeneous" in the terms I developed in Chapter 2) and intended to represent defined communities of interest.[6]

The VSA would have allowed states to increase the size of their territorial districts, but the territoriality of the district itself would have remained secure, even under the provisions of paragraph 2. Further, the historical record does not support the assertion that territorial districts were coterminous with communities of interest at the founding. In short, territorial districting in the United States is such a habit of mind that it is not seriously challenged in a bill that would have allowed widespread experimentation of electoral law on the state level, and it was based on historical claims that are not true.

Why are U.S. congressional districts (electoral constituencies) defined territorially? Where did they come from? The question of origins is important because of the recent debate about electoral systems and more prominently in the districting debates that have raged in the United States over the last forty years. With the Supreme Court's decision to hear districting cases in 1962, territorial districting became a battleground of political controversy and activism.[7]

---

years after the founding when states experimented with electoral systems. See Andrew Hacker, *Congressional Districting: The Issue of Equal Representation* (Washington, DC: Brookings Institution Press, 1963), pp. 40–2; Rosemarie Zagarri, *The Politics of Size: Representation in the United States 1776–1850* (Ithaca, NY, and London: Cornell University Press, 1987), pp. 105–24.

[5] Theodore S. Arrington, "One Page Summary of Testimony," Subcommittee on the Constitution, Committee on the Judiciary, United States House of Representatives, 23 September 1999. Copied from http://www.house.gov/judiciary/arrio923.htm. A complete record of the testimony appears at http://www.house.gov/judiciary/con0923.htm.

[6] See section 1.3.2.

[7] *Baker v. Carr* began the "reapportionment revolution" in 1962 by overturning the Court's finding in *Colegrove v. Green* that such cases concerned "political questions" and thus were not for the court to decide. *Colegrove v. Green*, 328 U.S. 549 (1946); *Baker v. Carr*, 369 U.S. 186 (1962). The "one-person, one-vote" standard was only later applied in *Reynolds v. Sims*, 377 U.S. 533 (1964). The districting question has been controversial since just after the founding of the United States. But the recent wave of controversy was begun first by the Supreme Court's insistence on strict equality among districts and then with the enforcement of the Voting Rights Act (VRA) of 1965 and its extension through the 1970s and in 1982. The literature on the districting cases and the VRA is now voluminous. For a good history of the early cases, see Robert G. Dixon, Jr., *Democratic Representation: Reapportionment in Law and Politics* (New York: Oxford University Press, 1968); see also Richard C. Cortner, *The Apportionment Cases* (Knoxville, TN: University of Tennessee Press, 1970). For the VRA, see Bernard Grofman and Chandler Davidson, eds., *Controversies in Minority Voting: The Voting Rights Act in Perspective*

Absent from those decisions, as from most contemporary considerations of voting reform, is the question of the origins of the territorial district itself.

In this part of the book, I give an historical account of the origins of the territorial district in the United States, and, more importantly from the viewpoint of a philosophical project of reconciliation, an account of its original justification.[8] Beginning with the emergence of representative institutions in thirteenth century England, territorial constituencies were justified by the centrality of local communities to political representation. What Arrington termed "geographically defined communities of interest" did indeed explain the motivations for using territorial districts in colonial and state governments through the eighteenth century. But we should not confuse the justification for colonial and state systems with that of the national system, even at the founding: The importance of residency does not explain why, at the founding, the United States used territory to define electoral constituencies for the U.S. House of Representatives. The stated hope (and fear) of the federal system at its founding was to neutralize, not promote, local communities of interest through the use of very large electoral districts. Once the size of the district became immense, the fact of territory and residency ceased to matter. Territorial constituencies were important, then, not because they were an end in themselves. Rather, they were important only because they enabled certain features of democratic life within the nation.

The U.S. case is useful for analysis for three reasons. First, like most legislatures in the world, the U.S. House uses territorial constituencies, and thus its history provides the necessary context for the evaluation of them in the U.S. system. The second reason for looking at the American case is that the heated debates about political representation have largely ignored the use of territory to define constituencies, and the founders largely ignored it even as they justified so many other political institutions. Finally, though not specific to the United States, the historical exegesis that follows over the next three chapters is meant to illustrate the role of normative theory in institutional design, a point I will develop in this chapter.

A study of this kind faces several substantive and methodological problems, and the purpose of this chapter is to explain how we can proceed in the face of these problems. First is the apparent anachronism of the historical questions themselves: If territorial districting was a "habit of mind" or was simply a necessary part of political representation in the eighteenth century because of the technological limitations of the day, it might seem to make the historical

(Washington, DC: Brookings Institution Press, 1992). For a more recent analysis, see Keith J. Bybee, *Mistaken Identity: The Supreme Court and the Politics of Minority Representation* (Princeton, NJ: Princeton University Press, 1998).

[8] As noted in Chapter 1, the project of justification as undertaken over these four chapters serves the purpose of Hegelian reconciliation as mentioned by John Rawls. See John Rawls, *Justice as Fairness: A Restatement* (Cambridge, MA: Harvard University Press, 2001), p. 4.

questions of this book, and the expectation that I would find answers to them, anachronistic.

As I argued earlier in section 1.3.2, advocates for voting reform claim that the territorial district was originally intended to represent communities of interest. Without the question, "did the founders, in fact, hope to represent 'communities of interest' through territorial districts for Congress?" it is hard to imagine how to evaluate these contemporary claims. If the question were instead, "why *didn't* the founders consider Internet deliberation (or other impossible plans) at the founding?" that *would be* an anachronism. But the historical questions I am asking deal with what was accepted for use, not what was rejected. And here, it is unclear to me why we should *not* expect to find robust justifications ever for necessary institutions. After all, the most robust justifications for any political institution at the founding of the United States came for the most necessary one of all: political representation itself. That early generation made arguments in order to rescue popular sovereignty and legitimacy from the fact that, to use Thomas Paine's image, we could not all meet under the same tree. The fact that something is necessary does not preclude finding justifications for it.

There is a second problem, not of anachronism, but of silence. Despite the possibility of finding justifications for necessary institutions and practices, I found no explicit justifications for using territory for electoral constituencies in the U.S. Congress. How can we proceed to make claims about what the justifications were if nothing was explicitly justified? The answer is to proceed indirectly, and negatively, considering justifications that are quite plausible, rejecting them if they are inconsistent with normative positions or empirical expectations that were widely held on all sides of the founding debates. In section 3.2, I will develop a list of plausible justifications, and in section 3.3 I will explain how we can use this indirect approach to form critical tests of these plausible justifications.

Finally, in section 3.4, I address two potential substantive problems that arise from limiting the scope of my analysis to the founding debates. First, I ignore the role of federalism in the U.S. founding. Second, I do not take up postfounding events, neither how the states responded to the federal constitution nor the developments of the twentieth century, both of which profoundly affected what happened to the institutions once begun. At the end of this chapter, I will explain this choice in detail.

3.2 PLAUSIBLE JUSTIFICATIONS FOR TERRITORY

Why would a nation want to define constituencies for political representation by where its citizens live, or along some other dimension? It seems to me there are five plausible reasons for defining constituencies by territory for the House of Representatives or any national body: interest representation; attachment to a large polity; protection of property; enabling consent to the constituency; and enabling democratic values within a constituency.[9] In addition to being plausible, they reverberate with the themes and values of the founding generation.

Before developing these justifications, I should mention briefly two points about this list. First, it is not an exhaustive list of *possible* reasons to choose territory. Consider these two other reasons: "the symbolic importance of land" and "because Beverly wants it to be territory." In contrast to these two bad reasons, the five justifications I take up are the most plausible group to justify a normative account. Second, while these five reasons may justify territory, they may not be the most persuasive reasons to define a constituency. That is, "defining a constituency such that it elects the smartest person" may be a more important principle than any of these five, and it may also require nonterritorial constituencies. Or as many recent theorists have emphasized, defining constituencies such that minority, oppressed, or disadvantaged voices get elected may very well be a more important way of defining constituencies.[10] But I need to operate slightly backwards here – trying to reconstruct justifications for an ever-present institution – even as I do not yet cede the more important question: What is the best way to define constituencies? It is a question I put off until Part III of this book.

Let me spell out what each of these justifications for territorial representation entails. (For the sake of prose, I have abbreviated "means of constituency definition" as "CD.")

Interest representation. Territory may be valuable as a CD because people live and work in patterns that define communities of interest, and territorial lines can be drawn around these residential or work patterns. Philadelphia is different from New York, and both are different from rural Ohio, in ways relevant to the interests of each area's residents. Other interest-based reasons connect more directly to the geography of the area, through human needs for exploitation of natural resources.[11] These communities need a voice and advocate in the House, and thus organizing citizens by where they live promotes the ends of interest representation.

Attachment to a large polity. When a nation becomes very large it is difficult for citizens to feel any attachment to the larger polity. Territory as a CD might encourage local attachment and a spirit of fellow-feeling toward a nation whose seat of government is often hundreds if not thousands of miles away.

Protection of property. Government's role in the protection of property was well articulated in the political thought of Hobbes, Locke, and Hume, as well

---

[9] See section 7.1 for a discussion of how the function of political representation will help determine how we justify its rules.

[10] See the extended discussion in section 2.5.

[11] They may be wants or desires instead of needs. I am grateful to Emma Greenberg Rehfeld for clarifying this point.

as known to the founders.[12] Many formal institutions, particularly those that regulated political representation, were structured to enhance real property ownership; the most apparent of these were property qualifications for office and voting. To the extent that property is "real" and located in particular territorial locations, territory as a CD may protect this property more readily because constituency lines might be drawn around real estate.[13]

Enabling consent to the constituency. Territorial constituencies might serve the purpose of enabling citizens to choose their own electoral constituencies by changing their residence. Unlike the other three, this justification treats territory for its logistical usefulness – it is not territory, per se, but the fact that it enables a point of consent to the system.[14] (The argument might be thought of as a normative adaptation of Charles Tiebout's work on the allocation of public goods.[15])

Enabling democratic practices within the constituency. If territorial constituencies are used, citizens who live near each other are far more likely to be represented by the same representative or group of representatives than people living far apart. Territorial constituencies then enable citizens to participate in three democratic practices that would be much harder to facilitate were voters not physically proximate to each other:

- Local information: Physical proximity between voters may make it easier for the legislature to collect relevant information about local matters throughout a large nation.[16]
- Deliberation: Physical proximity between voters may make it easier for voters to discern "virtuous" representatives because such selection depends on between-constituent deliberation about a candidate.[17]
- Voting as a symbolic moment of consent: Physical proximity between voters may enable voting days to become important symbolic moments of consent.

---

[12] The importance of government to protect property long predates these social contract theorists. These social contract theorists are more proximate ones to the founders, and property rights arguably play a central (if not *the* central) justification for government in these accounts.

[13] The protection of property justification is simply this protective function tied to the concerns expressed in variants of liberal political theory, and is thus distinguishable from interest representation per se.

[14] I am grateful to an anonymous reviewer from Cambridge University Press for emphasizing this point.

[15] Charles Tiebout, "A Pure Theory of Local Expenditures," *Journal of Political Economy*, 64, October 1956: 416–24.

[16] Local information is simply the information about the many parts of a nation that any national legislature needs to govern well. This is importantly different from the "interest" justification which stipulates that local interests *ought* to be pursued. Here, I mean to emphasize the *having* the information without the corresponding normative obligation to act on it.

[17] This corresponds closely to the kinds of benefits discussed in Nancy L. Schwartz, *The Blue Guitar: Political Representation and Community* (Chicago: University of Chicago Press, 1988). See particularly Chapter 8 of that book.

Absent from the preceding list is any justification based on historical precedent. First, history – the fact that "that's just the way it's always been done" – does not favor territory qua territory. By definition, history cannot be a *founding* reason to do something. Rather, it accrues to the status quo whatever the status quo happens to be. Indeed, the use of territorial constituencies in the United States emerged from a long history of their use in state and local representative institutions in the Anglo world. This continuity and stability may well favor *any* status quo for the reason that change is costly. If a change between the status quo and some new plan does not seem likely to result in significant benefits, the status quo might be favored. But this is not a principled reason to favor any particular object of the status quo. It is a fact about institutions that they exist in certain configurations. "History" does not create a justification for their use, only for their *continued* use.[18] In the American case, showing that the American system adopted a British (or even American colonial) institution simply moves the question back one step: Why did systems of representative government in England organize constituents by territory at their birth?

Second, and more importantly, at moments of a nation's birth, especially a birth as self-conscious as that of the United States, its founders grapple with those most deeply imbedded institutions, whether or not they were rejected or continued. As we will see, the most surprising fact about this debate is that territorial constituencies were so deeply imbedded in the minds of Anglo-American theorists and politicians of the seventeenth and eighteenth century that the question of how to define constituencies was not an issue for them. At precisely the moment representative government as a purportedly new species of government was being created, territorial constituencies were mostly ignored.

It may be noteworthy to contemporary readers that "identity" is absent from the preceding justifications even though some people today feel we should organize electoral constituencies on the basis of people's identity. It is precisely on the matter of representing identities that a good deal of the literature on voting and democratic theory has critiqued the status quo in favor of advocating

---

[18] For a good account of these issues, see Cass Sunstein, *The Partial Constitution* (Cambridge, MA: Harvard University Press, 1993). On history and institutions see Robert E. Goodin, "Institutions and Their Design," in *The Theory of Institutional Design*, ed. Robert E. Goodin (Cambridge, UK: Cambridge University Press, 1996), pp. 1–53. A slightly different form of the historical argument might be to endorse the CD because it "stands the test of time," a position I take to be essentially in line with Edmund Burke's and which I address in Chapter 5. Such an evaluation, though, requires us to ask, "what test is that?" and then we'd have to specify a substantive standard – perhaps something like, "people are happy with it," or "it works well." Whatever the "test of time" might be, it does not seem particular to territory, but rather to anything that happens to be used for a while. If territory were the only kind of constituency that could be used over time, then it would become a necessary condition to achieve this value. I am grateful to Larry May for raising this issue.

gender, race, class, or issue representation. Identity is not a particularly strong justification for territorial constituencies today because people tend not to view their congressional district as a locus of identity. More importantly, identity in the way it is currently understood was not particularly salient during the founding of the United States. To the extent local identity is just a kind of interest that can be territorially concentrated and thus represented, then it is already captured by the interest representation justification. So identity just does not form a particularly strong justification for the use of territorial constituencies, even though, again, a desire for identity representation may be a reason to reject territorial constituencies.

In the following three chapters (4–6), I argue that of these five plausible justifications, only the last – that territory enables democratic practices within the electoral constituency – received support at the founding of the United States. The founders did not view the other four plausible justifications as relevant to how citizens were grouped for national representation. There was widespread agreement that congressional districts would be too large to define distinct interests for representation. There was similar agreement that territorial districts for Congress would fail to foster attachment to the federal system. Critics of the constitution thought that district size was too large to achieve either of these goals; supporters agreed and looked to other institutions to secure interest representation and citizen attachment. The justification that territory somehow helped protect citizens from government encroachments on their property turns out to be a phantom, and thus cannot be said to have justified territorial use. And although fixed territorial lines would enable citizens to consent to which constituency they belonged, the high costs of moving, even with the great migrations through the United States in its early years, made territorial districts a poor means to that end.

Yet the last justification – that organizing citizens by where they lived enabled the efficient transmission of local information to the national legislature, citizen deliberation, *and* the tradition of elections as being tangible moments of consent – resonates with the concerns repeatedly expressed in the literature. In the end, the founders gave constituency division by territory per se no normative anchor. It simply functioned as an important means to these other democratic ends.

Before I present the evidence that supports these conclusions, I need to explain the method by which I arrive at them. I take this up in the next section.

3.3 AN INDIRECT METHOD OF VERIFICATION: NORMATIVE AND EMPIRICAL FOUNDATIONS

To answer the questions I have set forth, I look to both history and ideas: the historical context from which territorial constituencies were drawn, and the particular way they were treated by theorists at and around the founding of the new nation. I thus focus on the American founding debates and situate them in the political and intellectual history of their times.

The fact that there was no explicit discussion at the founding of the United States poses a difficult problem for our inquiry. But we can proceed indirectly based on the relationship between political institutions and their normative justifications. A political institution is a set of rules that govern the political sphere, and these rules are often established to achieve normative aims, that is, to achieve ends that are in some ways good, right, or just. Similar to what Claus Offe has described "the dual nature of institutions," when aiming at these normative goals, political institutions can be justified only when two conditions are met:

- Normatively, the aim of the rule or set of rules, is endorsable (it is purportedly, good, right or just).[19]
- Empirically, the rule or set of rules, is reasonably likely to achieve its normative aim.

By this account, when I claim that an institution is "justified" for a particular reason, I mean first that the particular reason is a normatively endorsable one, and second that the institution itself is likely to achieve the goals specified by the justification.[20] Similarly, when I claim that an institution was *historically* "justified" for a particular reason, I mean that its supporters found the justification to be normatively endorsable and that they also believed that the institution was likely to achieve the goals specified by that justification.

For example, consider what it means to justify the rule that sets the U.S. voting age at eighteen. If we claim that rule is justified, we are claiming first that the rule aims at a normatively endorsable goal, and second that the rule itself is empirically likely to achieve that goal. Historically, this describes exactly how the argument was made. Prior to 1971, men between the ages of eighteen and twenty-one were drafted to serve in the army and go to war without ever having a chance to vote for the leadership that decided their fate.[21] The normative aim of having a younger voting age was thus to give those who would risk their lives more control over their own fate, and in fact, setting the voting age at eighteen achieves this normative goal.

---

[19] This is the same as the first condition of justification (substantive) I described in section 1.2.

[20] Similarly, Offe claims that institutions must make normative sense to those who use them *and* be fit to accomplish that which they set out to accomplish. Claus Offe, "Designing Institutions in East European Transitions," in *The Theory of Institutional Design*, pp. 199–207. I agree, but make these two features more explicit. Further, the present framing of the normative dimension is, contra Offe, sociological or descriptive only when we evaluate the historical origins of the institution. In the historical case, we care what was consistent with the framers' norms. Beginning in Chapter 7, however, we will depart from this sociological framing and treat this as a forward-looking tool to answer normative questions about how we ought to define constituencies today.

[21] The voting age had been twenty-one for over two hundred years, and attempts were made during every American war of the twentieth century to reduce it to eighteen. Vietnam, however, changed the political opportunity. See Alexander Keyssar's terrific account. Alexander Keyssar, *The Right to Vote: The Contested History of Democracy in the United States, with a New Afterword* (New York: Basic Books, 2000).

It might seem, then, as if the justification for a rule rests only on its normative aim, and the empirical condition is simply redundant: Having provided a good normative reason for eighteen-year-olds to have a vote, they should have the vote. What then does the empirical condition add?

By itself the normative aim obscures the fact that, for various pragmatic and political reasons, most institutions aim only indirectly at normative goals. Even in this apparently clear case, the normative aim of extending the suffrage to those at risk of service would have justified (in 1971) only the extension of the vote to healthy males between eighteen and twenty-one, not to all citizens eighteen to twenty-one. Still, we correctly say that the lowering of the voting age was justified by the risk of service of men because lowering the age is empirically very likely to achieve this endorsable goal. Only by separating the normative and empirical claims can we attend to the way that rules are over and under inclusive of their own normative ends.

The fact that institutions do not perfectly achieve their purported normative aims illustrates the fact that institutions often have multiple justifications. In this present case, the normative "risk of service" argument would not justify extending the vote to eighteen-year-old women and unhealthy males. Instead, young women and young unhealthy males might be justified in receiving a vote because of the (purportedly endorsable) equal protection clause of the Constitution: If you give the vote to some eighteen-to-twenty-one-year-olds, then you must give it to all eighteen-to-twenty-one-year-olds. Or its extension to those outside of the "risk of service" group might be justified pragmatically: There was no political way a narrowly defined voting rule would actually be endorsed whether or not it was constitutional.

Returning, then, to the case of territorial constituencies, a complete answer to the question or why electoral constituencies are defined by territory will include both an account of the normative aims of those who established them *and* an account that explains why territorial constituencies are a means to these aims. Thus, each proposed justification will involve a particular normative goal and a corresponding empirical expectation about the role of territory in political representation.

For example, when we say that territorial constituencies were justified on the basis of interest representation, we imply the following normative claim and empirical expectation:

Normative claim:	Local political interests ought to be represented in the national legislature.
Empirical expectation:	Territorial congressional districts were expected to be coterminous with local political interests.

Thus, the only way the founders could have coherently justified territorial constituencies by this justification is if they thought territorial constituencies *would be* coterminous with local political interests *and* they believed that local political interests ought to be represented in the national legislature.[22] If the founders rejected either of these two claims, then we can conclude that they did not support the communities of interest justification. In this particular case, the founders (the Federalists, at least) disparaged interest representation of the sort described in the "normative claim," *and* they believed that the district would be too large to define any coherent set of interests. Using similar logic, we will be able to conclude with some confidence that territorial constituencies could not have been justified on the basis of any of the first four justifications, despite the lack of any explicit discussion of the matter.[23]

Because I have been unable to find any sustained discussion of territorial constituencies at the founding, our falsifying conclusions will be strongest: We will be most certain in our rejection of a justification because it is contradicted by normative or empirical claims. By contrast, our positive conclusions in Chapter 6 will be suggestive, broadly consistent with the evidence of the founding, but simply not at the level of certainty with which we can reject the justifications. This follows for reasons closely related to the logic of falsification. In general terms, these normative and empirical claims are necessary conditions for the justification to stand, and thus showing their absence is enough to reject the justification. But they are not sufficient claims; for example, the founders might have endorsed both normative and empirical parts of the communities of interest justification, but still have thought that there were more important communities of interest (perhaps racial, religious, gender, and so on) to represent than ones apt to be defined by territory. My approach, then, will be strongest in rejecting reasons for using territory (Chapter 5) and merely suggestive in supporting the positive claims that I will make in Chapter 6.

This account of justification is meant to be a political (theoretical and historical) approach rather than a strictly philosophical one. By this, I mean to distinguish three things. First, the fact that one rule might be justified by a number of different normative claims may make the justification incomplete and problematic, but it explains politically how any political institution can have multiple justifications for one rule.

The second point in which this is a political rather than philosophical distinction is that in practice, justifications are applied to the same institution even when they are logically inconsistent with each other. To use the earlier example, the normative aim of extending the vote to young men in the "risk of service" group was to give those who are at risk a voice and consent over the leaders who make the decisions that put them in harm's way. Yet this is explicitly undermined

---

[22] For a further refinement, see Chapter 7.

[23] Because I am interested in how the founders understood themselves, I am interested only in whether or not they believed these claims to be true, and not whether they turned out to have been correct beliefs.

by the overly broad rule that extends the vote to all eighteen-to-twenty-one-year-olds, because lowering the voting age for everyone leads to giving the vote to a larger number of non–"risk of service" people who can vote. The counterargument may be that younger people are more likely to feel sympathy for their eighteen-year-old "risk of service" brethren than would older people. But this is a different argument (and every person in the "risk of service" group already has two parents who presumably already feel sympathy for them and could vote). The justification thus hinged on an appeal to the consent of those who were directly affected by a policy, not for those who had sympathy with those who had a direct stake in the policy.

Finally, any philosophical account of justification would explain what it means to be "endorsable (purportedly good, right, or just)," and what qualifies as "reasonably likely" to bring it about. I will not take up these important matters, because our historical claims concern the expectations of the political actors at the time rather than an evaluation of their expectations: We care what the founding generation took to be endorsable and what they thought were reasonably likely outcomes. Second, the contemporary critique will be at a broad enough level that a thoroughgoing definition of these terms would be a distraction. In short, I acknowledge the complexity of the terms "endorsable" and "reasonable." Nevertheless, using this method, I hope to illustrate the structure of how normative questions of the good, right, and just are involved in the establishment of political institutions.

3.4 IGNORING FEDERALISM AND POSTFOUNDING DEVELOPMENTS

Two substantive problems arise from the scope of my analysis. First, I do not take up the issue of federalism except in passing. Second, I do not focus on postfounding developments, where the issues of gerrymandering, and thus constituency definition, loom large in legislative and public deliberation. I will take each in turn.

As I mentioned in the opening of this chapter, the U.S. Constitution gives the power to control electoral mechanisms to the states. It thus represents an instance of federalism – of the balance of power between states and the national government. Yet I do not take up the issue of federalism in any sustained way because federalism does not provide much insight into the more specific problem to be addressed. Federalism explains why the founders delegated the power to draw district lines to the states. It does not explain why the founders themselves expected territorial districts would be used. Nor would a study of federalism explain why states did or did not use territorial districting of representatives during the first fifty years of the United States. Federalism may explain why the power to draw lines was given to the states but not why the founders expected the states to use territory as a districting principle.[24]

---

[24] There is the further point that districting was a limited case of federalism. Congress retained the constitutional right to legislate in this arena, which they have done many times.

The fact that this power was given to the states raises a final problem of limiting the scope of this analysis to the founding period. Why look at the founding debate to seek intentions on this subject when the states themselves were famously laboratories of democracy? Why not look to the immediate response of the states to discover how they justified the use of territory for political representation?

Three factors argue for looking to the national debate at the founding. First, the literature has already adequately addressed what happened *post*founding.[25] Second, as I described in Chapter 1, the historical answer I am investigating is a broadly held assertion about the founders' justifications for territorial districting. Third, the intentions of those who shaped the new political landscape should not be confused with what happened in response to that landscape once formed, even if subsequent events are independently important to know. The more familiar case of political parties provides a useful analog. Although political parties were relatively quick to form, historians have underscored the importance of the fact that they were not anticipated by the founders. A similar methodological point is applicable to this case. There is no reason to expect that the states were conforming to the founders' expectations, and every reason to want to know what the founders were thinking, regardless of what actually ensued.

Given the history of districting cases in the United States, it may also be surprising that I do not focus on them in what follows. Although I will comment briefly on them at the end of Chapter 6, there are two reasons I do not discuss such cases in detail here. First, the contemporary districting debates seldom questioned the use of residency for constituency definition. The debates during the first half of the twentieth century centered around rural/urban population disparities. In the early 1960s, the Supreme Court's requirement of equal population for electoral constituencies, coupled with the Voting Rights Act of 1965, turned districting into a tool for racial justice (or injustice, depending on your politics). In neither case, however, was the question of *residential* constituency definition ever seriously questioned; and little from those debates speaks to the underlying issues of the present work. Contemporary districting debates were

---

[25] See Zagarri, *The Politics of Size*, pp. 105–24, for a good account of state response to the electoral laws after the founding. Among her findings is that "Politicians began to realize that the method used to elect congressmen would play a large part in determining who was ultimately elected" (p. 107). Thus, whether states chose territorial districts or a multimember system after ratification can be understood at least in part as political manipulation rather than based on principled ideas of representation. The crux of my study, however, questions her more important conclusion that there were principled differences between large and small states concerning their theories of representation. "The district system gave representation to the full variety of interests contained within a state – a variety more likely to be found in larger states." Yet the difference between small and large states may be explained by this alternative hypothesis: If representation required close physical proximity between voters, large states would have to be subdivided to accomplish this goal; by contrast such division would be less necessary for small states. Thus interests and their variety, and different theories of representation, may not explain the difference between large and small states.

responding to the fact that districts were already territorially defined and thus do not address the deeper theoretical issues that animated the choice of territory in the first place.

What did animate the founders' choices? The historical analysis of the next three chapters begins at the time of Robin Hood in the first decades of thirteenth century England, and ends about the time Rip Van Winkle awoke from his slumber almost six centuries later.

4

The English and Colonial Origins of Territorial Constituencies in the United States

> The intimate and familiar propinquity group is not a social unity within an inclusive whole. It is, for almost all purposes, society itself.
>
> –John Dewey[1]

Why were modern representational institutions in England and America organized around territorial constituencies? A good first guess begins with Dewey's description of early human history, and emphasizes the decidedly local social and political structure of early modern England and the American colonies. Before the modern institutions of representative government were formed, the basis of life was decidedly local, small, and static. Geographic and social mobility were not the norm – indeed there were significant impediments to each – and as such it was difficult to attach strong sentiments to things not locally based. Even as late as the seventeenth century, communities sent delegates to English parliament because it was by local communities that individuals primarily organized their lives. Territorial representation *was* originally used to represent territorially distinct communities.[2]

The nature of territorial representation quietly changed when district lines no longer matched existing communities – when small jurisdictional lines ceased to define a distinct constituency for national representation. This happened in England and the American colonies when the population grew (or was depleted by migration) and geographical mobility increased. As this happened during the seventeenth century in England (and during the eighteenth century across the Atlantic), the justification for territorial representation changed. The change

---

[1] John Dewey, *The Public and Its Problems* (USA: Swallow Press, 1954), p. 42.

[2] By the American Revolution, differentiation between local communities was not only imagined, it was explicitly articulated and formed the basis of the more heated debates on the nature of representation in the years immediately following. For a particularly good example of this see Theophilus Parsons, "The Essex Result," in *American Political Writing during the Founding Era*, eds. Charles S. Hyneman and Donald S. Lutz (Indianapolis, IN: Liberty Press, 1983 [1778]), pp. 481–522.

was inadvertent, because the founders (in the United States) took the existing system of territorial representation and massaged it to serve the more important ends of newly developing theories of political representation, particularly the idea that persons, and not places, were to be represented. Habits of mind begin with known facts that creep slowly into the background until they are out of sight. When each town defined a constituency, territorial lines provided a coherent rationale for using territory – local communities had defined local interests for representation. As constituency size grew (so that representative bodies would not be too large), large towns and counties had to be divided and combined (so that district population would be roughly equal), and the justification for using territory to define constituencies changed.

This chapter sets up the historical context for the founding period by illustrating the extremely local nature of political and social life in England and America prior to the founding of the United States. It illustrates the English origins of territorial districts (section 4.1), their development in American Colonial legislatures (section 4.2), and finally their state at about the time of American independence (section 4.3).

4.1 ENGLISH ORIGINS

Colonial institutions, the seeds of the American system, grew out of various parts of the seventeenth century English parliamentary system, even as writers of the American Revolution would appeal to the institution's ancient constitution as the source of their rights. The seeds of English parliament date to the thirteenth century, when membership in the *Curia Regis* or great council of the king was expanded to include knights of each shire, burgesses from each county, and some lesser clergy.[3] The expansion was occasioned by the need to raise money, and these new taxes required appeals to lower classes of citizens.[4] The "model parliament" of 1295 included clergy, barons, and lesser landholders (burgesses and knights). During the next century, the clergy withdrew to form their own body, and the two remaining classes (the barons and the lesser landowners) developed into what are now the House of Lords and the House of Commons.

The expansion of the King's council was important because it expanded the representational "constituency" downward toward the knights and burgesses to expand the representational body. But these people were each drawn from

---

[3] Provisions for the social expansion of the council appear as early as 1215 in a version of *Magna Carta*.

[4] As Pasquet observed, "The king was supposed to 'live of his own'" so aid was considered "a quite exceptional gift." D. Pasquet, *An Essay on the Origins of the House of Commons* (Connecticut: Archon Books, 1964 [1925]), p. 11. The overspending of Kings Richard I and John due to failed military conquest and maladministration preceded the institutional developments of the thirteenth century and parallel in obvious ways the early Stuart monarchs and the more dramatic changes four hundred years later.

separate local communities within England due to the essentially local life of people in thirteenth century England. Even calling it "territorial representation" is deceiving: We should probably call this early form "town representation" or "county representation," as territory was that which bounded the existing community. The fact that territory defined a town was as trivially important to political representation as the fact that skin defines the limits of one's body.

Local communities defined English life during this period to such an extent that the Crown treated delegates as independent actors rather than meeting with them as a unified body. As described by D. Pasquet, "The representatives of a county are not the representatives of England, but the attorneys of their county, empowered to speak and enter into engagements only in the name of that county and capable of accepting liabilities different from those of other counties."[5] That they did not meet as a collective group was indicative of the independence of the communities from which they came. Geographical mobility was not yet widespread and transportation was difficult; communities were stable and unchanging. To the extent there was an "England," it was created through a union of these smaller existing communities.[6] Early parliament drew representatives from local communities because that is where and how people defined themselves.

The independence of these representatives was also due to the very different nature of political representation during this period. Unlike *democratic* representation, early modern political representation did not imply the active "acting for" or structures of accountability and authorization that are at the forefront of Hanna Pitkin's influential account.[7] Instead, representatives were simply stand-ins for a community (or a class within the community) designed to give the "compulsory consent" of the people to the King's taxes.[8] These representatives were thus agents of their home communities, to whom they were closely tied.[9] As agents they also provided the King with information on abuses of "local sheriffs, bailiffs or others" in addition to communicating information from the King back home.[10] This early function of petitioning from local bodies would become one of the central arguments for the residential requirements

---

[5] Pasquet, *Origins of the House of Commons*, p. 29.

[6] "The men of the village had upon the whole more contacts with one another than they had with outsiders." George C. Homans, *English Villagers of the Thirteenth Century* (Cambridge, MA: Harvard University Press, 1941), quoted in Thomas Bender, *Community and Social Change* (Baltimore, MD: Johns Hopkins University Press, 1978), p. 61.

[7] Hanna Fenichel Pitkin, *The Concept of Representation*. (Berkeley, CA: University of California Press, 1967). On the development of representation and consent in early modern England see Constantin Fasolt, "Quod Omnes Tangit Ab Omnibus Approbari Debet: The Words and the Meaning," in *In Iure Veritas: Studies in Canon Law in Memory of Schaefer Williams*, eds. Steven B. Bowman and Blanch E. Cody (Cincinnati, OH: University of Cincinnati College of Law, 1991).

[8] Fasolt, "Quod Omnes Tangit," pp. 21–55. This early modern sense of representation is exactly consistent with Hobbes' use of the term in Chapter 16 of *Leviathan*.

[9] Pasquet, *Origins of the House of Commons*, passim.

[10] Ibid., p. 31.

for representatives in England and the United States in the eighteenth century.[11]

As the demands of the King increased from the thirteenth century to the end of Elizabeth's reign in 1603, parliament changed its *composition* and its *function*. Compositionally, the Commons and Lords emerged as a two-class system in the way just described. By the close of the fifteenth century, the Lower House of parliament was more unified socially. Though not a House of Commons by today's meaning of "commons," this Lower House became the body that represented the interests of the people at large, compared to that of the Lords, which embodied the aristocracy. *Functionally*, the Lower House was a more recognizably modern legislature, becoming the originator of petitions to the King. This petitioning increased the King's access to information and provided some protection from arbitrary rule.[12] Still, the House of Commons did not have the authority to propose legislation and enact law until after the myriad crises of the seventeenth century.[13]

Even as social distinctions collapsed in parliament, and its function changed from providing compulsory consent to crafting legislation, representation remained grounded on territory. Territory was a seemingly "natural" part of representation even as representational theories and theories of consent were beginning to change dramatically.

4.2 COLONIAL ORIGINS

During this transformation of English parliament, the King granted the first colonial charters that established the political institutions of the new American colonies. The political reforms and aftermath of the Commonwealth variously affected these charters. James Harrington and John Locke had an indirect influence on the charters for Pennsylvania and the Carolinas.[14] The founders

---

[11] Charles de Secondat, baron de La Brède et de Montesquieu, *The Spirit of the Laws* (New York: Cambridge University Press, 1989 [1748]), Book 11, Chapter 6; Hamilton, Madison, John Jay and James, *The Federalist*, ed. Jacob E. Cooke (Middletown, CT: Wesleyan University Press, 1961 [1987–8]), essays 35 and 52; Herbert Phillips, *The Development of the Residential Qualification for Representatives in Colonial Legislatures* (Cincinnati, OH: Abingdon Press, 1921).

[12] The initial role of the commons as a restraint against the crown has been widely discussed. For one example, see John Philip Reid, *The Concept of Representation in the Age of the American Revolution* (Chicago: University of Chicago Press, 1989), p. 7.

[13] On the changing role of parliament in the seventeenth century, see Fasolt, "Quod Omnes Tangit"; Gordon Wood, *The Creation of the American Republic* (New York: Norton, 1993 [1969]), p. 26.

[14] It is controversial what role either man played in the actual writing of the documents, but their indirect influence is well established. Harrington was a close personal friend of William Penn, who claims to have modeled his constitution on *Oceana,* and he famously influenced John Adams. Ralph Lerner, *The Thinking Revolutionary: Principle and Practice in the New Republic* (Ithaca, NY: Cornell University Press, 1988), p. 25; J. G. A. Pocock, "Introduction," in *The Commonwealth of Oceana and A System of Politics*, ed. J. G. A. Pocock (New York: Cambridge University Press, 1992); J. R. Pole, *Political Representation in England and the Origins of the*

knew of, and in many cases studied carefully, Algernon Sidney and Baron de Montesquieu. In this way, Bernard Bailyn and J. R. Pole have observed, the English system of the seventeenth century was the parent of *two* polities: latter day England and the United States.[15]

The sparse settlements of the early colonial Americans resulted in lives that resembled the close-knit localness of medieval English life. From the first settlements in Virginia and Plymouth, small towns and plantations isolated and defined the spectrum of life throughout the colonies. In New England, for example, "local community had a closed quality that is evident even in the physical layout. Whether built upon the ribbon or the cluster pattern, the town plan and the manner in which land was distributed suggest limited expectations for growth, surely nothing of the spirit one finds in town promotions in the middle and late nineteenth century."[16] In his summary of the vast literature on colonial America, Darrett B. Rutman concurs: "For most families, the distance spanned by the network of relationships in which they were enmeshed was short and the relationships themselves were multi-stranded in the sense that one dealt with the same group of 'others' over and over again and in a variety of ways."[17]

The closeness and *closed-ness* of town life manifested itself in both political and social ways. Politically, "decisions were made through 'discussion' and consensus rather than through interest-group conflict. Votes were seldom recorded in the minutes of town meetings. When decisions were made, the town records indicate simply that they were reached 'by general agreement.'"[18]

American Republic (New York: St. Martin's Press, 1966), pp. 11–12, 78. Similarly, Locke was the recording secretary for the commission that wrote the constitution of the Carolinas, and his influence, if not his writing, seems clear enough. For example, the *Fundamental Constitutions of Carolina* of 1669 bears Locke's view that the protection of property was an important, perhaps the central, aim of governance. Unlike any other constitution or charter among the thirteen colonies, each of which began with the establishment of familiar institutions of government (a legislature, executive and the courts, for example), the first twenty-six paragraphs of the Carolinian constitution define property rights. Only in paragraph 27 is a government institution finally established. And even there, it is the courts whose first appearance is for the purpose of protecting property owners and adjudicating between their claims, thus reflecting, at the very least, Lockean sympathies. Ben Perley Poore, ed., *The Federal and State Constitutions, Colonial Charters, and Other Organic Laws of the United States, in Two Parts*, 2nd ed. (Washington, DC: Government Printing Office, 1878).

[15] Bernard Bailyn, *The Ideological Origins of the American Revolution, Enlarged Edition* (Cambridge, MA: Belknap Press, 1992). The regaining of English rights perceived to have been lost becomes an explicit point among the American revolutionary writers and forms much of the justification for the Declaration of Independence. See also Hyneman and Lutz, *American Political Writing*.

[16] Bender, *Community and Social Change*, p. 65.

[17] Darrett Rutman, "Assessing the Little Communities of Early America," *William and Mary Quarterly*, 43, 2 April 1986: 167.

[18] Bender, *Community and Social Change*, p. 67. See also footnote 56 for Bender's references. The fact that town records report that decisions were made by "general agreement" well expresses the close, local political culture of New England, but it probably underestimates the underlying

Socially, New England towns were similarly unified:

The town was essentially homogeneous: It had one religious belief, a unified political vision, even a fairly even distribution of wealth and a narrow range of occupations. It was a remarkably undifferentiated society, and it was difficult to draw the line between family and community, private and public.[19]

Edward Cook's study of leadership in New England towns extends this point to the limited number of individuals who rotated from one political office to another.[20] And Pole emphasizes the suspicion of strangers in New England towns, which would contribute to a closed society:

Town records tell of many times when strangers who had come into the town without permission were warned to leave; when householders were rebuked for entertaining strangers without permission and ordered to dismiss them. The governing fear was that people might, without visible means of support, become charges on the town.[21]

While life "in the small communities of Anglo-America was, in brief, lived 'face to face' and on a scale reasonably described – as small, intimate, and essentially

conflict, and leads us to overstate the level of consensus on any given issue. Instead, reporting that a decision was reached by "general agreement" might be a way to demonstrate unity despite substantive disagreement. This is consistent with the practice through the mid-eighteenth century, in which English parliament deliberated and voted a first time behind closed doors to decide an issue. Following the initial vote, the matter would be introduced again for a second vote in which the first result was given unanimous support, even if it had been closely decided. Thus, the body could report that it unanimously supported or rejected a particular measure, thereby strengthening the institution of parliament (and the principle of majority rule) even when there were deep disagreements. Returning to New England, the fact that the public town records show "general agreement" thus says little about the level of disagreement that may have been ignored for the sake of communal stability. J. R. Pole, *The Gift of Government: The Richard Russell Lectures, Number One* (Athens, GA: University of Georgia Press, 1983), Chapter 5. The distinction between actual conflict within a body and the public show of stability during this time may thus be mischaracterized as idyllic moments of consensus. See, for example, Jane J. Mansbridge, *Beyond Adversary Democracy* (Chicago: University of Chicago Press, 1981), p. 2. Further, even if there were general agreement on measures in the town meetings, Bender's description ignores how interests regularly play out in deliberative settings, even though participants and advocates of deliberation want to contrast these settings to raw appeals to power. See Mansbridge, *Beyond Adversary Democracy*; Lynn Sanders. "Against Deliberation," *Political Theory*, 25, no. 3, June 1997: 347–76.

[19] Bender, *Community and Social Change*, p. 68. See also Robert J. Dinkin, *Voting in Provincial America: A Study of Elections in the Thirteen Colonies 1689–1776* (Connecticut: Greenwood Press, 1977). Of New England towns, he writes, "Unanimity was considered a highly valued goal by the majority of the inhabitants. Conflict over public issues was something to be avoided or at least played down as much as possible." But see the previous note on the role of conflict and reported unanimity.

[20] Edward M. Cook, Jr., *The Fathers of the Towns: Leadership and Community Structure in Eighteenth-Century New England* (Baltimore, MD, and London: Johns Hopkins University Press, 1976), pp. 12–17.

[21] Pole, *Political Representation*, p. 40. On page 41, Pole acknowledges the "collective responsibility for the spiritual and economic welfare" of town members as a corollary to this suspicious attitude.

cooperative,"[22] there was regional variation. In southern communities, the "county" served as the relevant sphere, sparsely settled and more economically stratified compared to the northern town.[23] According to Jefferson, in 1787, Williamsburg, the seat of Virginia's colonial government until 1780, "never contained above 1800 inhabitants; and Norfolk, the most populous town we ever had, contained but 6000."[24] By 1790, Charleston, South Carolina, had a population of fifteen thousand, dwarfed by the northern cities of Philadelphia, New York, and Boston with their combined population of ninety-three thousand people.[25]

In the South, social life was also more economically stratified, but still intensely local.[26] As Bender observes, the research on this period

... reveals the importance of locality-based social patterns of community there. The backcountry was comprised of intensely parochial and clannish settlements established by various cultural groups. While it is true that the more developed tidewater region lacked the compact towns or villages characteristic of New England, the county seems to have served as the basic unit of a vigorous community life in the South. Within this context, with the courthouse as the geographical and social core, one finds a clear pattern of intimate social relationships, kinship networks, and the regular routine of rituals that provide symbolic meanings for such localized and basically oral communities... my point here is that it is possible to argue that life was lived in local communities, not only in the colonial North, but given some variation, in the colonial South as well.[27]

---

[22] On the county and the South, see Rutman, "Assessing the Little Communities," p. 167. On economic stratification, see ibid., at p. 174; Pole, *Political Representation*, p. 137.

[23] Donald Lutz, *Popular Consent and Popular Control: Whig Political Theory in the Early State Constitutions* (Baton Rouge, LA, and London: Louisiana State University Press, 1980), pp. 153–4. However, in North Carolina there was more localized sentiment. In the early eighteenth century, there was agitation about drawing representatives from the county "and the people were well pleased when an act of 1716 provided that the parish instead of the county should be the election district." Cortland F. Bishop, *History of Elections in the American Colonies* (New York: Columbia College, 1893), p. 42. But, as Bishop notes, the act was repealed, causing a revolt that led to the proprietors selling their interest to the Crown, which in turn established local representative institutions. See also Thomas Jefferson, *Notes on the State of Virginia*, ed. Merrill D. Peterson (New York: Library of America, 1787), p. 233 (Query XII). Originally, the Virginia settlement extended north to include the Chesapeake Bay. In addition to navigable passages, the availability of rich soil and farmland provided more usable land on which to settle. In New England, for example, the geography did not permit such wide use of land and necessitated closer habitations that subsequently developed into towns.

[24] Jefferson, *Notes on the State of Virginia*, p. 233.

[25] According to the first federal census in 1790, Philadelphia had 42,000, New York 33,000, and Boston 18,000 people.

[26] Pole, *Political Representation*, p. 137. Rutman concurs on this stratification. Rutman, "Assessing the Little Communities," p. 174.

[27] Bender, *Community and Social Change*, pp. 70–1. Bender bases this on the work of Carl Bridenbaugh and, more recently, Darrett Rutman and Rhys Isaac. See Carl Bridenbaugh, *Myths and Realities: Societies of the Colonial South* (New York: Atheneum, 1965), pp. 131–2; Rhys Isaac, "Dramatizing the Ideology of the Revolution: Popular Mobilization in Virginia, 1774–1776," *William and Mary Quarterly*, 33, 1976: 375–85; Darrett Rutman, "The Social Web: A Prospectus

The social character of the other colonies differed from New England in intensity, but was still essentially local.[28]

Political life was similarly local. Although provincial governors appointed by proprietors or the British Crown governed eleven of the colonies,[29] local matters demanded local attention, and local institutions sprung up alongside the central colonial structures established in London.[30] Even against English attempts "to reduce the areas of local jurisdiction in the colonies, local provincial autonomy continued to characterize American life."[31] This autonomy came from a certain necessity of local communities to deal with decidedly local matters, to maintain "law and order" administering "justice in the colonies":

And it had in fact been local bodies, – towns and counties in the first instance, ultimately the provincial Assemblies – that laid down the rules for daily life; rules concerning the production and distribution of wealth, personal conduct, the worship of God – most of the ways in which people deal with the world, animate and inanimate, about them.[32]

By the end of the seventeenth century, every colony had a representative assembly composed of representatives of the towns and counties of a colony.[33] Electoral constituencies in colonial assemblies were coextensive with local political subdivisions because of the importance of these subdivisions to the lives of their inhabitants.[34] "The corporate method of representation presumed that physical

---

for the Study of Early American Community," in *Insights and Parallels*, ed. William L. O'Neill (Minneapolis, MN: Burgess, 1973), pp 57–123.

[28] The debate over the social diversity of early America tends to take localism as a given, questioning instead the similarity or differences between these local groups and how they interacted. See, for example, Bernard Bailyn, "A Domesday Book for the Periphery," in *Diversity and Unity in Early North America*, ed. Philip D. Morgan (New York: Routledge, 1993), pp. 11–42; Jack P. Greene, "Convergence: Development of an American Society, 1720–80" in *Diversity and Unity in Early North America*, ed. Philip D. Morgan (New York: Routledge, 1993), pp. 43–72; Rutman "Assessing the Little Communities." It would be an overstatement to say that local groups were radically homogeneous, whatever that would mean. But I take as well established that identity and community were based in local communities during the colonial period.

[29] Rhode Island and Connecticut were the exceptions. Dinkin, *Voting in Provincial America*, p. 5.

[30] "[T]he original settlers in New England came to found colonies, not towns, but the colonists soon found themselves scattered into separate pockets within the same colony." Lutz, *Popular Consent*, p. 154.

[31] Bailyn, *Ideological Origins*, p. 203.

[32] Ibid., pp. 203–4.

[33] Bishop, *History of Elections*, p. 16; Rosemarie Zagarri, *Politics of Size: Representation in the United States 1776–1850* (Ithaca, NY, and London: Cornell University Press, 1987), p. 37. Jack Rakove observes that, "New communities had generally received representation as they were organized...," thus reducing the English problem of "rotten boroughs." Jack Rakove, *Original Meanings: Politics and Ideas in the Making of the Constitution* (New York: Knopf, 1996), p. 212.

[34] Bailyn makes a similar connection between medieval English representation and that of the colonies. Bailyn, *Ideological Origins*, p. 162. By "local political subdivision," I mean a political and social community defined independently of its role as constituency for the colonial legislature. In the colonies, such territorial units were called "town," "parish," or "county," each of

proximity generated communal sentiment. Each geographic unit was thought to be an organic, cohesive community, whose residents knew one another, held common values, and shared compatible economic interests."[35] But the development was also based on availability: When representative government in the colonies coalesced by the early eighteenth century, there were defined local institutions on which to build. "By 1650, the various colonies were composed of towns, each governed by its inhabitants through a town meeting, with a board of elected selectmen running affairs between meetings but still remaining subordinate to the majority at the town meeting."[36] In the South, sparse population deprived its inhabitants of a central meeting place, so the county court served as local administrators.[37] "As elsewhere in the colonies, political power flowed upward from county or town to province rather than outward from the provincial government."[38]

With the population growth of the colonies during the eighteenth century, centralized government became more necessary, even as localism continued to define the political culture. Thus:

The colonial towns and counties, like their medieval counterparts, were largely autonomous, and they stood to lose more than they were likely to gain from a loose acquiescence in the action of central government, provincial or imperial; and when they sought favors from higher authorities they sought local and particular – in effect private – favors. Having little reason to identify their interests with those of the central government, they sought to keep the voices of local interests clear and distinct; and where it seemed necessary, they moved – though with little sense of innovating or taking actions of broad significance, and nowhere comprehensively or systematically – to bind representatives to local interests.[39]

Colonial governments, though originally dictated from England, were quickly affected by the development of internally homogeneous local units. As King John had originally done when calling for the knights and burgesses from each town four hundred years earlier in England, colonial government in America grew up on local divisions. Territory distinguished one locale from the other and thus one representative unit from another. "The town, not the individual, was the basic unit of political representation."[40] Territorial constituencies for representation in the colonial legislatures neatly mapped onto the local social and political structure of the day.

---

which denoted different objects. Rutman makes a similar observation on the difference of these terms. Rutman, "The Social Web," p. 165.

[35] Zagarri, *Politics of Size*, pp. 37–8. Georgia was not established until 1732.

[36] Lutz, *Popular Consent*, p. 155.

[37] Ibid., p. 159.

[38] Ibid., p. 160. See also Rakove, *Original Meanings*, p. 213, on the "localness" of colonial legislatures.

[39] Bailyn, *Ideological Origins*, p. 164.

[40] Bender, *Community and Social Change*, p. 67.

4.3 INDEPENDENCE AND THE UNITED STATES

Colonial legislatures remained more or less stable through the first half of the eighteenth century. That would change, of course, with the coming independence of the American colonies. On May 10, 1776, the Continental Congress called on the colonies to issue new constitutions to replace their charters, a bold statement of political independence anticipating the formal declaration later that summer.[41] The resulting documents established the political institutions of the newly forming states and used territory to define constituencies because each "town or county, with its unique characteristics, ... was the primary focus of political and social attachment for its inhabitants."[42] However, the concept of equal representation of persons was beginning to take hold: The towns and counties were assigned representatives to the state legislatures in very rough proportion to their populations.

With independence from England, the challenge of creating a nation confronted the thirteen colonies: how to create a union that at once respected the localness of the towns and counties upon which colonial governments had been structured while giving to the new union enough power to be effective? In 1781, with Maryland's accession, the Articles of Confederation were ratified, creating a weak federal union that ceded veto power to each state over the decisions of the whole.[43] Of note to us here is that constituencies for the Continental Congress were now *political* rather than *communal*: Representatives were elected from the state legislatures to the Congress rather than being elected by the territorially defined communities they represented.[44]

The weakness of the Articles of Confederation famously proved their undoing and the need for a stronger federal government occasioned calls for revising the Articles. In the summer of 1787, a new federal constitution was proposed that would strengthen the national government in part by denying states veto power over legislation. The practice of representing the states as political bodies continued in the U.S. Senate, as senators would be elected by their state legislatures and not the people themselves. But in the House of Representatives, the people of each state would directly elect their own representatives to the national legislature.

The House posed novel problems and opportunities for constituency definition. On the one hand, the new Constitution left the matter of constituency definition up to the states. In theory, states could simply use the local towns, counties, and parishes that formed the constituencies for their state legislatures as the basis of constituencies for the House of Representatives. The problem

---

[41] Wood, *Creation*, pp. 131–2.
[42] Lutz, *Popular Consent*, p. 76.
[43] Rakove, *Original Meanings*, pp. 25–8; Wood, *Creation*, pp. 463–7.
[44] It is not surprising, then, that local politics were viewed with higher esteem and importance than their colonial and national counterparts. For a nice description of this, see Ralph Lerner, "Giving Voice," Giornate Atlantich Di Storia Constituzionale, Laboratorio di Storia Constituzionale "Antoine Barnave" Universita degli Studi di Macerata, 13–15 September 1995, p. 15.

was that the small size of the new House of Representatives, combined with a commitment to rough population equality among districts meant that each electoral constituency for the House would be vastly larger than the electoral constituencies that had been used within many of the state governments. The local communities that constituted electoral constituencies in the *state* legislatures would thus have to be combined into larger constituencies to elect representatives to the House.

The fact that individual towns, boroughs, and counties would not comprise their own electoral constituencies for national representation occasioned great concern. Local communities had already expressed worry when their boundaries were occasionally broached for representation in state legislatures following independence. In 1776, for example:

> ...rebellious inhabitants of the Connecticut River valley in their vigorous opposition to representational schemes blurring town lines only voiced what many in all states of the region assumed to be the nature of the town. 'To unite half a dozen or more towns together, equally privileged, in order to make them equal to some one other town, is a new practice in politics. We may as well take the souls of a number of different persons and say they make but one, while yet they remain separate and different.'[45]

While the federal Constitution affirmed the localness of representation by leaving to states the implicit determination of the manner of election of national representatives,[46] localism was denied by the very size of the representational districts. With the creation of a relatively small House of Representatives, the U.S. Constitution thus ensured that its electoral constituencies would be distinct from the communities that were combined to form them, or, in very few cases of large cities, that were divided by them.

The Constitution of the United States established that each state would receive no more than one representative for every thirty thousand people. In 1790, when the first census was taken, there were roughly 4 million inhabitants in the United States, about 20 percent of whom were slaves.[47] Philadelphia, the largest city in the United States, had a population of forty-two thousand, and in New York thirty-two thousand people resided, roughly the size of a single electoral constituency. The "great" city of Boston numbered only eighteen thousand, only 60 percent the size of a new congressional district.

The sparseness of population in the South (Virginia, the Carolinas, and Georgia) meant that the problem there was even more acute. Charleston was the

---

[45] Wood, *Creation*, p. 192, quoting from "Instructions of the Freeholders of Buckingham County, VA" (May 1776), Force, ed., *American Archives*, 4th Ser., VI, 458–9 (Wood, *Creation*, p. 192, n. 51).

[46] Qualifications for electors of U.S. representatives are constitutionally defined to match those of the electors of "the most numerous branch of the State Legislature" (U.S. Constitution, Article I, Section 2).

[47] The U.S. population in 1790 was 3,929,214. U.S. Bureau of the Census, *Statistical Abstract of the United States: 1998*, 118th ed. (U.S. Bureau of the Census: Washington, DC, 1998), p. 8. State and local population figures in this paragraph are drawn from John S. Bassett, *The Federalist System* (New York: Cooper Square, 1968), pp. 163–77.

largest town in the South with fifteen thousand people. Virginia's largest city was Richmond (thirty-six hundred inhabitants), and only three other towns had a population exceeding two thousand.[48] There were no towns even of this size in North Carolina. Observing county population is also revealing. Of the seventy-four counties in Virginia whose militia population in 1780–1 Jefferson records, only eleven could muster militias over one thousand strong.[49] As Jefferson notes, "Every able-bodied freeman, between the ages of 16 and 50, is enrolled in the militia."[50] Even counting the non-able-bodied, women, and slaves, the entire population of that state (the largest in the Union in 1790) was 747,000, or an average of 10,000 per county. Had the population been evenly distributed (and it was not), national representation would require three counties to be combined for each representative sent to the House.

Electoral constituencies for political representation in the Anglo-American world had been based on where people lived because local communities were the central features of their lives. The sheer size of the new federal system of the United States necessitated the combination of these local divisions to create extremely large electoral constituencies undermining the local basis of political representation. The "constituency," though technically territorial, no longer mapped onto the local communities in which people lived. In the next chapter, we will consider what this meant for the founders of the new system.

[48] They were Norfolk, Petersburg, and Alexandria. Bassett, *The Federalist System*, p. 168.
[49] They were the counties of Accomac, Amelia, Bedford, Berkeley, Fauquier, Frederick, Halifax, Henry, Loudon, Mecklenburg, Monongalia, and Montgomery. Jefferson, *Notes on the State of Virginia*, p. 215, Query IX.
[50] Ibid., p. 216, Query IX.

5

Origins, Part 1

What Territorial Representation Was Not Meant To Do

> The history of representation in England, from which we have taken our model of legislation, is briefly this[:] before the institution of legislating by deputies, the whole free part of the community usually met for that purpose; when this became impossible, by the increase of numbers the community was divided into districts, from each of which was sent such a number of deputies as was a complete representation of the various numbers and orders of citizens within them; but can it be asserted with truth, that six men can be a complete and full representation of the numbers and various orders of the people in this state?
>
> – Cato, no. 5, Fall 1787[1]

At the founding of the United States, territorial electoral constituencies were an institutional habit of mind so ingrained in thought and practice that almost no argument about them appears in the literature. Further, territory was the basis (often paired with wealth, religion, or literacy) of representation in all colonial charters and their subsequent state constitutions at the founding. It is not discussed in any depth by those authors who influenced the writers and "ratifiers" of the Constitution: James Harrington, David Hume, Algernon Sidney, John Locke, or Montesquieu. Nor does it appear in the writings of the era, those of Edmund Burke, James Madison, Alexander Hamilton, Thomas Jefferson, or Thomas Paine, in other prominent primary sources[2] nor in the writings of the

---

[1] Herbert Storing, *The Complete Anti-Federalist*, 2.6.38, in *The Founder's Constitution* (hereafter *FC*), eds. Philip B. Kurland and Ralph Lerner, Vol. 2, Article 1, Section 2, Clause 3, no. 6 (hereafter 1:2:3, no. 6), p. 115.

[2] In addition to these, see John Adams, "Thoughts on Government," in *American Political Writing during the Founding Era*, eds. Charles S. Hyneman and Donald S. Lutz (Indianapolis, IN: Liberty Press, 1983), pp. 401–9; Anonymous, "Four Letters on Interesting Subjects," in *American Political Writing*, pp. 368–90; Anonymous, "Rudiments of Law and Government Deduced from the Law of Nature," in *American Political Writing*, pp. 565–605; Carter Braxton, "A Native of This Colony," in *American Political Writing*, pp. 328–9; *FC*, Vol. 1, pp. 382–423, and Vol. 2, pp. 41–68, 86–145; Theophilius Parsons, "The Essex Result," in *American Political Writing*, pp. 328–9.

Anti-Federalists. In only one place is another method of constituency definition even hinted at: professional class.[3]

Yet the founders were well aware that given the small size of the new House of Representatives, its electoral constituencies would have to be much larger than state legislative districts were. As we saw in Chapter 4, members of the House would have to represent multiple communities at once, altering the practice of local community representation that had been followed in the state legislatures. It was this fact that worried Cato and other opponents of the Constitution. Supporters countered that large electoral districts could be defended on the basis that persons, not places, deserved representation. But this familiar defense obscured the fact that people would still be represented by where they lived.[4] The large size of the district would matter far more than the fact that these districts were drawn territorially. Territory itself mattered only insofar as it enabled the achievement of other important deliberative, democratic ends.

In this chapter, I argue that the founders implicitly rejected the first four justifications for territory that I offered as plausible reasons in section 3.2. Both sides of the debate agreed that:

- Territorial districts would not *or* should not represent local communities of interest.
- Territorial districts would not *or* should not protect real property interests.
- Territorial districts would not *or* should not foster attachment to the national government.
- Territorial districts would not *or* should not enable citizens to consent to their electoral constituency.

To summarize these findings, first, supporters of the Constitution were wary of replicating interests within Congress and thought the large district would support these normative aims by undermining local communities of interest. Critics agreed that congressional districts would be much too large to represent particular interests in the national legislature, but for them this was a damning feature. Thus both sides agreed that no local community would have a particular voice in Congress, even if they disagreed about whether this was good or bad. Second, neither supporters nor critics of the Constitution thought the district would foster attachment to the national government. Instead, supporters argued that *local* attachment would provide a bulwark against national tyranny – attachment to the federal system being conditioned on its good behavior, not on "localness" of congressional districts. Critics agreed on the empirical assessment – districts would not foster attachment toward the national

---

[3] Alexander Hamilton, *The Federalist*, ed. Jacob E. Cooke, Essay 35 (hereafter *Federalist 35*) (Middletown, CT: Wesleyan University Press, 1961 [1787–8]), p. 219.

[4] James Madison provides a notable exception, presciently suggesting that states could use statewide multimember districts and avoid territorial divisions altogether. Nevertheless, this does not appear to have been his expectation. (See James Madison, "Notes," 9 August 1787, *FC*, Vol. 2, 2.2.3), p. 96.

government – but were less sanguine about alternative possibilities. Third, territorial constituencies were not justified as a means of protecting property primarily because there were other, more effective ways designed to protect it. Fourth, the fact that territorial districts enabled people to consent to one district or another did not receive any attention, even indirectly.

In this chapter, I present the textual evidence to support these findings, proceeding through an examination of the empirical and normative claims that each of these justifications imply. Recall the method discussed in section 3.3: We proceed indirectly looking for an endorsement of the normative aim and the expectation that, empirically, territorial districts could achieve that aim.

In what follows, I test the first three justifications for territory against the history and ideas of the founding period: that territorial districts would protect property (section 5.1); that they fostered attachment to the large national government (section 5.2); and that they were meant to define communities of interest for representation (section 5.3). The fourth justification of consent is not examined in any detail because of the lack of direct or indirect debate about using electoral constituencies as a method by which citizens could actually consent to their representatives. I thus reject it out of hand.[5] In Chapter 6, I present the evidence for the fifth justification of the last chapter: that territorial constituencies enabled various normative features of democratic politics.

5.1 TERRITORIAL DISTRICTS AND PROPERTY PROTECTION

The idea that territorial constituencies might have been intended to protect property resonates strongly with Lockean readings of the founding. The state, this story goes, was established to protect property rights. One of the most important of these interests was land itself, which might best be protected by organizing electoral districts along territorial lines. This justification entails the endorsement of the following claim, along with its empirical expectation:

Normative claim: Property rights ought to be protected.
Empirical expectation: Territorial electoral constituencies were expected to protect property rights.

The founders clearly supported some form of the normative claim, whether or not protection of wealth can be understood as *the* motivating factor of the revolution. The empirical expectation, however, explains why this justification fails: The founders did not expect territorial constituencies to protect property

---

[5] While it is true that people could choose to move from one district to another to get better representation (whatever that would mean), I found no discussion that such movement would actually take place. Although migration throughout the states was fluid during this period, I assume no one used this argument for the same reason few would find it persuasive today: The costs of moving are simply too high compared to the questionable marginal benefits of living in one different *congressional* district X versus another. I take up this argument in contemporary context in Chapter 7.

rights. Three facts illustrate this. First and most tellingly, state voting and office-holding qualifications at the time of the founding were based on *where voters lived* and not *where they owned property*. Second, by the eighteenth century, the concept of "property" had spread beyond land ownership to other forms of wealth. Finally, other rules – qualifications for voting and officeholding – *were* used to keep the very poor out of politics, but for more complicated reasons than simply to keep property rights secure. I will take each of these in turn.

First, if territorial representation were intended to protect property, we should expect that the right to vote *in a particular district* was conditioned on ownership of property *in that same district*. Yet, by 1787, only New York and Virginia had such requirements. In Massachusetts, Maryland, and South Carolina, property ownership in the district was merely one way to be quali-fied, residency the other. The other states made no such connection at all. The territorial district defined where people lived, not primarily where they owned property.[6]

Second, we can reject the empirical expectation because "property" meant far more than land even by the time of the founding period. Territorial districting involves drawing lines on the ground, and because somebody owns that ground, it might seem natural that territorially defined districts are related to the pro-tection of property. By the eighteenth century, however, the concept of property had broadened well beyond land to include more portable goods and rights.[7] By the fall of 1787, Madison wrote in *Federalist 10* that the "property interests" that "have ever formed distinct interests in society" are immediately expanded to "creditors and debtors, landed, manufacturing, mercantile and monied interests."[8] Or as Gordon Wood argued, "Eighteenth-century Whiggism had made no rigid distinction between people and property. Property had been

---

[6] Andrew Rehfeld, "Constructing the Nation: Territorial Representation and the 13 Original State Constitutions," paper presented at the American Political Science Association Annual Meeting, Washington, DC, 1997.

[7] The extension of "property" from land and goods into broader rights goes back to England in the early seventeenth century. Clive Holmes, "Parliament, Liberty, Taxation, and Property," in *Parliament and Liberty from the Reign of Elizabeth to the English Civil War*, ed. J. H. Hexter. (Stanford, CA: Stanford University Press, 1992), pp. 122–54; Ralph Lerner, *The Thinking Rev-olutionary: Principle and Practice in the New Republic* (Ithaca, NY: Cornell University Press, 1988), pp. 10–16; John Philip Reid, *The Concept of Representation in the Age of the American Revolution* (Chicago: University of Chicago Press, 1989), p. 41.

[8] The expansion of property to non-land-based forms was central to Madison's argument of pitting faction against faction. As Martin Diamond observes, "Publius sees in the large commercial republic the possibility for the first time of subordinating the difference over the amount of property to the difference over kind of property. In such a republic the hitherto fatal class struggle is replaced by the safe, even salutary struggle among different kinds of propertied interests." Martin Diamond, "The Federalist," in *History of Political Philosophy*, eds. Leo Strauss and Joseph Cropsey (Chicago: University of Chicago Press, 1987), p. 677. On Madison's expectation that commercial and manufacturing interests would overshadow traditional landed, agrarian interests, see Robert J. Morgan, "Madison's Theory of Representation in the Tenth Federalist," *Journal of Politics* 36, November 1974: 852–85.

defined not simply as material possessions but, following Locke, as the attributes of a man's personality that gave him a political character."⁹ If protecting property justifies territorial districting, it does so only when "property" means "land." Given the expansion of its meaning, there is little evidence of a connection here.

Finally, other political institutions were designed as more efficient and direct ways to secure property rights.¹⁰ First, property qualifications for voting and officeholding were originally justified because they purportedly secured voters and candidates who had a proper stake in society; only people with property should vote or serve in office because it was their property that would be affected by legislation. Property qualifications also were a signaling device for virtue and independence.¹¹ The wealthy man, the argument went, had proven by his industry or maintenance of his inheritance that he was worthy to vote or to hold office. Wealth was also a signal for independence of mind. As Montesquieu described, "In choosing a representative, all citizens in the various districts should have the right to vote except those whose estate is so humble that they are deemed to have no will of their own."¹² The financially secure voter (or representative) would be less easy to influence improperly than would be the poor citizen.¹³ Not surprisingly, qualifications for officeholding were thus higher than qualifications for voting. Protections of property were also proposed through the construction of a second house of the legislature that was explicitly designed to protect such interests. Famously, the U.S. Senate transformed from an aristocratic institution into a body representing the states

---

⁹ Gordon Wood, *Creation of the American Republic* (New York: Norton, 1993 [1969]), p. 219. See also Elbridge Gerry's remarks in convention that the commercial interests ought to check the landed interests "without which oppression will take place..." (FC 1:3:1, 2, Vol. 2, p. 186).

¹⁰ See for example the provision in Article 1, Section 9 of the U.S. Constitution. Donald Lutz offers a nuanced argument of the connection between property and territorial interests. "There was also the important fact that the towns in the interior were poorer, and generally speaking, had few wealthy people, if any. Therefore, the property requirement also had geographical implications." Donald Lutz, *Popular Consent and Popular Consent: Whig Political Theory in the Early State Constitutions* (Baton Rouge, LA; and London: Louisiana State University Press, 1980), p. 114. Yet these geographical variations were not prominently noticed in the debates over the Constitution, by which time property requirements had been dramatically lowered throughout the states. As Lutz notes in the same passage, "That property requirements were only slightly reduced and not eliminated does not so much reflect a negative attitude toward popular programmatic consent – although there was a substantial amount of negative sentiment – as it reflects the general irrelevancy of the requirement."

¹¹ These justifications appear in various pamphlets throughout the period. For useful discussions of property and representation, see Lutz, *Popular Consent*, pp. 100–6; Reid, *The Concept of Representation in the Age of the American Revolution*, pp. 31–42; Wood, *Creation*, pp. 214–22.

¹² Charles de Secondat, baron de La Brède et de Montesquieu, *The Spirit of the Laws* (New York: Cambridge University Press, 1989 [1748]), 2:11:6, p. 160.

¹³ Good ideas die hard. Ross Perot's 1992 United States presidential campaign employed this rationale as an appeal to voters who were told that his vast wealth would enable him to act independently of special interests.

in the national government, even if today it might be taken as representing an oligarchic interest.[14] Although the territorial district could logically be added, these protections were well tended to in other ways by the institutions of the proposed Constitution. For these reasons, we can say that the use of territory to define House electoral districts had little to do with the protection of property.

5.2 ATTACHMENT TO NATIONAL GOVERNMENT

The proposed federal government would establish a republican form of government over a vast territorial expanse. In Montesquieu's opinion, history showed that republican forms required the close attachment and engagement of citizens to and with their government. Government at a distance would break these bonds of attachment leading to instability and harm.

The attachment justification for territory thus begins from this fact: It is hard for citizens within large, representative governments to form "strong chords of sympathy" toward their national government. Defining electoral constituencies territorially, the justification goes, may help foster these chords. This justification can be parsed into its supporting parts:

Normative claim: Attachment to the national government ought to be fostered.
Empirical expectation: Territorial constituencies were expected to facilitate local attachment to the national government.

At the founding, we can say that Federalists and Anti-Federalists (that is, the supporters and opponents of the proposed Constitution) rejected the attachment justification because neither side expected territorial districts to foster such attachment. Both sides agreed that people would be strongly attached to their local communities. But neither side expected territorial congressional districts to foster local attachment because they were so large. The size of each constituency would undermine its ability to attach citizens to their government, even while people would attach to the things closest at hand.

Agreeing with Montesquieu that large republics could not generate citizen attachment from afar, the Federalists also rejected the normative claim, turning it on its head: Local and state governments were an important protective check against the inroads of adventuresome national politicians. Even further, they argued, the large district transcending many local communities might have the salutary effect of undermining local ties.[15] They thus created a novel solution to the problem of attachment in large republics: The federal government would have to *earn* its citizens' attachment. By contrast, Anti-Federalists endorsed

---

[14] I am indebted to Ralph Lerner for this point. For a forceful argument about the aristocratic nature of elections, see Bernard Manin, *The Principles of Representative Government* (New York: Cambridge University Press, 1997), passim.

[15] I am grateful to an anonymous reviewer at *Studies in American Political Development* for suggesting this point. It is closely related to the argument about communities of interest developed in the next section 5.3.

the normative claim because they believed citizens should be attached to the government that rules them. The fact that citizens could not be so attached within a large republic provided them good reason not to endorse the proposed constitution.

To understand these arguments, we begin with a brief discussion of Montesquieu because of his relevance and influence on the founders (5.2.1), Edmund Burke because of the conceptual clarify he brings to the issue (despite his writing after the founding) (5.2.2), and finally in section 5.2.3, the arguments of the founders themselves.

5.2.1 Montesquieu's Argument

In an argument that animated both sides of the ratification debate, Montesquieu warned that large republics encouraged factions because "the common good is sacrificed to a thousand considerations; it is subordinated to exceptions; it depends upon accidents. In a small one, the public good is better felt, better known, lies nearer to each citizen; abuses are less extensive there and consequently less protected."[16] Organizing constituents in a large republic was not a sustainable possibility because it was contrary to the nature of republican forms of government.

Montesquieu's observations are commensurate with the nesting idea of local attachment. To the extent that government of large territorial areas is to be undertaken, one must respect and honor not just the local political distinctions but the social mores, habits, *and* laws of the locale. Small republics will tend to be internally strong but unable to resist foreign incursions. "If a republic is small, it is destroyed by a foreign force; if it is large, it is destroyed by an internal vice." The federal republic is the only solution, an association of smaller groups. "It is a society of societies that make a new one, which can be enlarged by new associates that unite with it."[17] Representation in such republics should ideally be by town and population.[18]

Indeed, Montesquieu argues that town representation is useful for practical reasons:

One knows the needs of one's own town better than those of other towns, and one judges the ability of one's neighbors better than that of one's other compatriots. Therefore, members of the legislative body must not be drawn from the body of the nation at large; it is proper for the inhabitants of each principal town to choose a representative from it.[19]

Montesquieu's point is not however, a defense of territorial representation, per se. Rather, it is a defense of the principle that representatives should be drawn

---

[16] Montesquieu, *Spirit of the Laws*, 1:8:16, p. 124.

[17] Ibid., 2:9:1, p. 131.

[18] Ibid., 2:9:3, p. 133.

[19] Ibid., 2:11:6, p. 159. Note that Montesquieu's argument presupposes territorial districts that are coextensive with a defined community.

from their constituencies however they are defined – a principle not then accepted in England. The logic of Montesquieu's general point can be applied to other kinds of constituencies: Doctors should represent doctors, the wealthy should represent the wealthy, blacks should represent blacks, and so on.

Montesquieu offers little on which to base a theory of local attachment within the large republic, primarily because he was skeptical that such a republic could survive. Large republics fail in part because their size inhibits citizen attachment to the public good; they just deteriorate into faction. He agrees that individuals will attach to local groups more readily than large ones.[20] Most of the cases he cites emphasize the importance of generating local loyalties to the ruler. But, excepting the passage from Book 11 just quoted, local constituencies in the context of representative government are not offered as a way to foster local attachment within large republics. It is entirely likely that Montesquieu *would* endorse territorial constituencies as long as they were coextensive with local jurisdictions, because they would help foster attachment to the head of government. However, there is no such explicit argument within *Spirit of the Laws*, nor are such "locally based" electoral constituencies consistent with the necessities of a large republic.

5.2.2 Burke's Reflections

To be attached to the subdivision, to love the little platoon we belong to in society, is the first principle (the germ as it were) of public affections. It is the first link in the series by which we proceed toward a love to our country and to mankind.

– Edmund Burke[21]

In contrast to Montesquieu, we find in Edmund Burke's *Reflections on the Revolution in France* the clearest articulation of the attachment justification for territorial representation. Published in 1790, and thus obviously not known to the founders, Burke's argument establishes the justification for grouping constituents for the purpose of inculcating love of country and obedience to law. At the same time, Burke rejects the revolutionary plan of drawing new territorial districts into exact geometrical units. In Burke we find someone who valued territorial groupings only because communities had local, that is territorial, bases. His arguments help us understand the theoretical dimensions of the argument that we will find in the debates at the founding of the United States. So we proceed here as a way to clarify and illustrate the meaning and appeal of the attachment justification using a source from the same era as the founders.

---

[20] For other examples, see his discussion of the Germanic peoples (ibid., 6:28:2, p. 535); the interplay of local customs and Roman law (ibid., 6:28:12, p. 547); and the use that Charlemagne made of local loyalty when governing a vast empire (ibid., 6:31:19, p. 699).

[21] Edmund Burke, *Reflections on the Revolution in France*, ed. J. G. A. Pocock (Indianapolis, IN: Hackett, 1987), p. 41.

Burke began by criticizing the new French system of representation designed to provide territorial representation according to exact geographical lines:

The French builders, clearing away as mere rubbish whatever they found and, like their ornamental gardeners, forming everything into an exact level, propose to rest the whole local and general legislature on three bases of three different kinds: one geometrical, one arithmetical, and the third financial....[22]

Burke is critical of using "the metaphysics of an undergraduate and the mathematics and arithmetic of an exciseman to structure government," a system that owes more to human nature than Euclid.[23] Thus, it is not that nesting per se was problematic, but rather that artificial divisions violated those "inconveniences for which use had found remedies, and habit had supplied accommodation and patience. In this new pavement of square within square, and this organization and semi-organization, made on the system of Empedocles and Buffon, and not upon any politic principle, it is impossible that innumerable local inconveniences, to which men are not habituated, must not arise."[24] The problem was that new divisions – however perfect they were on a map – ignored the political world on which France had been built:

They have attempted to confound all sorts of citizens, as well as they could, into one homogenous mass; and then they divided this their amalgama into a number of incoherent republics. They reduce men to loose counters, merely for the sake of simple telling, and not to figures whose power is to arise from their place in the table.[25]

The nested French system also kept representatives too disconnected from the people. "There must be many degrees, and some stages, before the representative can come in contact with his constituent... these two persons are to have no sort of communion with each other."[26] Though Burke was the most famous supporter of virtual representation, the legislator still needed contact with his constituents so that he could know those interests he was virtually and actually representing:

The electors and elected throughout, especially in the rural *cantons*, will be frequently without any civil habitudes or connections, or any of that natural discipline which is the soul of a true republic. Magistrates and collectors of revenue are now no longer acquainted with their districts, bishops with their dioceses, or curates with their parishes.[27]

Burke rightly saw that the lack of attachment had practical effects on the operation of government. Nesting need not disconnect the elected from the people,

---

[22] Ibid, p. 152.

[23] Ibid., p. 162. As Pocock notes, Burke's comments on the geometrical formation of France's system were apparently erroneous. Ibid., p. 225, note lxxxviii. Burke's theoretical points still hold.

[24] Ibid., p. 152.

[25] Ibid., p. 162.

[26] Ibid., p. 153.

[27] Ibid., p. 161.

though by Burke's light there were too many impermeable layers for the French system to operate properly.

The result of improper nesting was a citizenry who failed to develop a love of their nation, and in this way the attachment justification emerges with clarity:

It is boasted that the geometrical policy has been adopted, that all local ideas should be sunk, and that the people should no longer be Gascons, Picards, Bretons, Normans, but Frenchmen, with one country, one heart and one Assembly. But instead of being all Frenchmen, the greater likelihood is that the inhabitants of that region will shortly have no country. No man ever was attached by a sense of pride, partiality, or real affection to a description of square measurement. He never will glory in belonging to the Chequer No. 71, or to any other badge-ticket. We begin our public affections in our families. No cold relation is a zealous citizen. We pass on to our neighborhoods and our habitual provincial connections. These are inns and resting places. Such divisions of our country as have been formed by habit, and not be a sudden jerk of authority, were so many little images of the great country in which the heart found something which it could fill. The love to the whole is not extinguished by this subordinate partiality.[28]

Contra Montesquieu, keeping electoral constituencies small enough to foster local attachments made representative government over a large nation possible. And thus the new French system, these new "colonies of the rights of men," in Burke's derision of Thomas Paine, bears striking similarity to Tacitus' observations of the "declining policy of Rome" in establishing military colonies:

...[N]o longer were entire legions led off, as once they were, with their tribunes, and centurions, and soldiers grouped in their own distinct centuries, in order to constitute a state by their concord and mutual affection; but, strangers to each other, were brought in of different companies, without a leader, without mutual attachment, suddenly gathered together, as if from any other class of men, a crowd rather than a colony.[29]

Without attachment on a human scale, the general good of the nation was unlikely to be realized.

Burke's observations crystallize the attachment argument and its relevance to territory. First, there was nothing inherent to territorial distinctions, nothing magical about territorial constituencies, except insofar as they corresponded to existing administrative units or communities. Thus the French had erred not by using territory in drawing their geometrical districts, but by ignoring what were in Burke's assessment "natural" distinctions. Second, and reflecting Montesquieu's argument previously, territory directly aids attachment by making it easier for communication between the representative and his constituents. Both of these conceptual issues were subjects of debate around the time of the federal convention and the ratification of the Constitution.

---

[28] Ibid., p. 173.
[29] Tacitus, *Annales* 1.14, sect. 27, in Burke, *Reflections*, p. 161, n. 46, trans. J. G. A. Pocock, ibid., pp. 225–6.

5.2.3 Attachment to the United States

The idea that nested communities could foster attachment in a large republic was articulated in America at least as early as the 1770s. Towns and counties, after all, constituted the states, and though not as large as the confederation would be, the states were nonetheless historically large republics. As Gordon Wood has documented, Jefferson and the radicals of Pennsylvania were both impressed by the role that local involvement in politics played in attaching citizens to government. "Men became concerned about government because they participated daily in the affairs of their tithings and towns, not only by paying taxes but by performing public duties and by personally making laws."[30] In 1778, each colony faced a fundamental constitutional question of attachment: If England was the source of its political existence, what justified the colony's authority over its citizens now that it was independent? In New Hampshire, the response was to nest themselves:

When the Crown's authority was rejected, "*the people made a stand at the first legal stage, viz. their town incorporations*," miniature constitutions that made everyone of the towns "a State by itself," able to justify binding its minority by the majority. So convinced now were these rebellious westerners that a corporate charter was needed to establish and make legal a body politic that they recommended in 1778 to all towns not already incorporated that they "forthwith incorporate themselves."[31]

By the time of the federal convention, the animating concern had shifted, in Benjamin Franklin's words, from the "excess of power in the rulers" to the "defect of obedience in the subjects."[32]

Supporters of the Constitution thus faced the problem of large territorial government that we saw foreshadowed by Montesquieu and afterward developed by Burke. How could individuals attach themselves and be loyal and compelled to obey government at a distance? Both Hamilton and Madison accepted that attachment naturally arose to things physically nearer to one's gaze,[33] a political adaptation of David Hume's moral theory.[34] In the eyes of Hamilton and

---

[30] Wood, *Creation*, p. 228.

[31] Wood, *Creation*, p. 288, quoting from *A Public Defence of the Right of the New-Hampshire Grants . . . to Associate Together, and Form Themselves into an Independent State* (Dresden, VT, 1779), in Nathaniel Bouton, et al., eds., *Documents and Records Relating to New Hampshire, 1623–1800*, 40 vols. (Concord and Manchester, NH: NH State Printer, 1867–1943), X, pp. 312–13.

[32] Benjamin Franklin, *Boston Independent Chronicle*, 10 May 1787, quoted in Wood, *Creation*, p. 432.

[33] Concerning the strength of the New York constitution, and the argument that it should have served as a "standard for the United States," Hamilton wrote, "I answer that it is not very probable the other states should entertain the same opinion of our institutions which we do ourselves. It is natural to suppose that they are hitherto more attached to their own, and that each would struggle for the preference." Hamilton, *Federalist 83*, p. 571. More explicit arguments follow later in this chapter.

[34] "Virtue, placed at such a distance, is liked a fixed star, which though to the eye of reason, it may appear as luminous as the sun in his meridian, is so infinitely removed, as to affect the

Madison, this tendency to attach to local objects was a mixed blessing. On the one hand, local attachment would protect citizens from federal intrusions into their liberties. On the other hand, local attachment encouraged and enabled the worst sort of demagoguery. Attachment to a large republic thus needed to be generated in ways that did not depend on local attachments. Characteristically, *The Federalist* argued that citizens would be attached to their national government only when it pursued the public good. The federal system would thus demand and earn the obedience of its subjects depending on its good behavior.

Anti-Federalists were less sanguine. Montesquieu, in their view, was essentially correct: Large republics *were* tyrannies waiting to happen in large part because it was too difficult for citizens to be attached to them. Martin Diamond's description of the Anti-Federalist position reflects Montesquieu's worry that any large republican government is doomed to despotism:

> To preserve their rule, the people must be patriotic, vigilant, and informed. This requires that the people give loving attention to public things, and that the affairs of the country be on a scale commensurate with popular understanding. But in large countries the people are baffled and rendered apathetic by the complexity of public affairs, and at last become absorbed in their own pursuits.

Critics of the Constitution rejected large republics and saw a limit to the possibilities of nesting. State government – itself an admittedly nested system – was as large a republic as could be effectively instantiated. Larger republics had to "respect the primacy of the member states," and thus critics rejected the proposed Constitution "as resting on a novel and false view of republican union."[35]

Because of the large size of the electoral constituency, neither side expected congressional districts to foster attachment to national government. As we'll see, the federal system was to be three-tiered, with citizens at its base, the state (either as legislators or electors) at its center, and the federal government at the head. State and local jurisdictions, along with the good works of the national

---

senses, neither with light nor heat. Bring this virtue nearer, by our acquaintance or connexion with the persons, or even by an eloquent recital of the case; our hearts are immediately caught, our sympathy enlivened, and our cool approbation converted into the warmest sentiments of friendship and regard." David Hume, *An Enquiry Concerning the Principles of Morals*, ed. J. B. Schneewind (Indianapolis, IN: Hacket, 1983), Section V, p. 50. Hume also praises Harrington's *Oceana* for its nested system of government, though not explicitly for the attachment this nesting expected to accrue to its head. See David Hume, "Idea of a Perfect Commonwealth," in *David Hume, Essays: Moral Political and Literary*, ed. Eugene F. Miller (Indianapolis, IN: Liberty Fund, 1987), pp. 512–29. Hume ultimately endorses nesting in government for both the attachment it engenders and the hesitation it builds into the actions of government. See Hume, "Of Some Remarkable Customs," in *David Hume, Essays*, pp. 366–76. Also see Epstein's treatment of Hume and Madison. Epstein, *The Political Theory of the Federalist*, pp. 101–2.

[35] Diamond, "The Federalist," pp. 663–4. In his discussion of *Federalist 14*, Diamond rightly notes even the states "were not small republics as that term had been traditionally understood; they were already *extensive* republics" (p. 667). Even Rhode Island was larger than what had been considered a "small" republic.

system, provided the arenas for attachment to occur. Some territorial units *were* meant to facilitate attachment, but those units were not districts for the House of Representatives.

Hamilton's observations in *Federalist 17* establish the centrality of physical proximity to the concept of attachment:

It is a known fact in human nature that its affections are commonly weak in proportion to the distance or diffusiveness of the object. Upon the same principle that a man is more attached to his family than to his neighbourhood, to his neighbourhood than to the community at large, the people of each State would be apt to feel a stronger byass towards their local governments than towards the government of the Union; unless the force of that principle should be destroyed by a much better administration of the latter.

The conditional establishes Hamilton's expectation that the federal government would be better administered and more highly respected than the obviously troubled if not failed local democratic experiments. However, local institutions, particularly the "ordinary administration of criminal and civil justice," will be "the most powerful, most universal and most attractive source of popular obedience and attachment." These local institutions will provide "[t]his great cement of society...." So much so, Hamilton argued against his critics, that the states will be "not unfrequently dangerous rivals to the power of the Union." His goal was to calm opponents' fears that a federal government could easily lay claim to the loyalties of its citizenry at the expense of the states, by agreeing in clear and forceful terms: The most natural attachment of individuals to political societies does indeed occur at the local level.[36]

Madison agreed that citizens would initially attach themselves to local and state governments in favor of the federal authority so much so that it would provide an important balance to federal power.[37] Critics of the Constitution, argued Madison, ought not to fear the federal government's authority to raise an army, for example. Such an army would be necessarily limited and weak and "would not yield in the United States an army of more than twenty-five or thirty thousand men. To these would be opposed a militia amounting to near half a million citizens with arms in their hands, officered by men chosen from among themselves, fighting for their common liberties, and united and conducted by governments possessing their affections and confidence." Local attachments to "subordinate governments" thus formed a "barrier against the enterprizes of ambition, more insurmountable than any which a simple government of any form can admit of."[38] These local bonds formed a crucial bulwark against tyranny, precisely because they would fail to attach the citizen to the federal republic.

---

[36] Hamilton, *Federalist 17*, p. 107.

[37] "Many considerations, besides those suggested on a former occasion, seem to place it beyond doubt, that the first and most natural attachment of the people will be to the governments of their respective States." Madison, *Federalist 46*, p. 316.

[38] Ibid., p. 321–2.

But these strong local commitments had a dark side. Even as it provided a shield against tyranny, Hamilton argued, local attachment could also lead to demagoguery, ambitious individuals "seizing the opportunity of some casual dissatisfaction among the people." Thus, a strong union across a large territory would allow the promotion of public felicity, and this would serve to attach the people properly to their government. There is, wrote Hamilton:

... an obvious distinction between the interest of the people in the public felicity, and the interest of their local rulers in the power and consequence of their offices. The people of America may be warmly attached to the government of the Union at times, when the particular rulers of particular States, stimulated by the natural rivalship of power and by the hopes of personal aggrandisement... may be in a very opposite temper.[39]

What then for the Federalists would serve as the source of attachment to the federal system? As foreshadowed by Hamilton's preceding statement, attachment between citizens and the federal government would be conditional given only when the government *earned* the affections of its people. Madison later emphasized that the love of liberty would strike attachment among men toward "the Union of America, and be able to set a due value on the means of preserving it."[40] Most decisively he wrote:

[If] the people should in future become more partial to the federal than to the State governments, the change can only result, from such manifest and irresistible proofs of a better administration, as will overcome all their antecedent propensities. And in that case the people ought not surely to be precluded from giving most of their confidence where they may discover it to be most due....[41]

Madison also argued the corollary, that unstable government will cause a "diminution of attachment and reverence which steals into the hearts of the people, towards a political system which betray so many marks of infirmity, and disappoints so many of their flattering hopes. No government anymore than an individual will long be respected, without being truly respectable, nor be truly respectable without possessing a certain portion of order and stability."[42]

As advocated in so much of *The Federalist*, the goal of the federal system was to redirect the actions of individuals toward the public good. Here, the system would redirect a natural sentiment to attach to close objects (such as local demagogues) toward the more distant republic. To inculcate that love, the federal government would have to be brought closer to its citizens.[43] A good government

---

[39] Hamilton, *Federalist* 59, p. 402.

[40] Madison, *Federalist* 41, p. 273.

[41] Madison, *Federalist* 46, p. 317.

[42] Madison, *Federalist* 63, p. 422.

[43] See also Jay, *Federalist* 2, p. 12, in which Jay argues that the people's "universal and uniform attachment to the cause of the Union, rests on great and weighty reasons." His support of the Union (versus various confederations) continues in Jay, *Federalist* 5, pp. 23–7.

affects the lives of citizens through its ordinary operations, bringing its own virtues close to the hearts of its subjects:

> ... [T]he more the operations of the national authority are intermingled in the ordinary exercise of government; the more the citizens are accustomed to meet with it in the common occurrences of their political life; the more it is familiarised to their sight and to their feelings; the further it enters into those objects which touch the most sensible cords, and put in motion the most active springs of the human heart; the greater will be the probability that it will conciliate the respect and attachment of the community. Man is very much a creature of habit. A thing that rarely strikes his senses will generally have but little influence upon his mind. A government continually at a distance and out of sight, can hardly be expected to interest the sensations of the people. The inference is, that the authority of the Union, and the affections of the citizens towards it, will be strengthened rather than weakened by its extension to what are called matters of internal concern; and will have less occasion to recur to force in proportion to the familiarity and comprehensiveness of its agency. The more it circulates through those channels and currents, in which the passions of mankind naturally flow, the less will it require the aid of the violent and perilous expedients of compulsion.[44]

Policy thus emerged as the preferred means to generate citizen attachment to their national government, without the pernicious effects or local attachment. It is not especially through the connection of local representatives, though this can admittedly help. However, Hamilton emphasized the right of the federal system to involve itself in local matters as a way of fomenting public attachment. Territorial constituencies would be critical to achieving this aim only to the extent they facilitated communication from representatives to their constituents.

What role, then, do members of the House of Representatives play in attaching citizens to their national government? Their function is twofold, and neither directly justifies territorial representation. First, only by the election of the best representatives is the output of the federal system likely to be of the best quality, and thus deserving of attachment. Expanding on his argument in *Federalist 10*, Madison famously argued that large districts will tend to elect better representatives, in turn producing better federal governance. And in *Federalist 57*, he writes, "Reason ... assures us, that as in so great a number, a fit representative would be most likely to be found, so the choice would be less likely to be diverted from him, by the intrigues of the ambitious, or the bribes of the rich."[45] It is *size of the constituency* and not its territoriality that increases the likelihood that the best representatives would be elected. The effect of local constituencies on attachment is thus indirect and not related to territory, except insofar as it happens to promote the election of the most virtuous. As we will see in Chapter 6, limits of communication and promotion of virtue required territorial proximity in order to elect the best representative. But attachment to the national system did not justify territorial constituencies per se.

---

[44] Hamilton, *Federalist 27*, pp. 173–4.
[45] Madison, *Federalist 57*, p. 388.

Second, representatives stood as protection against any possible aristocratic tendency of the Senate that would foster bad government:

Against the force of the immediate representatives of the people, nothing will be able to maintain even the constitutional authority of the senate, but such a display of enlightened policy, and attachment to the public good, as will divide with that branch of the legislature, the affections and support of the entire body of the people themselves.[46]

Attachment to the system is the result of a good system. Not only did the federal constitution weaken Burke's idea of nesting platoons of soldiers and close affections of citizens; the Federalists looked upon the idea with great suspicion. The natural tendency of man to attach upward through local affections was turned on its head. Attachment to the federal system would be conditional by good behavior. The good behavior of the government was only ensured through the election of the best representatives, a need that only incidentally justified local constituencies.[47]

In sum, neither supporters nor opponents of the Constitution expected territorial constituencies to generate attachment to the national government. Whether or not this was praiseworthy or lamentable was, as we have seen, precisely the point of disagreement.

5.3 TERRITORIAL DISTRICTS AND COMMUNITIES OF INTEREST

We arrive now at perhaps the most compelling reason for using territorial constituencies: There seems to be something about where people live that should be made present (represented) in the national legislature. The representative assembly, John Adams wrote, "should be in miniature an exact portrait of the people at large."[48] In particular, if local interests were something worth representing, then defining constituencies by where citizens lived made more sense than defining them along some other dimension. This justification implies that the founders endorsed the following normative claim and had the following empirical expectation:

Normative claim: Local political interests ought to be represented in the
                         national legislature.

---

[46] Madison, *Federalist 63*, p. 431.

[47] Gordon Wood argues that *social* nesting was part of *The Federalist*:

For as Hamilton's social analysis in *The Federalist*, Number 35, suggested, what justified elite rule, together with the notion of virtual representation and the idea of the homogeneity and unity of the people's interest, was the sense that all parts of the society were of a piece, that all ranks and degrees were organically connected through a great chain in such a way that those on the top were necessarily involved in the welfare of those below them (Wood, *Creation*, p. 498).

While I concur with this argument, it obviously contributes nothing to a justification for territorial representation.

[48] John Adams, "Thoughts on Government," in *American Political Writing*, p. 403.

Empirical expectation: Territorial congressional districts were expected to be coterminous with local political interests

Although these claims might seem to be precisely why territorial constituencies were used for political representation, there is evidence that no one expected territorial constituencies to be coterminous with local political interests: Both supporters and opponents of the proposed constitution thought that the new electoral constituencies would be much too large for that. In addition, the Federalists explicitly rejected the normative claim, arguing for a vision of political representation that kept interests out of the legislature in service to the public good. Anti-Federalists did endorse the normative claim, arguing that national representation should indeed be about representing local community interests. So the "communities of interest" justification failed for both sides *only* because neither side expected territorial constituencies to be conterminous with local interests.[49] The judgment that this failure was a good thing entailed the rejection of the normative claim, a rejection only *endorsed* by the Federalists while lamented by their opponents.[50]

I present the evidence for these arguments first with a discussion of Madison and Hamilton's arguments (section 5.3.1) followed by the debate at the convention and the Anti-Federalist response (section 5.3.2).

5.3.1 The Arguments of Madison and Hamilton

Madison and Hamilton were wary of institutionalizing faction in any way that would subvert the public good. Their approach to congressional districts is thus illuminating because both of them expected that territorial constituencies would be the norm. For Madison, local districts had been a primary source of faction in the state legislatures during the confederation, and therefore of great

---

[49] The practice of equalizing district population for the purpose of "fair" representation even when town and county boundaries are not respected provides little support, for two reasons. Population equality and representation of place are not logically incompatible. In fact, during the 1770s and 1780s, states provided representation to their towns (counties or parishes) based both on location and population, allocating more representatives to larger towns. Thomas More's plans in *Utopia* provide another way to achieve population equality and representation of place: The state could move citizens from one town to another to maintain roughly equal population between towns. This, of course, would have violated just about every underlying principle of liberty and freedom that fueled the revolution. The point is that it is not *impossible* to achieve these two aims. See Thomas More, *Utopia*, eds. George M. Logan and Robert M. Adams, Cambridge Texts in the History of Political Thought (Cambridge, UK: Cambridge University Press, 1993 [1516]), pp. 55–6.

[50] Robert J. Dinkin makes the reasonable argument that the Federalists originated as "Cosmopolitans" and the anti-Federalists as "Localists." Robert J. Dinkin, *Voting in Revolutionary America: A Study of Elections in the Original Thirteen States 1776–1789* (Westport, CT: Greenwood Press, 1982), p. 8. For the Anti-Federalists' concerns that a large republic would eviscerate local concerns and thus undermine the rights of individuals, see Herbert Storing, *What the Anti-Federalists Were For: The Political Thought of the Opponents of the Constitution* (Chicago: University of Chicago Press, 1981).

concern. The largeness of electoral districts for the House would answer his concerns about the localism that had erupted there. Similarly, Hamilton worried about the improper influence of particular interests on national legislation, but believed these would be randomly distributed among electoral constituencies throughout the republic. We can illustrate this by tracing each author's argument that would appear in *The Federalist*.

In the spring of 1787, Madison famously prepared for the coming convention in Philadelphia. Among his many worries, his concern that localism would improperly influence the new national legislature was particularly keen. In Madison's view, local electoral constituencies had been a corrupting influence on state legislatures during the confederation: "We find the representatives of Counties and corporations in the Legislatures of the States, much more disposed to sacrifice the aggregate interest, and even authority, to the local views of the Constituents: than the latter to the former."[51] Local interests were among the more potent forces against the advancement of the public good.[52]

Given his concerns about localism, it should surprise us that in *Federalist 10* – Madison's essay on the intermingling of faction and government in the extended republic – Madison does not explicitly mention the congressional district or even the local community as a source of faction. Their absence from the enumerated causes of faction in a large republic is all the more surprising because local districts were explicitly listed among the sources of faction in his earlier drafts of the essay that focused on the problems of small republics. The absence of local districts in *Federalist 10* provides suggestive evidence that in the federal system, Madison believed the large district would help neutralize local interests rather than replicate them within Congress. We can make this claim because the earlier versions of *Federalist 10* were addressed to the problems of the state legislatures while, in contrast, *Federalist 10* was a defense of the proposed national system. The U.S. congressional district – as compared to the state legislative district – would thus not serve to define any particularity at all.

Madison's advocacy of large representative districts is now famous, but in many cases for different reasons than those I am presenting here. However, the following analysis turns a common reading of Madison's argument on its head.

---

[51] James Madison, "Letter to Thomas Jefferson," 24 October 1787, in *Papers of James Madison*, eds. William T. Hutchinson, William M. E. Rachal, Robert Rutand, et al. (Chicago: University of Chicago Press, 1962–91), Vol. 10, p. 211. (Hereafter, PJM, Vol. 10, p. 211.)

[52] Although local communities defined the electoral constituency, not all local communities received representation for purely political reasons. Rosemarie Zagarri, *Politics of Size: Representation in the United States 1776–1850* (Ithaca, NY, and London: Cornell University Press, 1987), p. 43. Also, "[b]y 1787, only five states continued to use towns as the apportionment unit, five used the county, and four used the county plus the few major cities." Lutz, *Popular Consent*, p. 167. States changed to larger districts as their populations grew, towns multiplied, and their legislatures thus grew unwieldy.

Instead of minimizing the effects of factions by multiplying them *within* the legislature, it supports the view that Madison's concern was to allow faction to counter faction *among constituents* so that factions based on local interests would be less likely to enter the national government. Facing multiple local interests, the elected representative would then not be beholden to any particular one; rather, he would be able to pursue the public interest free from partisan factionalism within the district. Such an account treats representation as a trust that voters place in a more independent agent ready to deliberate with other representatives and reconsider upon reflection.[53] When permanent majorities are descriptive of a constituency, they will tend to elect representatives who are precommitted to particular programs – a loose form of the rejected practice of instructions that lived a brief life during the confederation. By comparing his other contemporaneous statements on faction and interests with the argument that wound up in *Federalist 10*, I can demonstrate that Madison did not expect local district interests to be directly represented within the national council.[54]

Madison rehearsed the essay that became *Federalist 10* three times before its publication. In April 1787, he penned a memorandum entitled "Vices of the Political System of the United States."[55] Probably begun in February of that year, it was a follow-up to his "Notes on Ancient and Modern Confederacies," written in the spring of 1786. His speech to the federal convention on June 6 and his letter to Jefferson later that fall after the convention, complete the preliminary set.[56] Each contains versions of what would become paragraph seven in *Federalist 10*, the paragraph in which Madison enumerates what he believes will be the sources of faction. In each of these rehearsals, Madison's list is quite similar. Yet the specific causes of faction are not quite the same between

[53] In the terms described by Hanna Pitkin, Madison's view had more in common with Burke and the trustee model than with others who promoted a delegate model in which representatives were closely beholden to their constituents. See Hanna Fenichel Pitkin, *The Concept of Representation* (Berkeley, CA: University of California Press, 1967). Pitkin nevertheless views Madison differently, attributing to him a pluralist and delegate view. See Pitkin, *The Concept of Representation*, pp. 191–6.

[54] According to Dinkin, for about half of the colonial period, elections to colonial legislatures were uncontested. When, in the early eighteenth century, they became more contested and then contentious, personal animosity was most often to blame. Although policy disputes were more frequent, they were not made an issue for voters during elections until midcentury. Political leaders "thought that their ends could best be achieved by using their persuasive powers over the other representatives during the legislative sessions rather than out on the stump." Dinkin, *Voting in Provincial America*, p. 10. It seems likely that Madison wished to foster heterogeneity within the district as a way of reducing factionalism among voters, in addition to moderating party faction *within* the legislature. He was thus hearkening back to earlier colonial times, in keeping with his humbling experience of having lost an assembly seat to a tavern keeper for want of campaigning. For more on *Federalist 10*, see Alan Gibson, "Impartial Representation and the Extended Republic: Towards a Comprehensive and Balanced Reading of the Tenth Federalist Paper," *History of Political Thought*, Vol. 12, no. 2, Summer 1991: 263–304.

[55] PJM, Vol. 9, p. 355.

[56] PJM, Vol. 10, pp. 33, 213.

essays.[57] A comparison of these lists shows that the electoral district forms a "source of faction" in the context of state systems but falls out at the federal level. (See Table 5.1 for a comparison summary of these versions.)

In "Vices," Madison wrote:

All civilized societies are divided into different interests and factions, as they happen to be creditors or debtors – rich or poor-husbandmen, merchants, or manufacturers – members of different religious sects – followers of different political leaders – *inhabitants of different districts* – owners of different kinds of property, etc.[58]

In his remarks at the Constitutional Convention on June 6, 1787, Madison restated this with only slight difference, beginning to resemble that of *Federalist 10*:

All civilized Societies would be divided into different Sects, Factions, & interests, as they happened to consist of rich & poor, debtors & creditors, the landed the manufacturing the commercial interests, *the inhabitants of this district or that district*, the followers of this political leader or that political leader, the disciples of this religious Sect or that religious Sect.[59]

In both cases, districts and local inhabitants form as powerful a faction as any other kind.[60]

Later that month Madison's argument began to change. Responding to Luther Martin's extended speech on the rights of states, Madison implied that the only relevant distinctions between the people of the forthcoming

---

[57] See Douglass Adair. "That Politics May Be Reduced to a Science: David Hume, James Madison and the Tenth Federalist," in *Fame and the Founding Fathers*, ed. Trevor Colbourn (Indianapolis, IN: Liberty Fund, 1974), p. 144, note 6; David F. Epstein, *The Political Theory of the Federalist* (Chicago: University of Chicago Press, 1984), pp. 206–7. As Epstein notes, Madison's letters to Washington, 16 April 1787, and to Lafayette, 20 March 1785, are also relevant, if not exactly versions of *Federalist 10*, which the other three clearly are. The writings that prefigured *Federalist 10* have received some attention, but I have found few that discuss the historical development of the particular paragraph concerning the sources of faction. Epstein is an exception, noting the development of the "opinions" that Madison cited through an analysis of these previous versions (ibid., p. 76; p. 210, n. 52). But Epstein does not mention the presence or absence of "district" nor its role to diminish factions directly, even as he refers to "Madison's previous versions of the argument of *Federalist 10*" (ibid., p. 86), and provides a comparison of the four works in terms of religious opinion. See also ibid., p. 206, n. 2.

[58] PJM, Vol. 9, p. 355, emphasis added.

[59] PJM, Vol. 10, p. 33, emphasis added.

[60] One reason that the present analysis is only suggestive is that from this context it is impossible to know for certain whether the "districts" to which Madison refers are electoral districts, as compared to "regions" or "areas" more generally. In Madison's time, the term "district" was used in both senses. (For an example of district as "region," see *Federalist 56*; of district as "area," see *Federalist 41*.) Two facts do support the claim that Madison had electoral districts in mind. First, the term "district" drops out of the final argument even though Madison still worried that *regional* differences might constitute a source of faction in the national system. Second, state electoral districts, in Madison's view, had had a corrupting influence on state legislatures during the confederacy. The salient situation for Madison was the aftermath of Shay's Rebellion.

TABLE 5.1. *Enumerated Causes of Faction in* Federalist 10 *and Its Precursors[a]*

Likely Source of Faction	"Vices" *April 1787*	Convention *June 6, 1787*	Letter to Jefferson 24 October 1787	Federalist 10, November 22, 1787
Creditors or debtors	✓	✓	✓	✓
Rich or poor	✓	✓	✓	Implied
Profession	✓[b]	✓[c]	✓[d]	✓
Property	✓[e]	✓[f]	✓[g]	✓[h]
Religion	✓[i]	✓[j]	✓[k]	✓[l]
Politics	✓[m]	✓[n]	✓	✓[o]
Districts	✓[p]	✓[q]	?[r]	Not Mentioned
Other	✓[s]		✓[t]	✓[u]

[a] Except for district interests, the interests likely to be the source of faction remain the same when reviewing the state systems (the first two statements) with the consideration of the federal system (the last two documents).

[b] "Husbandmen, merchants, or manufacturers."

[c] "[T]he landed the manufacturing the commercial interests."

[d] "[A] landed interest, a monied interest, a mercantile interest, a manufacturing interest."

[e] "[O]wners of different kinds of property."

[f] "[T]he landed the manufacturing the commercial interests."

[g] "These classes may again be subdivided according to the different productions of different situations & soils."

[h] "Those who hold, and those who are without property, have ever formed distinct interests in society," and "A landed interest, a manufacturing interest, a mercantile interest, a monied interest, with many lesser interests, grow up of necessity in civilized nations, and divide them into different classes, actuated by different sentiments and views."

[i] "[M]embers of different religious sects."

[j] "[T]he disciples of this religious Sect or that religious Sect."

[k] "In addition to these natural distinctions, artificial ones will be founded, on accidental differences in political, religious or other opinions, or an attachment to the persons of leading individuals."

[l] "A zeal for different opinions concerning religion...."

[m] "[F]ollowers of different political leaders."

[n] "[T]he followers of this political leader or that political leader."

[o] "A zeal for different opinions...concerning Government...an attachment to different leaders ambitiously contending for pre-eminence and power...."

[p] "[I]nhabitants of different districts."

[q] "[T]he inhabitants of this district or that district."

[r] "These classes may again be subdivided according to the different productions of different situations & soils."

[s] "[E]tc."

[t] "In addition to these natural distinctions, artificial ones will be founded, on accidental differences in political, religious or other opinions, or an attachment to the persons of leading individuals."

[u] "Different circumstances of society."

United States that *might* be found were those of the sort existing between the three largest states (Massachusetts, Pennsylvania, and Virginia). "If there possibly can be a diversity of interest, it is in the case of the three large states. Their situation is remote, their trade different." Two weeks later, in the debate over representation of persons in the House of Representatives, property begins to assume the central place it would in *Federalist 10*. Madison's view was "that population & wealth were not measures of each other … however … in the U. States it was sufficiently so for the object in contemplation" – that is, for the establishment of the House on the principle of representation by population.[61] His justification was the sufficient uniformity of the whole of the United States. "Altho' their climate varied considerably, yet as the Govts. the laws, and the manners of all were nearly the same, and the intercourse between different parts perfectly free, population, industry, arts and the value of labour, would constantly tend to equalize themselves."[62] Madison, moving toward representation as a means of achieving the public good, saw the sufficiently large constituency as capturing this unity. Nevertheless, there are still vestiges of localized interests.

In the letter to Thomas Jefferson written that fall, after the convention but before *Federalist 10* was published, the enumerated interests become those of class, wealth, and opinion. The purpose of listing the causes of faction now is to show why the federal system would be superior to the state systems. Here the only vestige of locality is in the "situations and soils" that likely differed according to physical location:

In all civilized Societies, distinctions are various and unavoidable. A distinction of property results from that very protection which a free Government gives to unequal faculties of acquiring it. There will be rich and poor; creditors and debtors; a landed interest, a monied interest, a mercantile interest, a manufacturing interest. These classes may again be subdivided according to the different productions of *different situations & soils*, & according to different branches of commerce, and of manufactures. In addition to these natural distinctions, artificial ones will be founded, on accidental differences in political, religious or other opinions, or an attachment to the persons of leading individuals.[63]

With his eye on the federal system rather than the states, the closest Madison comes to viewing electoral districts as a source of faction is the term "different situations & soils," and it is unlikely that Madison expected them to correspond neatly to congressional districts. First, neither Madison nor anyone else proposed drawing congressional district lines around these situations and soils. More importantly, Madison was clearly concerned about how these "situations & soils" are *transformed* to create wealth, and not with the soil itself.[64]

[61] PJM, Vol. 10, p. 99.

[62] Ibid.

[63] PJM, Vol. 10, p. 213, emphasis added.

[64] The transformation of land into wealth through our labor of course echoes Locke's argument. John Locke, *Second Treatise of Government*, ed. Peter Laslett, Cambridge Texts in the History of Political Thought (Cambridge, UK: Cambridge University Press, 1988 [1690]). See Chapter V,

Nevertheless, to be charitable, we might envision *some* connection between specific land and specific districts, as unlikely as it is.

In the published version of *Federalist 10*, however, the local district is completely absent from the sources of faction listed. In the seventh paragraph, Madison writes that the "latent causes of faction are thus sown in the nature of man," and that we will "see them everywhere brought into different degrees of activity, according to the different circumstances of civil society." After listing the "zeal" and "propensity" of man to "attach" to different kinds of opinions, Madison then enumerates the sources of faction likely to arise in the federal system:

But the most common and durable source of factions has been the various and unequal distribution of property. Those who hold and those who are without property have ever formed distinct interests in society. Those who are creditors, and those who are debtors, fall under a like discrimination. A landed interest, a manufacturing interest, a mercantile interest, a moneyed interest, with many lesser interests, grow up of necessity in civilized nations, and divide them into different classes, actuated by different sentiments and views. The regulation of these various and interfering interests forms the principal task of modern legislation, and involves the spirit of party and faction in the necessary and ordinary operations of the government.[65]

In this final version of the argument, Madison has eliminated the local constituency as a source of faction at all.

What explains the omission of local districts among Madison's enumerated sources of faction from the final version of the essay? The difference between the early versions and the final essay is their subjects: The former concerned the state governments, whereas *Federalist 10* concerned the proposed union. As I argued in the previous chapter, state legislative districts were indeed mostly coterminous with existing political and social communities, the voting population of which often numbered in the low hundreds and seldom extended to the several thousands. In the proposed national system, congressional districts would be *much* larger and drawn in ways that would combine local communities into single congressional districts. The Constitution provided representation in the House for every thirty thousand people. Indeed, until the day of signing, the draft Constitution stipulated a ratio of one to forty thousand.[66] There is good reason to believe that Madison left the district out of *Federalist 10* because

---

in particular paragraphs 27 and 32. For a detailed discussion of Locke's Chapter V and this section of *Federalist 10*, see Epstein, *The Political Theory of the Federalist*, p. 73.

[65] Madison, *Federalist 10*, p. 59.

[66] George Washington's support of Nathaniel Gorham's last minute plea for such an increase broke Washington's silence at the convention and forced the alteration of the final document. Jack Rakove, *Original Meanings Politics and Ideas in the Making of the Constitution* (New York: Knopf, 1996), p. 228. Madison preferred an even smaller fraction, and thus even larger electoral constituencies.

the sheer size of constituencies in the federal system would prevent them from being a source of faction.[67]

Madison thus viewed the local districts as more dangerous at the statewide level, but less likely to be the source of faction in the national government because of their size. This distinction is also found later in *Federalist 10* as Madison compares federal and state systems. He argued that the ideal size of a representative body will be some constant number regardless of the size of a republic – large enough "to guard against the cabals of a few," but small enough "to guard against the confusion of a multitude." When republics increase in size, the proportion of representatives to constituents must therefore decrease. And thus in state government, where smaller districts (that is, towns and counties) define constituencies, there will be closer attachment to these interests that would not occur, in Madison's opinion, at the national level. "By enlarging too much the number of electors, you render the representative too little acquainted with all their local circumstances and lesser interests; as by reducing it too much, you render him unduly attached to these, and too little fit to comprehend and pursue great and national objects." The Constitution, allowing both federal and state systems, "forms a happy combination in this respect; the great and aggregate interests being referred to the national, the local and particular, to the state legislatures." The national system would not be prone to factions from local *communities*, because the electoral district was just too big.[68]

Elsewhere in *The Federalist* we can see additional evidence of Madison's view. In *Federalist 46*, Madison explicitly established the tripartite nesting of the federal system, with citizens at the foundation, states at the next level, and the federal government at the head. Importantly, congressional districts as such are not part of this nested scheme. "The *States* will be to the [federal legislature] what counties and towns are to the [state legislatures]."[69] Madison intended to alleviate the concerns of the Anti-Federalist opposition. As we will see, they preferred small, localized systems of government, and were deeply concerned that the federal plan would run roughshod over state interests. The more local representation, the stronger his argument would have been. But Madison knew

---

[67] It is difficult to explain the causes of an event that occurred. It is much more difficult to explain some act of omission. Yet, the local district is the only source of faction explicitly mentioned in Madison's precursors to this essay that is not included in the final version. Madison paid a great deal of attention in writing his first contribution to what became *The Federalist*. So we ought at least to wonder why he left it out, even if the reasons I provide can only be suggestive. But also note that Madison saw slavery as the source of a particularly strong set of interests even as he does not explicitly mention it in these passages. See Madison's remarks in convention as recorded by him, 30 June 1787. Reprinted in *FC*, Vol. 2, 1:2:3, no. 2, p. 98. The change in Madison's rhetoric may be similarly attributed to politics – remaining silent about the origins of factions in the local district would be an effective strategy against Anti-Federalist concerns. This seems unlikely, however, because of direct attacks on the problems of state government throughout *The Federalist*, problems that Madison did not shy away from.

[68] Madison, *Federalist 10*, p. 63.

[69] Madison, *Federalist 46*, p. 318, emphasis added.

that even the House of Representatives would not represent local interests as such, owing to the large size of its districts.[70]

Hamilton shared Madison's view that large districts would not be a significant source of faction in the national system, reinforcing Madison's position that wealth and class, not localism, were bound to corrupt the new large republic. Hamilton, however, did not differentiate between state and federal systems. Instead, emphasizing Madison's concerns, Hamilton argued that wealth and property would be randomly distributed throughout the republic. Thus, any particular district could not serve as the source of faction. The larger the district, the more likely this would be.

We find Hamilton's argument in *Federalist 59* and *60* concerning the power to regulate elections of representatives to the House of Representatives.[71] Although the new government could alter the manner of elections, appropriate interests would not be defined by district and thus this power was unlikely to be a source of federal abuse.[72] In *Federalist 59*, Hamilton argued that states should have the initial but not ultimate authority to regulate such elections. Moreover, in *Federalist 60*, Hamilton dismissed the concern that vesting ultimate authority in the federal government would lead to abuses. The discussion is crucial, for it establishes Hamilton's expectations that relevant interests would be randomly distributed among congressional districts.[73]

Hamilton began *Federalist 59* by debunking the claim that elections would provide the opportunity for a particular sort of deviousness: "[I]t is alleged as to promote the election of some favourite class of men in exclusion of others; by confining the places of election to particular districts, and rendering

---

[70] Additional evidence from Madison's writing in *The Federalist* appears in essays 37 and 46, particularly as concerns the relationship between the states and the federal government. By 1791, Madison supported a Pennsylvania law "that every Citizen throughout the State shall vote for the whole number of members allotted to the State." His support was tied to the quality of representative he expected would be elected, consistent with his arguments at the convention and in *The Federalist*. "James Madison to Thomas Jefferson," 1791, in *FC*, Vol. 2, 1:2:1, no. 17, p. 61.

[71] Hamilton, *Federalist 59–60*, pp. 397–410.

[72] Hamilton was responding to the Anti-Federalist concern that such control over elections, might, in the words of Timothy Bloodworth of North Carolina, "destroy representation entirely." Cecilia Kenyon, ed., *The Anti-Federalists* (New York: Bobbs-Merrill, 1966), pp. lxv–lxvi.

[73] Remember that I am investigating the expectations and normative claims of people, not the truth of these claims per se. This is not to deny that there is a truth of the matter – surely, Hamilton was either correct or mistaken that interests were randomly distributed among districts. Nevertheless, the empirical information would be unimportant to understanding Hamilton's argument unless it could be shown that he willfully misrepresented his opinion. If Hamilton (or other philosophers) purposely manipulated facts in this way, then strictly speaking, the objects of my analysis are only the arguments these individuals make, and not the writers themselves. Speculation about their intentions is an interesting and important aspect of intellectual history, but not part of this analysis. As far as I know, there is no reason to doubt Hamilton's intentions on this point.

it impracticable to the citizens at large to partake in the choice." He first dismissed this concern by appealing to its unlikelihood, and the resistance to such a scheme built into the system. It is "inconceivable and incredible" that such an event would occur, "without occasioning a popular revolution." However, Hamilton continued, the difference of representatives owed to the "sufficient diversity in the state of property, in the genius, manners, and habits of the people of the different parts of the union to occasion a material diversity of disposition in their representatives towards the different ranks and conditions in society." The Federalists were thus concerned about these ranks and conditions, and not those interests defined by territorial districts. The greatest institutional check was to embody these different interests in different parts of government: the people in the House, the states in the Senate, and a third, less-defined group (the electors), electing the president.[74]

Hamilton listed the specific interests that should be of concern to the federal system:

But what is to be the object of this capricious partiality in the national councils? Is it to be exercised in a discrimination between the different departments of industry, or between the different kinds of property, or between the different degrees of property? Will it lean in favor of the landed interest, or the monied interest, or the mercantile interest, or the manufacturing interest? Or to speak in the fashionable language of the adversaries of the Constitution; will it court the elevation of the "wealthy and the well born" to the exclusion and debasement of all the rest of the society?[75]

Hamilton's response, similar to Madison's, was that the real distinction was between "landed men and merchants." Further, these concerns must be even greater at the local level, where these interests were more likely to be a problem.[76] Why was it more of a problem at the local level? Because:

[In] proportion as either [interest] prevails, it will be conveyed into the national representation, and for the very reason that this will be an emanation from a greater variety of interests, and in much more various proportions, than are to be found in any single state, it will be much less apt to espouse either of them, with a decided partiality, than the representation of any single state.[77]

Here Hamilton echoes the "pluralist" reading of Madison's *Federalist 10* – large numbers of interests within the legislature would cancel each other out. Crucially, Hamilton expected that the election of senators by state legislatures

[74] Hamilton, *Federalist 60*, pp. 403–5.
[75] Ibid., pp. 405–6.
[76] Hamilton and Madison regularly countered Anti-Federalist objections to the proposed Constitution by showing that a purported objection was drawn from practices of the state, practices that their opponents regularly praised. See Rakove, *Original Meanings*.
[77] Hamilton, *Federalist 60*, p. 406.

would render the Senate, but not the House of Representatives, a battleground of state interests.

Having established the proper representation of merchant and agricultural interests, Hamilton considered how federal meddling in elections might come to affect the concentration of these important interests. He argued that even if the federal government meditated upon which interests to manipulate, control of the places of elections (again, for the House) would be ineffective because the interests of concern were scattered and, most importantly, unrelated to place:

> But upon what principle is the discrimination of the places of election to be made in order to answer the purpose of the meditated preference? Are the wealthy and the well born, as they are called, confined to particular spots in the several states? Have they by some miraculous instinct or foresight set apart in each of them a common place of residence? Are they only to be met with in the towns or cities? *Or are they, on the contrary, scattered over the face of the country as avarice or chance may have happened to cast their own lot, or that of their predecessors?* If the latter is the case, (as every intelligent man knows it to be [*footnote*: Particularly in the Southern States and in (New York)]) is it not evident that the policy of confining the places of elections to particular districts would be as subversive of its own aim as it would be exceptionable on every other account?"[78]

If territorial constituencies were intended to channel particular interests into the House of Representatives, then Hamilton is being either inconsistent or disingenuous; neither appears likely. Hamilton admits that the states would be able to control and possibly manipulate the qualifications of electors and candidates, since the Constitution gives control of them to the states.[79] But the power to control "the regulation of the times, the places, and the manner of elections" would not likely lead to such abuse because he did not expect relevant interests to be defined by territory.

5.3.2 The Debate over the Constitution and the Anti-Federalist Response

But, my fellow-citizens, the important question here arises, who are this House of Representatives? "A representative Assembly, says the celebrated Mr. Adams, is the sense of the people, and the perfection of the portrait, consists in the likeness." – Can this Assembly be said to contain the sense of the people? – Do they resemble the people in any one single feature? – Do you represent your wants, your grievances, your wishes, in person? If that is impracticable, have you a right to send one of your townsmen for that purpose – Have you a right to send one from your county? Have you a right to send more than one for every thirty thousand of you?... Who is there among you would not start at being told, that instead of your present House of Representatives, consisting

---

[78] Ibid., p. 408, emphasis added.

[79] Article I, Section 2 states, "The House of Representatives shall be composed of members chosen every second year by the people of the several States, and the electors in each State shall have the qualifications requisite for electors of the most numerous branch of the State Legislature."

of members chosen from every town, your future Houses were to consist of but ten in number, and these to be chosen by districts?

– "John DeWitt," no. 3, Fall 1787[80]

There was, of course, opposition to the plan supported by Hamilton and Madison in *The Federalist*. The opposition is seen in the writings of the so-called Anti-Federalists and within the debates during the Constitutional Convention. In these debates, we find the empirical claim concerning communities of interest again rejected – constituencies were not expected to be coterminous with local communities – even as the normative claim that constituencies ought to represent communities of interest was endorsed. These arguments illustrate the deep suspicions of the Anti-Federalists toward any plan that failed to replicate local interests and protect citizens' rights in the national government. Reflecting Montesquieu, they argued that popular government could best operate on a small scale, where interests of a group were more homogeneous.[81] In a large national representative body, interests needed a place, and the opponents of the Constitution were concerned that the proposed system would not guarantee adequate representation of the full range of interests – very local, very territorial – present among the people.

Three topics can illustrate these points: 1) what the proper objects of government should be; 2) whether or not the congressional district, once formed, was expected to become its own community of interest; and 3) whether or not district lines were expected to be drawn around groups with similar interests, even if they were very large. In all three of these cases, we will see that the debate favors the view that territorial districts were not expected to represent local communities of interest and were therefore, for the Anti-Federalists, a good reason for concern.

Proper Objects of Government: People or States, Not the Congressional District. Among the more prominent debates during the federal convention was whether the newly forming government should regard the states or the people as its direct objects. Should, for example, the states pass laws that regulate individuals directly, or should their laws be aimed only at state governments? Some overlap was inevitable: A law that forbade the states from taxing tea might, in the end, make it cheaper for individuals to drink it. The debate was closely related to the Great Compromise establishing the states as electoral constituencies for the Senate and population-based representation in the House.[82]

---

[80] Storing, 4.3.14, in *FC*, Vol. 2, 1:2:1, no. 11, p. 51.

[81] See, for example, George Mason's speech during the Virginia Ratifying Convention, June 4, 1788, Elliot 3:29–35, in *FC*, Vol. 2, 1.2.3, no. 18, p. 137.

[82] The debate provides little insight on our present topic, see Andrew Rehfeld, "Silence of the Land: On the Historical Irrelevance of Territory to Congressional Districting and Political Representation in the United States," *Studies in American Political Development*, 15, no. 1, Spring 2001: 53–87, from which the present account is drawn. See also Rosemarie Zagarri, "Suffrage and Representation," in *The Blackwell Encyclopedia of the American Revolution*, eds. Jack P. Greene and J. R. Pole (Oxford, UK: Blackwell, 1994); Rakove, *Original Meanings*, Chapter IV.

For that compromise was one of principle: whether to represent the people as individuals or to represent them as they constituted themselves politically in the form of the states.

The Great Compromise, however, sheds little light on the question of territorial districting for Congress. The tension between representation of place and representation of people is at first a confirmation of the argument advanced here and then ultimately a distraction. The push for districts of equal population confirms that community and local interests were important in the historical formation of territorial representation. It also signals a weakening of the communal bounds and perceived homogeneity of communal interests that, as we saw in the preceding chapter, accompanied the use of territory to define constituencies. Once population equality became the central rule of representation upon which the House of Representatives rested, then the "why territory?" question looms even larger. After it was decided that people, not places, should be represented in the House of Representatives, what justified the use of territorial constituencies in that particular branch of Congress?[83] The fact that states were represented in the Senate provides no insight into the expectation that location would define constituencies in the House.

But the conceptual question, "should the national government take the states or individuals to be its object of governance?" provides some insight into our question because the possibility that congressional districts might form a new object of government was never discussed. Put differently, if the large territorial constituency was intended to represent communities of interest, we should expect to see an argument that the proper object of government ought to be a collection of these communities. The fact that there was no such argument provides further confirmation that territorial districts were not expected to represent communities of interest – even very large ones – in the national legislature.

An early disagreement among participants at the convention emerged between those who saw individuals as the object of the federal government and those who viewed the states as its end. In line with other Anti-Federalists, Luther Martin believed that the federal system should protect the state governments, which in turn had individuals as their objects. "A general government may operate on individuals in cases of general concern, and still be federal. . . . States will take care of their internal police and local concerns. The general government

---

[83] Even the most progressive suggestions about equal representation were territorially bounded. For example, David Brearly thought that states should have separate representation only if they were exactly equal:

Is it fair then it will be asked that Georgia should have an equal vote with Virga.? He would not say it was. What remedy then? One only, that a map of the U.S. be spread out, that all the existing boundaries be erased, and that a new partition of the whole be made into 13 equal parts.

David Brearly, recorded in Madison notes, 1:176, 9 June 1787, in *FC*, Vol. 2, 1.2.3, no. 2, p. 91. The accounts by Robert Yates (*Volume One* 1966 [1913], pp. 181–2) and King (*Records* 1966 [1913], p. 183) concur with Brearly's proposal.

has no interest, but the protection of the whole."[84] In contrast to Martin, Benjamin Franklin argued that individuals were the proper objects of government. Franklin ignored the intermediate position that a congressional district (or any substate jurisdiction) should be (or might be) the object of federal government. Yet, in making this argument, Franklin echoed Martin's point that *independent* political societies *were* the groups with any claims to representation. Districts and local communities were not viewed in any way as independent political groups but constitutive of them.

Finding David Brearly and William Patterson's proposal to redraw state lines to equalize population "an equitable one" that he would not be opposed to "if it might be found practicable,"[85] Franklin argued that the large electoral constituency would be irrelevant to national politics:

Formerly, indeed, when almost every province had a different Constitution, some with greater others with fewer privileges, it was of importance to the borderers when their boundaries were contested, whether by running the division lines, they were placed on one side or the other. At present when such differences are done away, it is less material. The Interest of a State is made up of the interests of its individual members.[86]

The problem with any territorial plan, Franklin understood, is that it would require frequent revision entailing "considerable difficulties" owing to population changes.[87] Franklin foreshadowed the politics of redistricting and suggested that the convention consider an innovative alternative that he thought "to be as equitable, more easily carried into practice, and more permanent in its nature."[88]

In his argument supporting the Constitution at the Pennsylvania Ratifying Convention, James Wilson similarly emphasized the different functions of the constituent district in state and federal systems:

[A] large number is not so necessary in this case as in the cases of state legislatures. In them there ought to be a representation sufficient to declare the situation of every county, town, and district; and if of every individual, so much the better, because their legislative powers extend to the particular interest and convenience of each. But in the general government, its objects are enumerated, and are not confined, in their causes or operations, to a county, or even to a single state.

---

[84] Yates describes the speech as "Diffuse" and "desultory." See Luther Martin, 27 June 1787, Yates' notes, in *Records* 1966 [1913], p. 439. See also at p. 441.

[85] Benjamin Franklin, 11 June 1787, in Madison's notes in *FC*, Vol. 2, 1:2:3, no. 2, pp. 92–3. Madison notes that Franklin's opinion was delivered by James Wilson, Franklin having "thrown his ideas of the matter on a paper" (ibid., p. 92).

[86] Ibid., p. 93.

[87] Ibid.

[88] Ibid. Franklin's plan was to have the "weakest State say what proportion of money or force it is able and willing to furnish for the general purposes of the Union." Other states being stronger or wealthier would match that amount and each state would then retain equal voting rights in the legislature *and* contribute equally to the government. According to Madison, immediately after Franklin's plan, the convention agreed to representation by "some equitable ratio of representation" as proposed by Rufus King and Wilson, thus paving the way for proportional representation.

Wilson continued, "No one power is of such a nature as to require the minute knowledge of situations and circumstances necessary in state governments possessed of general legislative authority."[89] Local districts, whether defined by town or county lines, were not intended to be represented or reproduced in the national legislature, as they were in the states. The objects of national legislation were simply different.[90]

Wilson Nicholas, a member of the Virginia Ratifying Convention, took up the argument even as he rejected the claim that the small number of representatives would leave Congress too little

> ... acquainted with the local situation and circumstances of their constituents. When we attend to the object of their jurisdiction, we find this objection insupportable. Congress will superintend the great national interests of the Union. Local concerns are left to the state legislatures. When the members compare and communicate to one another their knowledge of their respective districts and states, their collective intelligence will sufficiently enable them to perform the objects of the cognizance. They cannot extend their influence or agency to any objects but those of a general nature; the representatives will, therefore, be sufficiently acquainted with the interests of their states, although chosen by large districts.[91]

Again emphasizing the importance of individual interests in Congress, and not those of districts per se, Wilson concluded, "As long as people remain virtuous and uncorrupted, so long, we may fairly conclude, will their representatives, even at their present number, guard their interests, and discharge their duty with fidelity and zeal: when they become otherwise, no government can possibly secure their freedom."[92]

After the convention, Hamilton argued in *Federalist 17* that the different ends of government should quiet discontent over the feared power of the new federal government: "... all those things in short which are proper to be provided for by local legislation, can never be desirable cares of a general jurisdiction. It is therefore improbable that there should exist a disposition in the Federal councils to usurp the powers with which they are connected...."[93] The argument that federal and state governments have different ends thus leaves barren the

---

[89] James Wilson, Pennsylvania Ratifying Convention, 30 November 1787, from Elliot 2:442–3, in *FC*, Vol. 2, 1:2:3, no. 7, p. 116. See also Oliver Elseworth (Ellsworth), 10 July 1787, as recorded by James Madison, in *FC*, Vol. 2, 1:2:3, no. 2, p. 102.

[90] It is striking that in all the debate around the apportionment clause of the Constitution (Article I, Section 2, Clause 3, which establishes that there shall be one representative for every thirty thousand people) there is no argument that the ratio is too great because community representation would not be actuated. The tension was between individual and state representation. The local community – the origin of territorial representation – drops completely out of the debate.

[91] Wilson Nicholas, debate in Virginia Ratifying Convention, 4 June 1788, Elliot 3:11–14, in *FC*, Vol. 2, 1.2.3, no. 18, pp. 136–7.

[92] Ibid.

[93] Hamilton, *Federalist 17*, p. 106. See also his comments in *Federalist 16*: "The government of the Union, like that of each State, must be able to address itself immediately to the hopes and fears of individuals; and to attract to its support, those passions, which have the strongest influence upon the human heart." Hamilton, *Federalist 16*, p. 103.

claim that the congressional district was to represent interests in the national legislature. For either the end of federal government was to be the states – which it was agreed had definable interests – or it was to be the broad collection of individuals who would form a general public interest. In either case, the argument assumes that the congressional district as such would not form a separate object of government.

Congressional Districts Were Never Viewed as Part of the Nested Levels of Government. Congressional districts were never expected to be the object of national or state governments. But, like any other boundary, once drawn they might become a new locus of activity that itself would create a community of interest. While this would have contradicted the expectations of Madison and Hamilton, as well as the Anti-Federalists, it is nonetheless useful to see that the newly formed congressional district was never expected to create a new sublevel of government in itself.

Luther Martin's speech of June 27, 1787, quoted previously, began by noting the different ends of federal and state systems. But it ended in a manner that shows representation in large national systems to be rightly constructed by a nesting of governmental units that gives consent upward toward the top of the system. Men form initial societies within their states, and the national system must be an outgrowth of that. Although Martin does not state it, the consequence of his argument is clear: If political union depends upon the consent between territorial communities, then subsequent districts that violate these territorial lines violate these lines of consent.[94]

No one imagined that congressional districts would form political units by themselves, and thus it would have been surprising to find an argument tying distinct interests to them. Thus, William Samuel Johnson rejected the proposed representation of persons as threatening a basic principle of government. Since the convention would likely base the House on the principle of representation of people, the founders would have to base the Senate upon the existing political unit. "For whom are we to form a government? for the people of America, or for those societies? Undoubtedly for the latter. They must, therefore, have a voice in the second branch of the general government, if you mean to preserve their existence. The people already compose the first branch."[95] Clearly, congressional districts were neither envisioned nor considered political societies as such.

On June 29, 1787, Madison explicitly rejected the political society arguments of Martin and Johnson as artificial. Nevertheless, he endorsed the nested plan:

Some contend that states are sovereign, when in fact they are only political societies. There is a gradation of power in all societies, from the lowest corporation to the highest

[94] The nesting of political consent as a component of political representation is especially important in large nations and significantly undermines a normative basis for district line drawing done by third parties without a means for citizen consent. See Chapter 8.

[95] William Samuel Johnson, 29 June 1787, Yates' notes, *Records* 1966 (1913), p. 470.

sovereign. The states never possessed the essential rights of sovereignty. These were always vested in congress. Their voting, as states, in congress, is no evidence of sovereignty. The state of Maryland voted by counties – did this make the counties sovereign?[96]

But sovereignty and consent are different things – Madison knew that individuals could give consent to a political society but still not be sovereign over it.

Johnson made both responses explicit in his proposal for a mixed system:

> Those who contend for an equality of Votes among the States, define a State to be a mere association of men & then say these Associations are equal – on the other hand those who contend for a Representation in proportion to numbers, Define a State to be a District of Country with a certain Number of Inhabitants, like a parish or County, and then say, these districts shd. have an influence in proportion to their Number of Inhabitants – both reason justly from yr. Premises – we must then compromise – let both parties be gratified – let one House or Branch be formed by one Rule & & the other by another.[97]

The implication is that House electoral districts were only expected to function as a method of vote aggregation. Those "association[s] of men," that is the states, formed the justification for representation only in the Senate.

Other Ties That Bind: The Small Community, Constituent Relations, and Regional Interests.

As we close the discussion of the communities of interest justification, three brief issues remain. First, the Anti-Federalists, emphasized the small community as the locus of representation. Second, there is the matter of the Anti-Federalists' related but quite different argument for close connections between representatives and their constituents. And finally, I will end with a brief comment on the territorially bound *regional* interests that were described and expected to emerge.

George Mason, an outspoken Anti-Federalist, argued early at the convention that proper representation simply required congressional districts small enough so that they could transmit the sentiments and interests of the people directly to the national representative body. According to Madison:

> Mr. Mason argued strongly for an election of the larger branch by the people....It ought to know & sympathize with every part of the community; and ought therefore to be taken not only from different parts of the whole republic, but also from different districts of the larger members of it, which had in several instances particularly in Virga., different interests and views arising from difference of produce, of habits. &c &.[98]

The justification was common for Anti-Federalists: to provide for the rights of every individual in the new nation. But, as we have already seen, this argument at the district level could not be sustained, for it violated its own empirical

---

[96] James Madison, 29 June 1787, Yates' notes, in *Records* 1966 (1913), p. 471.

[97] Johnson, 29 June 1787, King, in *Records* 1966 (1913), pp. 476–7.

[98] Madison's notes, 31 May 1787, *Records* 1966 (1913), pp. 48–9.

assumption; incorrectly assuming that districts would be drawn small enough to define local interests. Even if local districts had independent interests, they would remain unprotected by the size of the national republic. Better to resort to the nested plan with the state government as a buffer for individual rights.

Similarly, the author of "the Cornelius Letter" challenged Hamilton's contention that interests would be randomly distributed. Urban and mercantile interests were concentrated in small areas allowing for "constant connection and intercourse between them." It would be relatively easy for them to "centre their votes where they please." By contrast, the landed interests were scattered in less dense settlements, putting them at an electoral disadvantage. "To concert uniform plans for carrying elections of this kind is entirely out of their way. Hence, their votes if given at all, will be no less scattered than are the local situations of the voters themselves."[99] As Cecilia Kenyon reports, "the Anti-Federalists feared . . . the superior opportunities for organized voting that they felt to be inherent in the more thickly populated areas . . . they wanted constituencies sufficiently small to render such organization unnecessary." More to the point, large districts would dilute the interests that were diverse (and more diverse in the country). "True representation – undistorted by party organization – could be achieved only where electoral districts were small."[100]

In this sense, the Anti-Federalists did not justify territorial constituencies in the national government because their large size would negate the normative claim that these interests ought to be represented. A related defense of the small district, however, emphasized its ability to enable ties between representatives and their constituents. The new system would sever these ties again because districts were too large.[101] In the eyes of its critics, the proposed system "would be a government of strangers."[102]

The Anti-Federalists viewed the issue of interest representation as closely related to that of the relationship between representatives and their constituents. It is important for us, however, to see the difference of these two arguments. The closeness of representatives to their constituents serves only as a second-order justification for territory, and properly falls under the set of "enabling justifications" I outlined in Chapter 2. Territorial representation as such is justified in service to "interest representation" just so long as territorial groupings form a relevant interest group whether or not that group had a close relationship to its representative. However closely the Anti-Federalists connected territorial representation to the interest justification, if there were ways other than living near

---

[99] "The Cornelius Letter," in Samuel Bannister Harding, *The Contest over the Ratification of the Federal Constitution in the State of Massachusetts* (New York: Green and Co., 1896), in *The Anti-Federalists*, p. liv, n. 35.

[100] *The Anti-Federalists*, p. lv. See also pp. cix–cx. Kenyon's analysis centers on the fear of political organizing that the Anti-Federalists correctly believed would arise if large districts were created. Though important, especially as a logistical justification for territorially small districts, this political organizing nevertheless is a different issue than the interest justification.

[101] *The Anti-Federalists*, pp. lvi–lxi. See also Rakove, *Original Meanings*, pp. 203–43.

[102] Ibid., p. lxi.

their representatives for voters to develop close connections to them, territory per se would not be necessary. The Anti-Federalists bear no criticism for failing to see how contingent these particular territorial arguments were. Rather, their failure shows how incidental territory was even for supporters of small districts. As part of their justification for the small district, advocates viewed territory as a means to an end of close relations between a constituent and a representative, rather than an end in itself.

Finally, there were regional matters that concerned the founders, but these were generally much broader than individual districts as such – in many cases, "region" referred to a collection of states or at least a collection of future districts. Gouverneur Morris expressed his concern at the federal convention that because of these regional differences, proportional representation would lead to the elevation of men neither good enough for the job nor committed to the general good. Responding to Mason's argument that the anticipated admission of the western states into the union "as equals" would not be damaging because "they will have the same pride & other passions which we have," Morris disagreed: "Among other objections it must be apparent they would not be able to furnish men equally enlightened, to share in the administration of our common interests. The Busy haunts of men not the remote wilderness, was the proper School of political Talents."[103] He continued, tying this problem of regional representatives with their constituents' interests:

> If the Western people get the power into their hands they will ruin the Atlantic interests. The Back members are always most averse to the best measures. [Morris] mentioned the case of Pena. formerly. The lower part of the State had ye. power in the first instance. They kept it in yr. own hands. & the country was ye. better for it.[104]

Morris equated the common good with Atlantic interests, but the point is well taken. Different regional areas will have interest often at odds with the public good. Morris's argument was not widely supported precisely because the maligning influence of localism did not seem especially different from place to place. As Madison notes, "To reconcile the gentln. with himself it must be imagined that he determined the human character by the points of the compass. The truth was that all men having power ought to be distrusted to a certain degree." It was the interests of men, not especially of place, that drew Madison's suspicion.[105]

Just as important, the interests that mattered to opponents of the federal plan were more often stated in the Madisonian terms of property and class rather than local community per se.[106] Thus, the opposition to the Constitution

---

[103] Morris here is concerned with the election of local representatives rather than the separable though related issue of organizing constituents on a local basis.

[104] James Madison, 11 July 1787, Madison's notes, in *FC*, Vol. 2, 1:2:3, no. 2, p. 105.

[105] George Mason, 11 July 1787, Madison's notes, in *FC*, Vol. 2, 1:2:3, no. 2, p. 103; Gouveneur Morris, 11 July 1787, Madison's notes, in *FC*, Vol. 2, 1:2:3, no. 2, p. 104.

[106] This may be an oversimplification. The Anti-Federalists were committed to small local government, and were often suspicious that the federal system would place the interests of the

expressed its concern that only "men of the most elevated rank in life, will alone be chosen. The other orders in the society, such as farmers, traders, and mechanics, who all ought to have a competent number of their best informed men in the legislature, will be totally unrepresented."[107] Martin saw the problem of conflicting territorially defined interests as occurring only on the federal level, where territory defined the states and not the smaller districts. Martin argued in support of equal votes for state equality in the federal system:

That the *adequacy of representation* is *more important* in a *federal*, than in a *State* government, because the members of a State government, the *district* of which is *not very large*, have generally such a *common interest*, that laws can scarcely be made by *one* part *oppressive* to the *others*, without *their suffering in common;* but the *different States* composing an *extensive federal empire*, widely distant *one* from the *other*, may have *interests so totally distinct*, that the *one* part might be be [sic] greatly *benefited* by what would be *destructive* to the *other*.[108]

Martin is clear that his concern for territorial equality is based on maintaining the *"distinct political individual existences"* of the states.[109] In the case of the House, a system of districting that transcended (and divided) existing political units could not be justified on a similar account, nor was it Martin's point to do so.

The framers of the Constitution did not justify territorial constituencies as a way to secure local interests in the national legislature, nor to facilitate attachment to the new republic. Supporters of the Constitution believed these facts were salutary; their opponents felt otherwise. Further, the role of government as a protector of property was unrelated to territorial organization. Finally, the idea that territorial constituencies would allow individuals to give voice or exit to a different well-defined location as a show of consent was neither discussed nor a practical option. Thus the first four justifications developed in section 3.2 can be rejected as explanations for why territory was used to define electoral constituencies. While there were no direct or "first-order" reasons for using territory to define constituencies, territory was the only way to enable other philosophical principles of democratic political representation, including deliberation among constituents. We turn now to this argument in the next chapter.

---

community in the hands of a small elite. But it is less clear that territorially defined interests, as compared with the more important securing of individual liberty, motivated their concern. See *The Anti-Federalists* and Storing, *What the Anti-Federalists Were For*, pp. 15–23.

[107] The Address and Reasons of Dissent of the Minority of the Convention of Pennsylvania to Their Constituents, 18 December 1787, Storing 3.11.34–7, in *FC*, Vol. 2, 1.2.3, no. 8, p. 117.

[108] Luther Martin, Genuine Information 1788, in *FC*, Vol. 2, 1.2.3, no. 9, p. 119, emphasis in the original.

[109] Ibid., p. 119, emphasis in the original.

6

Origins, Part 2

Territorial Representation as an Enabler of Democratic Values

> But when Americans spoke in the abstract about why representatives were responsible to the local electoral district rather than to the whole people, they were less interested in stressing obedience or accountability than knowledge ... American theory had always favored local representation. The doctrine was not devised to resist parliamentary legislation; it was the pragmatic explanation of American constitutional conditions.
>
> – John Philip Reid[1]

There was, as usual, a crowd of folk about the door, but none that Rip recollected. The very character of the people seemed changed. There was a busy, bustling, disputatious tone about it, instead of the accustomed phlegm and drowsy tranquillity. He looked in vain for the sage Nicholas Vedder, with his broad face, double chin, and fair long pipe, uttering clouds of tobacco-smoke instead of idle speeches; or Van Bummel, the schoolmaster, doling for the contents of an ancient newspaper. In place of these, a lean, bilious-looking fellow, with his pockets full of handbills, was haranguing vehemently about rights of citizens – elections – members of Congress – liberty – Bunker's Hill – heroes of seventy-six – and other words, which were a perfect Babylonish jargon to the bewildered Van Winkle.

The appearance of Rip, with his long grizzled beard, his rusty fowling-piece, his uncouth dress, and an army of women and children at his heels, soon attracted the attention of the tavern politicians. They crowded round him, eyeing him from head to foot with great curiosity. The orator bustled up to him, and, drawing him partly aside, inquired "on which side he voted?" Rip stared in vacant stupidity. Another short but busy little fellow pulled him by the arm, and, rising on tiptoe, inquired in his ear, "Whether he was Federal or Democrat?" Rip was equally at a loss to comprehend the question; when a knowing, self-important old gentleman, in a sharp cocked hat, made his way through the crowd, putting them to the right and left with his elbows as he passed, and planting himself before Van Winkle, with one arm akimbo, the other resting on his cane, his keen eyes and sharp hat

[1] John Philip Reid, *The Concept of Representation in the Age of the American Revolution* (Chicago: University of Chicago Press, 1989), p. 83.

penetrating, as it were, into his very soul, demanded in an austere tone, "what brought him to the election with a gun on his shoulder, and a mob at his heels, and whether he meant to breed a riot in the village?" – "Alas! Gentlemen," cried Rip, somewhat dismayed, "I am a poor quiet man, a native of this place, and a loyal subject of the king, God bless him!"

– Washington Irving[2]

So much of the political landscape had changed during Rip Van Winkle's slumber that Rip's innocuous huzzah for his majesty turned out to be anything but. Deliberation – or more accurately, the pressing of each other for account of where each stood – featured prominently in the political life of the new republic. Rip was surprised not just by the vigor of the debate; its very contours were unrecognizable to him. Despite these changes, the political and social life of citizens in the new republic remained very local.

In the previous chapter, I argued that at the founding there was little support for the first four justifications for territorial constituencies that I developed in Chapter 3. This was especially true in the case of the attachment and the communities of interest justifications. In these cases, where people lived was itself central to a normative theory of political representation. While I rejected these justifications for territory, I argue in this chapter that territorial constituencies were necessary and thus justified to enable three other democratic practices *within* the electoral constituency. First, they helped provide local information to the legislature through representatives. Second, they facilitated the *between*-constituent deliberation presumed necessary for the selection of virtuous representatives. Third, territorial constituencies allowed the polis to have an important moment of communal consent at each election.

This set of enabling justifications also provides a foundation for the claim that representative government as a whole was based on necessity or convenience. As Thomas Paine put it in *Common Sense*, "If the colony continue increasing ... it will be found best to divide the whole into convenient parts, each part sending its proper number."[3] The set of enabling justifications gets at the question that Paine leaves unanswered: If dividing the whole based on where they live is convenient, what is it convenient for?

In sections 6.1–6.3, I treat each of these three themes using the method, outlined in Chapter 3, of asking what were the empirical expectations of the founders as well as asking what normative claims they endorsed. I conclude in section 6.4 with some brief comments on the use of territorial constituencies since the founding of the United States. As a methodological reminder from section 3.3, although the evidence in this chapter supports the claims being made, it remains suggestive and may well be consistent with other explanations.

---

[2] Washington Irving, "Rip Van Winkle," in *American Fairy Tales*, ed. Neil Philip (New York: Hyperion, 1976 [1820]), pp. 22–3. I am grateful to Emma Greenberg Rehfeld for bringing this passage to my attention.

[3] Thomas Paine, "Common Sense," in *Thomas Paine Political Writings*, ed. Bruce Kuklick (Cambridge, UK: Cambridge University Press, 1989 [1776]), p. 5.

6.1 GETTING FACTS INTO THE LEGISLATURE

If territorial constituencies were justified because they enabled representatives to gather local information efficiently, that implies that the founders thought such local information was a good thing to have, and that they expected the territorial district to help gather this information. We can purse this argument in the terms developed in section 3.2:

Normative claim: The national legislature ought to have local information.

Empirical expectation: Territorial constituencies were expected to facilitate the transmission of local information into the legislature.

At the founding of the United States, national government served two primary ends: fostering commerce and providing national security. These activities required that the national legislature have information about local laws, opinions, practices, even geography, a fact that both opponents and supporters of the Constitution endorsed; thus all sides supported the preceding normative claim.[4]

Consistent with the preceding empirical expectation, Federalists publicly argued that representatives under the proposed Constitution would be sufficiently informed of these local conditions. Further, they would be able to "transmit" this information into Congress, a fact premised on their being elected from territorially defined constituencies.[5] However, we should not push this too far because the "local information" they thought relevant to national governance was actually information about states and larger regions. Still, having representatives of territorially defined constituencies would be a particularly efficient way to secure this information. By contrast, Anti-Federalists rejected the empirical claim, arguing again that the large size of the electoral district meant that representatives would be unable to transmit the needed information reliably

---

[4] Facts should be distinguished from interests that are purportedly specific to a local group. Loosely, by "interests" I mean those policies a group either desires or should desire to have enacted as law for reasons related to its own good. (See Chapter 7 for a more precise definition.) By contrast, "knowledge" is a set of facts about some group. Thus a group's specific interests will be among the set of facts that a representative needs to know. As George Mason distinguished the two, "The mode of levying taxes is of the utmost consequence; and yet here it is to be determined by those who have neither *knowledge* of our situation, nor a common *interest* with us, nor a fellow-feeling for us." George Mason, Debate in Virginia Ratifying Convention, 4 June 1788, in ed. Jonathan Elliot, *The Debates in the Several State Conventions on the Adoption of the Federal Constitution as Recommended by the General Convention at Philadelphia in 1787*, 5 vols, 2nd ed. 1888 (Reprint; New York: Bort Franklin, n.d.), Vol. 3, 29–35; "The Founders' Constitution," in *The Founders' Constitution* (hereafter FC), eds. Philip B. Kurland and Ralph Lerner (Chicago: University of Chicago Press, 1987), Vol. 1, Article 2, Clause 3, no. 18 (hereafter 1:2:3, no. 18), p. 137. (Emphasis added.)

[5] The notion of "transmission" is particularly well developed in Nancy L. Schwartz, *The Blue Guitar: Political Representation and Community* (Chicago: University of Chicago Press, 1988); see also the discussion of her argument in section 2.1.

into the legislature. (The Anti-Federalist argument closely parallels their arguments about attachment that I presented in section 5.3.2, so I will not elaborate on their defense of the normative claim.)

Before illustrating the Federalist position, I want to use the distinction developed in section 1.4 between "hard" and "soft" knowledge – knowledge of particular facts on the one hand and "ways of thinking" that purportedly differ between groups and help define that group (whatever be the cause of that difference – education, experience, genetics, culture, and so on). We might think of "hard knowledge" as any information that could easily be written down. Hard knowledge about a territorial constituency includes facts about its population and local geography; the kinds of businesses, religious, and social organizations that operate within its boundaries; and the particular state and local laws that govern its citizens. By "soft knowledge," I mean being able to process information in a manner that accords with how members of the constituency process information, think, and feel. Soft knowledge describes knowledge of how people might react to certain propositions and what they might think of some event.[6]

By its nature, it is difficult to have soft knowledge of a group unless one is a member of that very group. Once we frame soft knowledge in this way, we can see that we cannot secure soft knowledge of a group within a legislature simply by defining constituencies. We also must develop some electoral mechanism that reliably translates these purported perspectival features about constituents into electoral success. Sharing the perspective of members of some group is a fact about a representative, not the group that he or she represents.[7]

---

[6] By soft knowledge, I mean something akin to what some theorists have termed "perspectival knowledge." I am not defending the plausibility or existence of perspectives that cannot be reduced to a set of beliefs or propositions about the world. I am, however, defending the empirical claim that many people have thought that "perspectives," "ways of thinking," or *weltanschauung* more generally differ from sets of beliefs in ways that correspond to the "soft/hard" distinction I am making here. For some examples, Jane J. Mansbridge, "Should Blacks Represent Blacks and Women Represent Women? A Contingent 'Yes,'" *Journal of Politics*, 61, no. 3, August: 628–57; Anne Phillips, *The Politics of Presence* (New York: Oxford University Press, 1995); S. Laurel Weldon, "Beyond Bodies: Institutional Sources of Representation for Women in Democratic Policymaking," *Journal of Politics*, 64, no. 4, November: 1153–74.

[7] A central goal in creating majority African American districts is to promote the election of black representatives so that their voices (perspectives that only they could offer) were heard. For four very different examples, see Charles R. Beitz, *Political Equality: An Essay in Democratic Theory* (Princeton, NJ: Princeton University Press, 1989); Bernard Grofman and Chandler Davidson, eds., *Controversies in Minority Voting: The Voting Rights Act in Perspective* (Washington, DC: Brookings Institution Press, 1992); Bernard Grofman, Lisa Handley, and Richard G. Niemi, *Minority Representation and the Quest for Voting Equality* (New York: Cambridge University Press, 1992); Iris Marion Young, *Justice and the Politics of Difference* (Princeton, NJ: Princeton University Press, 1990). A more certain way to secure soft knowledge of a group would be to reserve seats in the legislature for that group, regardless of how constituencies are defined. This is increasingly being done for women throughout the world, most recently through the enactment of *Parité* in France. For more, see Lisa Baldez, "Elected Bodies: The Gender Quota Law for Legislative Candidates in Mexico," *Legislative Studies Quarterly*, 29, May 2004: 231–58.

Conceptually, the need for soft knowledge – the need to think and feel as the people thought and felt – was valued highly in the founding debates about political representation but it did not justify territory per se. Rather, the need for representatives to maintain these strong chords of sympathy with the people would have applied to any constituency definition. Even if constituency definition were the *only* way to secure one particular kind of perspectival knowledge within a legislature, we would still have to make an argument that a particular perspective – territory or profession or religion or economic class – ought to be present and we would be right back where we began wondering why territory was chosen.

There were purported perspectival differences that corresponded to territorial boundaries – those of towns, states, and regions – but the congressional district was either too large in the first case, or too small in the latter two to correspond to them accurately. As I discussed in Chapter 4, at the founding, local towns and counties were distinctive cultural and social aspects of American life, in the sense that people of "this town" did not seem fundamentally like people of "that town" – a sense that follows closely perspectival difference. States and regions were similarly the purported source of perspectival differences: To be a "Virginian" meant having (or believing one had) a distinctive worldview. To the extent "thinking like a southerner" or a Virginian was important, it would not justify smaller territorial electoral districts.

The need for hard knowledge, knowledge of facts and circumstances, provides a stronger justification for territory because Congress needed knowledge of local facts in order to legislate well, and territorially defined constituencies enabled the efficient transmission of this information from local communities to the national legislature. Having constituents who were defined by where they lived made data gathering and communication of these facts easier, even if the territorial district was not necessary for their dissemination.

The need for local knowledge justified the earliest cases of political representation as seen in *Magna Carta*. Article 45 states, "We will appoint as justices, constables, sheriffs, or bailiffs only such as know the law of the realm and mean to observe it well." And local *needs* (as compared to interests) were important for representation in Montesquieu's political theory, forming an apparent justification for territorial constituencies. "One knows the needs of one's own town better than those of other towns.... Therefore, members of the legislative body must not be drawn from the body of the nation at large; it is proper for the inhabitants of each principal town to choose a representative from it."[8] Indeed, Montesquieu rejects outright the idea of a republicwide constituency.

---

[8] Charles de Secondat, baron de La Brède et de Montesquieu, *The Spirit of the Laws* (New York: Cambridge University Press, 1989 [1748]), 11:6, p. 159. Along with knowing the needs of one's community, it is here that Montesquieu emphasizes the better judgment one's neighbors have regarding a candidate's ability to serve as representative, quoted in section 5.2. This only *apparently* justifies territoriality. Instead, the general principle is that representatives should be drawn by virtue of their membership in whatever has been defined as constituency. See the discussion in section 6.2.

Admittedly, the "local" facts that supporters of the Constitution thought were important for national representation at the founding were those of the state or the region. The need for knowledge within the national legislature turns out to be an argument for state representative delegations rather than for local, territorial ones within the state. Still, as we will see, territorially based constituencies were expected to enable the transmission of this information.

In *Federalist 10* we have Madison's acknowledgment that a district that is too large will undermine the ability of the representative to transmit facts into the legislature; if the district is too small, then the representative will be overly attached to its constituents:

> By enlarging too much the number of electors, you render the representative too little acquainted with all their local circumstances and lesser interests; as by reducing it too much, you render him unduly attached to these, and too little fit to comprehend and pursue great and national objects.

Madison's solution is in federalism – robust state governments will look out and protect local interests, while the national government will advocate for the whole. "The Federal Constitution forms a happy combination in this respect; the great and aggregate interests being referred to the national, the local and particular, to the state legislatures."[9]

Even with a federalist system there was still a need for local facts within the national legislature, especially for forming tax law. In *Federalist 36*, Hamilton argues that hard knowledge of local law within Congress would protect citizens from unjust taxation. The argument is an analogy to the states and exhibits both the usefulness of territorial constituencies and expanded scope of government at the national level. Because of its centrality, I quote it here at length:

> It has been asserted that a power of internal taxation in the national legislature could never be exercised with advantage, as well from the want of a sufficient knowledge of local circumstances, as from an interference between the revenue laws of the Union and of the particular States. The supposition of a want of proper knowledge seems to be entirely destitute of foundation. If any question is depending in a State legislature respecting one of the counties, which demands a knowledge of local details, how is it acquired? No doubt from the information of the members of the county. Cannot the like knowledge be obtained in the national legislature from the representatives of each State? And is it not to be presumed that the men who will generally be sent there will be possessed of the necessary degree of intelligence to be able to communicate that information? Is the knowledge of local circumstances, as applied to taxation, a minute topographical acquaintance with all the mountains, rivers, streams, highways, and bypaths in each State; or is it a general acquaintance with its situation and resources, with the state of its agriculture, commerce, manufactures, with the nature of its products and consumptions, with the different degrees and kinds of its wealth, property, and industry?[10]

[9] James Madison, *The Federalist*, ed. Jacob E. Cooke (Middletown, CT: Wesleyan University Press, 1961 [1787–8]), Essay 10 (hereafter *Federalist 16*), p. 63.
[10] Hamilton, *The Federalist 36*, p. 224.

Hamilton is arguing that the "knowledge of local circumstances, as applied to taxation" is *not* "a minute topographical acquaintance with all the mountains, rivers, streams highways and bypaths in each state." Rather, "it is a general acquaintance with its situation and resources." Indeed, the point is that large territorial electoral constituencies will be particularly helpful in the transmission of information into the legislature without bogging it down with irrelevant facts.

Once elected, representatives would need to have hard knowledge of the different laws throughout the land and this again is facilitated by the territorial constituency. In *Federalist 55*, Madison refutes the charge that the members of Congress "will not possess a proper knowledge of the local circumstances of their numerous constituents." And in *Federalist 58*, Madison puts forth three guiding principles of a legislature's size: safety, local information, and sympathy with society:

The people can never err more than in supposing that by multiplying their representatives, beyond a certain limit, they strengthen the barrier against the government of a few. Experience will forever admonish them that on the contrary *after securing a sufficient number of the purposes of safety, of local information and of diffusive sympathy with the whole society*, they will counteract their own views by every addition to their representatives.[11]

A final example comes in a discussion between Madison and George Mason during the Virginia Ratifying Convention. Both men agreed that it was a problem that national representatives would not have local information necessary for doing their jobs. For Mason, there is no solution; but for Madison, the solution is the nested system of state and local government. As Mason argued, "The gentleman" who praised this system, "must ... acknowledge that our federal representatives must be unacquainted with the situation of their constituents. Sixty-five members cannot possibly know the situation and circumstances of all the inhabitants of this immense continent."[12] Madison responded directly to this argument:

Let me observe, also, that, as far as the number of representatives may seem to be adequate to discharge their duty, they will have sufficient information from the laws of particular states, from the state legislatures, from their own experience, and from a great number of individuals; and as to our security against them, I conceive, sir, that the general limitation of their powers, and the general watchfulness of the states, will be a sufficient guard.[13]

Territorial districts would help ensure that representatives from each state had enough collective "experience" to generate information sufficient to do their

[11] Madison, *The Federalist 53*, p. 363; 55, p. 372; 58, p. 396. Emphasis in the original.

[12] George Mason, Debate in Virginia Ratifying Convention, 4 June 1788, Elliot 3:29–35, *FC*, 1:2:3, no. 18, p. 137.

[13] James Madison, Debate in Virginia Ratifying Convention, 4 June 1788, Elliot 3:29–35, *FC*, 1.2.3, no. 18, p. 139.

jobs. Again, the argument here is not decisive and there might be a case made that as long as districts were merely the size of the state, such information would be passed on. But along with the other evidence presented in this chapter, it suggests that the Federalists expected territorial districts to encourage and facilitate the transmission of *enough* local information for legislatures to do their jobs well.

6.2 VIRTUE AND THE VALUE OF CONSTITUENT DELIBERATION

Territorial constituencies were justified because they enabled deliberation between constituents. We can parse this into its two corresponding parts:

Normative claim: Constituents ought to deliberate with one another for the purpose of selecting better representatives.

Empirical expectation: Territorial constituencies were expected to enable such deliberation.

The empirical expectation gets at a purported benefit of territorial representation even today: There are few ways better than physical proximity to enable citizens to deliberate about politics (or anything else, for that matter). The normative claim is thus the more interesting one, and among other things, it forces us to specify just what exactly deliberation was meant to achieve.

Why was constituent deliberation of value to the founding generation? Local deliberation facilitated the selection and evaluation of political leadership, in particular whether or not a candidate had the virtue purportedly required for elected leadership. Local elections were thought to promote virtuous individuals because virtue was thought to be discerned locally. Even within a large district, connections between leaders of local communities would be important to ensure a virtuous choice. Were voters of a constituency dispersed throughout the nation, this reputational effect would not be secured. Indeed, the worries that dubious sorts of individuals would be known nationally lies at the very heart of the argument establishing the electoral college for the selection of a president.[14]

The view that local deliberation was critical to the discernment of the best sort of characters for office goes back to early modern English practice. I begin there, trace the view's development by James Harrington and Montesquieu (both of whom influenced the founders), and then follow the thread into the founding debates.

As I argued in Chapter 4, political and social spheres were enmeshed in early modern England. As Mark Kishlansky observed:

... in the early modern world there was no separation between the social and the political. Authority was integrated. Personal attributes, prestige, standing, godliness – were all implicit in office holding. Their presence qualified individuals for place, their absence

---

[14] Hamilton, *Federalist 68*.

disqualified them. Individuals represented communities by virtue of the possession of these qualities, not by reflecting the special interests or ideals of particular groups of constituents. In all but a handful of instances, most of which are extremely well documented, before 1640 ideology was absent from the process of parliamentary selection.[15]

Although the not uncommon practice of selecting a member of parliament from outside one's community may seem to go against this grain, it does not, for two reasons. First, nonresident candidates who were selected were those whose fame extended beyond their own community. Second, even in the case of the English system, where nonresident candidates were recruited, they were vouched for by eminent local leadership.[16] Local leaders essentially signaled virtue to members of a constituency.[17]

In *Oceana*, James Harrington developed the linking of virtue and local elections into a robust theory of filtration.[18] Harrington (as well as Algernon Sidney) argued that virtue in government would be secured through a three-stage process: The "elders" qualified for nominating and electing candidates; one elder randomly selected nominated candidates; and finally, the whole group voted on these already filtered candidates. The enfranchisement of the elders was meant to increase the odds that a good choice would be made. As J. G. A. Pocock described, "The democracy could discover the aristocracy by using its own modes of discernment, and there was no need to legislate its choice in advance; a theory of deference was usually invoked in order to democratize the polity."[19]

Local voting was particularly important to this process. Having emphasized land ownership through the agrarian law as a means of securing virtue in the citizen, Pocock observes, "When land was acquired, it was in order to bequeath it: to found families or *oikoi* based on a security of inheritance, which set the sons free to bear arms and cast ballots.... As with Aristotle, the end of land [ownership] is not profit, but leisure: the opportunity to act in the public realm or assembly, to display virtue."[20] One displayed virtue by choosing wisely, because elections were most often publicly held and seldom was a private ballot

---

[15] Mark Kishlansky, *Parliamentary Selection: Social and Political Choice in Early Modern England* (New York: Cambridge University Press, 1986), p. 16.

[16] Kishlansky describes this as a process of substitution: Those "vouching" for a candidate were often peers who would nominate civil servants since they were not eligible to stand themselves. The point remains the same. Kishlansky, *Parliamentary Selection*, p. 42.

[17] Hamilton, *Federalist 84*, p. 582. Hamilton's argument thus foreshadows the information and signaling effects of reputation in Congress (and outside) developed in Edward G. Carmines and James H. Kuklinski, "Incentives, Opportunities, and the Logic of Public Opinion in American Political Representation," in *Information and Democratic Processes*, eds. John A. Ferejohn and James H. Kuklinski (Chicago: University of Illinois, 1990), pp. 240–68.

[18] James Harrington, *The Commonwealth of Oceana an A System of Politics*, ed. J. G. A. Pocock. (Cambridge, UK: Cambridge University Press, 1992).

[19] J. G. A. Pocock, *The Machiavellian Moment: Florentine Political Thought and the Atlantic Republican Tradition* (Princeton, NJ: Princeton University Press, 1975), p. 515.

[20] Ibid., p. 390.

used; the public vote meant that voters could be held to account for their only substantive political act.

Institutions could only guide men toward virtuous choices; men still had to recognize virtue when they saw it. Harrington thus attached great faith to men's ability to recognize virtue.[21] But if, as Pocock has written, "the many can be trusted to know the talented few when they see them," that still requires that the many be in a position actually to *see* the few.[22] This is a problem for large nations, and Harrington's solution was, again, a nested system of choosing the choosers. Towns would choose men of virtue (he hoped) to be electors of a representative. These electors were to convene and presumably come to know each other enough to select a virtuous representative. Thus, in Harrington's plan, the selection of national representatives was a three-tiered event of choosing the choosers.[23]

Virtue took on a similarly local quality for Montesquieu. "The people are admirable for choosing those to whom they should entrust some part of their authority. They have only to base their decision on things of which they cannot be unaware and on facts that are evident to the senses."[24] These facts include who distinguished themselves in war and thus who should be elected a general; who has been "assiduous" as a judge "that many people leave the tribunal satisfied with him," and so could be elected a praetor [a judge of private suits]; and who would strike the citizen as magnificent or wealthy and thus be chosen an aedile [a supervisor of the police]. "All these things are facts that they learn better in a public square than a monarch does in his palace." Although Montesquieu was contrasting the people to the Crown on the issue of who is best suited to choose government officials, the localness of this knowledge is clear: ". . . one judges the ability of one's neighbors better than that of one's other compatriots."[25] Territorial proximity of voters, it was hoped, would facilitate the election of the best and the brightest.

For both Federalists and Anti-Federalists, knowing virtue depended on close proximity. Consider George Washington's first cabinet appointments as a case in point. With the British specter of Walpole looming over him, Washington took pains to give positions based on merit rather than blood or other nonmeritorious qualities. Such merit could be discerned only by the local communities before whom it was displayed. "'First Characters' were men who by virtue of their abilities and records of public service stood first, as it were, *in the respect of*

---

[21] Ibid., p. 394.

[22] Ibid.

[23] For a similar scheme, see David Hume, "Idea of a Perfect Commonwealth," in *David Hume, Essays: Moral Political and Literary*, ed. Eugene F. Miller (Indianapolis, IN: Liberty Fund, 1987), pp. 512–29.

[24] Montesquieu, *Spirit of the Laws*, 2:2, p. 11.

[25] This point may not be immediately obvious: Certainly Montesquieu's real concern is with how insulated the king qua king is from the knowledge of the people. But the king would also readily know any candidate who impressed voters far away from where he distinguished himself.

their neighbors," Stanley Elkins and Eric McKitrick wrote in their study *The Age of Federalism.* Evidence for these qualities "was to be found in personal merit, talent and prior public service...all of which added up to what Washington most wanted for his appointees, *the esteem of their fellow-citizens."*[26] But this merit could only be known locally.

The founders, particularly the Federalists, revised Harrington and Montesquieu's arguments about using institutions to secure virtue to apply to the new republic. While in the minds of the founders elections would not guarantee the selection of more virtuous candidates, electoral institutions could increase the probability of good outcomes.[27] In fact, both sides in the constitutional debate endorsed the normative claim that local proximity was crucial for the deliberation about virtue. Again, the disagreement centered on size of the district: Whereas the Federalists (particularly Madison in *Federalist 10*) thought that largeness would aid this selection,[28] the Anti-Federalists again thought the largeness of the district would undermine the ability for virtue to be discerned locally.[29] In either case, virtue was a local affair.

During the ratifying convention in Philadelphia, opponents of the Constitution claimed, in James Wilson's words, that "the representatives will not be known to the people, nor the people to the representatives, because they will be taken from large districts, where they cannot be particularly acquainted." Experience, Wilson countered, "demonstrates that the larger the district of election, the better the representation.... Nothing but real weight of character

---

[26] Stanley Elkins and Eric McKitrick, *The Age of Federalism* (Oxford, UK: Oxford University Press, 1993), p. 54, emphasis added.

[27] I thank Ralph Lerner for emphasizing this point to me.

[28] A large district, as Madison argued in *Federalist 10*, also increases the number of potential "fit choices"; that is, it increases the likelihood that a good candidate will be found. Yet, as David Epstein rightly notes, increasing the number of constituents would presumably also increase the likelihood of a bad choice; Madison did not appear to recognize this fact. David F. Epstein, *The Political Theory of the Federalist* (Chicago: University of Chicago Press, 1984). Many articles have been written on the relation between virtue and district size in Madison's thought. In addition to Epstein, see Douglass Adair, "The Tenth Federalist Revisited," in *Fame and the Founding Fathers*, ed. Trevor Colbourn (Indianapolis, IN: Liberty Fund), pp. 106–31; Alan Gibson, "Impartial Representation and the Extended Republic: Towards a Comprehensive and Balanced Reading of the Tenth Federalist Paper," *History of Political Thought*, 12, no. 2, Summer; Gary Wills, *Explaining America: The Federalist* (New York: Doubleday, 1981), pp. 263–304.

[29] For the Anti-Federalists, the possibility that the "most influential characters" would control elections was troublesome because it threatened to promote demagogues, and because it was more likely to promote an aristocracy. As Cecilia Kenyon summarizes:

... the prediction was based on the assumption that the ordinary voter, confronted with the choice of representative [sic] in a district so large that he could not personally know the candidates, would vote for someone who was outstanding – perhaps a demagogue or perhaps an aristocrat – or else seek advice from a leader, probably an aristocrat, in his own community.

See also the arguments of Patrick Henry and Men, quoted in Cecilia Kenyon, ed., *The Anti-Federalists* (New York: Bobbs-Merrill, 1966), pp. liii–liv.

can give a man real influence over a large district."[30] How exactly would the "weight of character give a man real influence over a large district"? Here is where the enabling benefits of territorial constituencies kick in: If good representation depended on voters following proven leaders, then at the founding this meant that voters had to be physically proximate to these leaders and thus to each other. The reason for this was exactly that which Hamilton articulated in *Federalist 84* (quoted in Chapter 5): Distance from Congress would necessitate a filtered and tiered system of communication. Voters stood at the base of that system and would take their direction from local leadership. So the need for voters to be territorially proximate was directly related to a substantive theory of political representation – namely, the desire to elect better representatives.

This then raises what is arguably the central benefit of territorial constituencies at the founding: Grouping voters in reasonably close physical proximity was required in order for them to choose their representatives wisely. It is an argument that we can find clearly expressed later in Alexis de Tocqueville's descriptions of nineteenth century America and as a normative argument fully developed by John Stuart Mill: Representative government entrusts citizens with the responsibility of electing their leadership, and this responsibility has a corresponding effect on their capacities as citizens. Representative government – as compared to monarchy or tyranny or even benevolent despotism – requires that citizens be educated *as* citizens. And if publicity is maintained, representative government facilitates its own beneficial effects. But until the age of the telephone and the Internet, deliberation demanded local contact between citizens. It demanded that voters within a constituency be enabled to discuss the affairs of the day with their neighbors, even if the electoral district comprised more than one neighborhood. So territorial districts were not simply the only way that representation could be done, they facilitated this central component of democratic theory: the development of a citizens' deliberative and political capacity.[31]

These deliberative effects were well known to the founders. Montesquieu's arguments about democracy rested on the territorial proximity of the people not only or mostly because the community or locale had particular interests to be represented, but because public and communal voting was a "fundamental law of democracy." Public voting was valued because of the influence that "eminent men" were expected to have in such elections. Such influence necessitated physical proximity of voters, as Montesquieu refers approvingly of the

---

[30] *FC*, 1:2:1, no. 12, pp. 51–2. Also note the end of Wilson's speech to confirm this:

> This is remarkably shown in the commonwealth of Massachusetts. The members of the House of Representatives are chosen in very small districts; and such has been the influence of party cabal, and little intrigue in them, that a great majority seem inclined to show very little disapprobation of the conduct of the insurgents in that state.

[31] See Schwartz, *The Blue Guitar*, for a particularly good development of how territorial proximity could develop the capabilities of citizens.

Athenian system of raising hands.[32] And, as Joseph Story summarized in his discussion on the debate over whether representatives should be directly elected by the people (or by the state legislatures as they were in the Senate), we see this effect of deliberation and discussion. The benefit of entrusting election directly to the citizens themselves was to create a culture of political civility and education, what might be called "republican civility" today:

The *indirect* advantages from this immediate agency of the people in the choice of their representatives are of incalculable benefit, and deserve a brief mention in this place. . . . In the first place, the right confers an additional sense of personal dignity and duty upon the mass of the people. It gives a strong direction to the education, studies, and pursuits of the whole community. It enlarges the sphere of action, and contributes, in a high degree, to the formation of public manners, and national character. It procures to the common people courtesy and sympathy from their superiors, and diffuses a common confidence, as well as a common interest, through all the ranks of society. It awakens a desire to examine, and sift, and debate all public proceedings, and thus nourishes a lively curiosity to acquire knowledge, and, at the same time, furnishes the means of gratifying it. The proceedings and debates of the legislature; the conduct of public officers from the highest to the lowest; the character and conduct of the executive and his ministers; the struggles, intrigues, and conduct of different parties; and the discussion of the great public measures and questions, which agitate and divide the community, are not only freely canvassed, and thus improve and elevate conversation; but they gradually furnish the mind with safe and solid materials for judgment upon all public affairs; and check that impetuosity and rashness, to which sudden impulses might otherwise lead the people, when they are artfully misguided by selfish demagogues, and plausible schemes of change.[33]

Note that the description reflects the invisibility of territorial districts – virtue, Story summarized, accrued to any citizen who had the vote. Story may have been optimistic, but we cannot escape the obvious: Having territorially proximate voters enabled the achievement of these aims. It was thus not merely *having* the vote, but having the vote *for the same representative* among a group of people likely to deliberate with one another about how to cast that vote. And this just meant territorial districts – whether single-member or large multimember state districts. None of these benefits would have accrued to a population geographically disparate.

6.3 ELECTIONS AS TANGIBLE MOMENTS OF CONSENT

The final justification for territorial constituencies as an enabler of other democratic values takes up communal consent: So long as voters were territorially proximate, elections could serve as tangible moments of consent. The argument for this last justification is the most speculative because territory is not so much

---

[32] Montesquieu, *Spirit of the Laws*, 2:2, p. 14. Public voting also kept "intrigues" out of the selections of officials, implying that people both publicly state their vote and do so when others are present to witness it.

[33] *FC*, 1:2:1, no. 20, pp. 65–8.

"justified" by this feature as it is consistent with elections that could operate as moments of consent.

This consent justification can be parsed into its two corresponding parts:

Normative claim: Elections ought to be symbolic moments of communal consent.

Empirical expectations: Territorial constituencies were expected to facilitate elections of this kind.

The evidence for the normative claim is indirect: It is consistent with the practice of public elections when viewed through the lens of consent theory. Territorial constituencies make communal, public voting easier, and the public nature of the vote had important symbolic significance to its participants. The empirical expectation is thus trivially true: If voting was expected to be a communal event, then given the technology of eighteenth century America, voters needed to live near each other. In what follows, I argue that communal public voting was valued as an expression of communal consent.

I should emphasize first that the justification applies only to elections that involve public gatherings of the constituency or a part thereof. We must begin, then, by differentiating this justification from the false claim that territorial constituencies made voting per se any more convenient than nonterritorial constituencies.[34] Defining constituencies by where people live does not make *casting* private votes any more or less convenient than any other constituency definition. As long as private ballots are used, members of the same electoral constituency could live hundreds of miles from each other and cast their vote by mail. Even if concerns of fraud and coercion necessitated casting private ballots in public places (as most citizens do on election day today), this concern would not require territorial constituencies. Instead, individuals could receive different ballots, corresponding to their nonterritorial constituency and cast them at a public polling location. The argument that a territorially proximate group of individuals should itself constitute a constituency is a different matter.

I turn first to the argument that communal elections were expressions of public consent, and then to illustrate the very communal, public nature of elections in the American republic.

As Bernard Manin recently argued, elections originally served a different purpose in ancient times than they did for moderns, tied as each was to very different notions of political equality.[35] In ancient Greece, equality meant the equal right to rule; for the moderns, equality means the equal right to choose

---

[34] "...[D]istributeth the people according unto the places of their habitation. For except the people be methodically distributed, they cannot be methodically collected, but the being of a commonwealth consisteth in the methodical collection of the people." James Harrington, "The Commonwealth of Oceana," in *The Commonwealth of Oceana and A System of Politics*, ed. J. G. A. Pocock, Cambridge Texts in the History of Political Thought (New York: Cambridge University Press, 1992 [1656]), p. 77. See also Paine, *Common Sense*, p. 5.

[35] This paragraph and the next are summaries of Bernard Manin, *The Principles of Representative Government* (New York: Cambridge University Press, 1997).

one's rulers.[36] The ancients selected their leaders through a random lottery of self-nominated "candidates." By contrast, representatives in the modern world were (and are) seen as a separate class of rulers elected by the people. Election in modern times is meant to promote the well-spoken, wealthy, and virtuous, and thus might be thought of as an aristocratic element within a democratic system. This hybrid is what we speak of as representative democracy, or "republican" government, as we know it today. As we saw in section 6.2, elections could filter "proper" candidates only when a fair amount of publicity surrounded them – that is, public deliberation about candidates and also public sanctioning of voters to encourage proper selection.

In addition to promoting "proper" sorts of candidates, voting and elections purportedly instantiate the consent of those governed. But how precisely do elections relate to the idea of consent? The answer may seem obvious – consent theory held that government could legitimately rule in part because individuals voluntarily consented to them. What kind of expression could be more explicitly consensual than an election in which the voters actually do choose who will wield the axe over them? These facts lead Manin to argue that the rise of consent theory also explains the use of election, rather than random selection, to choose political leadership – we need to authorize our leadership in order to legitimize it.

Historically, however, consent theory did not justify the use of voting per se; it purportedly legitimized a government's right to rule an individual citizen because that citizen voluntarily accepted the very general political conditions of the exercise of that force.[37] John Locke is the clearest example here: Individuals consent to leaving the state of nature and forming a political community with each other. Yes, they give their consent to use election as the selection rule for picking their leaders. But that does not make any particular outcome of an election itself the expression of consent;[38] elections were a very practical way of expressing the force of a community, and majority rule was a decision rule that

---

[36] The argument thus echoes the themes of Benjamin Constant, "The Liberty of the Ancients Compared with That of the Moderns," in *Benjamin Constant: Political Writings*, ed. and trans. Biancamaria Fontana, Cambridge Texts in the History of Political Thought, pp. 308–28 (Cambridge, UK: Cambridge University Press, 1988). Manin argues that lot was *not* considered at the time of the American founding *because* the concept of equality shifted from "right to rule" to "right to select." Although I think his description of this shift is correct, I do not see the evidence to support his claim that holding a particular view of equality *caused* anyone to ignore the use of lot. More plausibly, the founders were moving away from the control that local groups had on elections and thus consciously wanted to capture the aristocratic element of elections, as Manin calls it. This aristocratic element would, then, not be *caused* by the shift in notions of "equality," but rather entailed the shift post hoc.

[37] On the rise and dominance of consent theory in seventeenth century England, see Don Herzog, *Happy Slaves* (Chicago: University of Chicago Press, 1989). In practice, the theory is notoriously hard to realize in any thoroughgoing way. For an excellent critique, see A. John Simmons, *Moral Principles and Political Obligations* (Princeton, NJ: Princeton University Press, 1979).

[38] For a similar point, see Ruth Grant, *John Locke's Liberalism* (Chicago: University of Chicago Press, 1987), p. 118.

could be widely accepted.[39] Analytically, nonunanimous decision rules fail to meet the requirements that all individuals consent to their output. In the case of a simple majority rule election of two candidates, up to "half minus one" of the population explicitly withholds its consent to whichever candidate goes on to win. When plurality elections are used, the winner of an election can fail to win even a majority of votes.[40]

But elections do *feel* like an expression of consent – individuals are making purportedly voluntary choices about who will govern them. Further, if the community is thought to be a unity of some kind, then majority rule emerges as a way of giving the collective's consent. Elections then emerge as a moment of symbolic,[41] communal consent, rather than as a means for all actually to consent.

Consistent with others,[42] Manin agrees that this view accurately reflects the history of the time: The self-conception of late eighteenth century Americans involved consenting to the laws they passed because they collectively (rather than individually) had elected the rulers who made the laws. It grounded their understanding of why the government had the right to make and enforce laws. Consent also justified their obligations to government. Regardless of the philosophical problems with this position, Americans during the founding period perceived that consent through majority voting grounded political right as strong as earlier generations perceived that kings ruled by divine right.

The practice of elections during the founding period closely mirrored this communal symbolic expression of consent. For one thing, "elections" were extremely different events in eighteenth century America than they are now. "Competitive elections of any kind were not too common at the beginning of the Revolutionary period."[43] More importantly, they were local public events that demanded close territorial proximity between voters.

Territorial constituencies made voting convenient, but "voting" was not a matter of checking off someone's name on a ballot. In England, candidate selection in the early seventeenth century originally consisted of either a voice vote

---

[39] See Jeremy Waldron's discussion, though, on the physics of consent, in Jeremy Waldron, *The Dignity of Legislation* (New York: Cambridge University Press, 1999), Chapter 6.

[40] Plurality elections are those in which the top vote getter wins, no matter what the candidate's share of the vote actually is. Electoral college rules notwithstanding, a majority of voters voted against Bill Clinton in the 1992 and 1996 U.S. presidential elections and against George W. Bush in 2000.

[41] I say "symbolic" to suggest that communities do not in fact form a unity and to remind us that this is a different form of consent than that mandated by consent theories of government. Nothing hinges on the use of this term, nor on this assertion about the nature of groups.

[42] For two examples, see Constantin Fasolt, "Quod Omnes Tangit Ab Omnibus Approbari Debet: The Words and the Meaning," in *In Iure Veritas: Studies in Canon Law in Memory of Schaefer Williams*, eds. Steven B. Bowman and Blanch E. Cody (Cincinnati, OH: University of Cincinnati College of Law, 1991), pp. 21–55; Herzog, *Happy Slaves*.

[43] Robert J. Dinkin, *Voting in Revolutionary America: A Study of Elections in the Original Thirteen States 1776–1789* (Westport, CT: Greenwood Press, 1982), p. 8.

of the collective community or the public gathering for the purpose of giving a ballot, both of which require people to gather together.[44] The selection of a member for parliament was a public, communal event that drew the community physically together.

Consider Kishlansky's account of selection of parliamentary representatives in the early seventeenth century: They were often uncontested but always publicly – communally – approved.[45] Communities gathered to assent publicly to a candidate chosen by the town's social elite through a process that was diametrically at odds with modern-day competitive elections. "Communities were not used to contested choices in any sphere of social life and had only the most imperfect means of dealing with them."[46] Citizens did not mark a ballot to show approval, but gave their voices in support of candidates – a process "both anonymous and unanimous."[47] Even in the few cases where the process was contested, the selection was similarly public. For example, those supporting each candidate would assemble on different sides of a hill to express their support tangibly.

In the American colonies, election history was slightly different. A few colonies used the secret ballot only a few years after their establishment. The first secret ballot was used in Salem to select a church minister on July 20, 1629.[48] But the open ballot and voting *viva voce* were more common. In Virginia, for example, voice voting continued at least through 1785. At that point, an act was passed requiring a written ballot in cases where a public show of support was indeterminate.[49] Even in Massachusetts, the officers in New England "were at first elected by the view, or the showing of hands."[50]

The written ballot was introduced for two reasons, neither related to a desire for secrecy, and thus the need for voters to be physically proximate to one another remained. First, the written ballot was seen to be a more convenient way of voting.[51] Consider Spencer D. Albright's account of Massachusetts' ballots in the early nineteenth century. Following a ruling that political parties could

---

[44] There are various accounts of this period in both the American colonies and England. Spencer D. Albright, *The American Ballot* (Washington, DC: American Council on Public Affairs, 1942); Eldon Cobb Evans, "A History of the Australian Ballot System in the United States," Ph.D. Dissertation, University of Chicago, 1917; Kishlansky, *Parliamentary Selection*; J. R. Pole, *Political Representation in England and the Origins of the American Republic* (New York: St. Martin's Press, 1966); Charles S. Sydnor, *American Revolutionaries in the Making* (New York: Macmillan, 1952). For a terrific account of the history of voting that focuses primarily on America after the founding, see Alexander Keyssar, *The Right to Vote: The Contested History of Democracy in the United States, with a New Afterword* (New York: Basic Books, 2000).

[45] Kishlansky, *Parliamentary Selection*.

[46] Ibid., p. 55. For an account of the deep strains of social order in early seventeenth century England, see Herzog, *Happy Slaves*.

[47] Kishlansky, *Parliamentary Selection*, p. 11.

[48] Albright, *The American Ballot*, p. 14.

[49] Ibid., p. 18.

[50] Evans, "History of the Australian Ballot," p. 1.

[51] Ibid.

preprint ballots and distribute them to voters, "party leaders began to print the tickets . . . on colored paper so that they could be recognized some distance from the polling place. Thus there could be no secrecy."[52] In West Jersey in 1676, the governing board enacted the written ballot "to avoid noise and confusion, and not by Voices, holding up of the Hands, or otherwise howsoever."[53] Indeed, even the Massachusetts act of 1647 authorized the sheriff to collect such written ballots from "those freemen who remained at home and send them to the court of elections" was not intended to move voting to private venues.[54] Such proxy voting – that is, voting without attending the election meeting – was generally frowned upon. In Virginia, a law of 1646 forbade the practice, "requiring the election of Burgesses to be by a 'plurality of voices and that no hand writing shall be admitted.'"[55] As Albright indicates, such a law needed to be passed only where that practice existed; there may have been increasing unwillingness to be physically present for elections. Voting would still be a public event and not an isolated moment of political participation.

Through the mid-eighteenth century, communal meetings defined colonial American representative selection even when secret voting occurred – in Massachusetts through the town meeting, in Pennsylvania through church gatherings, and in Virginia at court houses.[56] So festive were southern elections that prohibitions were finally enacted forbidding candidates from providing alcohol on voting days.[57]

By 1789, no U.S. state constitution required *viva voce* voting, but that was a relatively recent development. As late as 1777, the newly written New York state constitution explicitly allowed for voice voting:

. . . if after a full and fair experiment shall be made of voting by ballot aforesaid, the same shall be found less conducive to the safety or interest of the State than the method of voting *viva voce*, it shall be lawful and constitutional for the legislature to abolish the same, provided two-thirds of the members present in each house, respectively, shall concur therein. And further, that, during the continuance of the present war, and until the legislature of this State shall provide for the election of senators and representatives in assembly by ballot, the said election shall be made *viva voce*.[58]

Only after such an experiment to see whether secret balloting would actually "preserve liberty and equal freedom" would voting *viva voce* be rejected.

[52] Albright, *The American Ballot*, p. 20.

[53] Cortland F. Bishop, *History of Elections in the American Colonies* (New York: Columbia College, 1893), p. 166. Quoted in Albright, *The American Ballot*, p. 16.

[54] Ibid., p. 15.

[55] Albert Edwin McKinley, "The Suffrage Franchise in the Thirteen English Colonies in America," Ph.D. Dissertation, University of Pennsylvania, 1905, p. 245. Quoted in Albright, *The American Ballot*, p. 17.

[56] Pole, *Political Representation*.

[57] Sydnor, *American Revolutionaries*, Chapter 4 ("Swilling the Planters with Bumbo").

[58] New York State Constitution (1777), Paragraph VI (retrieved 22 February 2004, from the Avalon Project at http://www.yale.edu/lawweb/avalon/states/ny01.htm).

Charles S. Sydnor's account of voting in Virginia is also illustrative of the period. As late as the mid-eighteenth century, candidates for the colonial legislature stood (or sat) for a vote behind a table. At one end was the sheriff to whom a constituent would report his vote. The fortunate candidate would extend his hand in thanks to the voter and wish him good health and prosperity. It is no coincidence that "drink" was eventually forbidden from these proceedings.[59] As concerns of corruption began to rise, the secret ballot was introduced. Even though a secret ballot would not require constituents to be territorially proximate, territorial constituencies still made the voting easier. Election days were often still celebratory occasions at a central location.

Returning, then, to Manin's observations of the role of consent that animated the choice of election over random selection, I believe we are justified in making a stronger point. The gathering to select a candidate on election day served not only the purpose of choosing the candidate but formed a tangible, if symbolic, moment of consent for the community, who were gathered to choose their representative. Such moments did not require territorial representation; everyone might receive a different ballot just in case he belonged to this constituency or that one. Nonetheless, territoriality enabled and made more likely the aim of bringing the community together for this tangible moment of communal consent.

6.4 EPILOGUE: POSTFOUNDING DEVELOPMENTS

On April 5, 1792, George Washington signed his nation's first presidential veto.[60] The decision must not have been an easy one for Washington. Aside from the obvious trappings of absolute power that the veto represented – trappings that Washington was famously loathe to take on – the decision lacked the decisiveness characteristic of the man. For one thing, he waited until the last moment to veto it, just before the bill would have automatically become law. According to Thomas Jefferson, then Washington's secretary of state, the first president appeared unexpectedly at Jefferson's residence for advice before breakfast that morning. Washington was still uncertain whether or not to support the bill.

After that morning meeting, Washington was leaning toward veto, and the first president requested that three of his close associates – Jefferson, Attorney General Edmund Randolph, and Representative James Madison – draft the document. It is only speculation, but perhaps the most compelling point to him was that the states were getting anxious that the veto had not yet been used. As an institutional matter, Jefferson, Randolph, and Madison explained, the states

---

[59] Sydnor, *American Revolutionaries*, p. 56.

[60] The following account comes from Edmund J. James, *The First Apportionment of Federal Representatives in the United States: A Study in American Politics* (Philadelphia, PA: American Academy of Political and Social Science, 1896).

of the new republic needed to see that the president could limit Congress. By the end of the day, Washington had vetoed the bill.

That bill was the first federal plan of apportionment for representatives passed by Congress. The plan would establish how many federal representatives each state would receive in Congress. The Constitution set an upper limit for the size of the House by ensuring that there would be no more than one representative for every thirty-thousand citizens. Using that ratio in 1792 could have produced a House of 120 members. But the matter was left to Congress to decide. In the debate, serious proposals wavered between a House of 82 and 112 members. In the end, Washington vetoed the bill that would have established a larger house. He later approved a plan that established the first apportioned Congress at 106 members.

The size of the House determined the number of constituents that a representative would represent.[61] And it was the size of this ratio that had threatened the proposed union of the thirteen original states because it was perceived as being too small to guarantee the close connection between government and its citizens. With the Constitution ratified, arguments about institutional design were replaced by arguments about politics in its more mundane guise. The use of territory to define electoral constituencies would never have a chance to emerge as a separate issue. Instead, the territorialness of the district famously became – and in the American context still is – a way of manipulating political representation for good or ill. .

The historical analysis of these last three chapters demonstrated that territorial constituencies were not recognized as the Constitution was ratified. But immediately after the ratification, the political landscape changed in unexpected ways. Perhaps the most unexpected development was the emergence of the national party system during the first decade of the republic and then particularly after the death of George Washington in 1799. By 1801, only a dozen years after ratification, Jefferson emerged as the commander in chief as well as the head of a political party. The landscape had indeed changed.

---

[61] I use the word "constituent" in this context cautiously. The method of counting population varied depending on the type of person counted. Free persons and those "bound to service for a term of years" were each counted individually. Indians not taxed would not count at all (though notice they would count if they were taxed) and "all other persons" would be counted as three-fifths of their normal number. All other persons were, of course, slaves. This is obviously an important symbolic offense, as ethically each slave should have been counted as fully human. As a practical matter, it was of course slavery and not the three-fifths clause that dehumanized Africans in America. Ironically, however, the problem with the three-fifths clause is not that it *devalued* slaves, but that it *overvalued* them, giving too much political power to their white owners. Had slaves been counted as full citizens ("fully human" according to the simplifying myths of American grade schools), southern white political strength would have increased further in the House of Representatives. The clause cut both ways because the cost of allowing southern states to count their slaves for increased political power was that they would face higher taxes. Indeed, this was part of the compromise that resolved a thorny problem at the Convention. The point remains: Viewing the three-fifths clause as proof of how the Constitution acquiesced to the dehumanization of slaves confuses the important difference between symbolic and actual political power.

Madison's expectations (partially explored in Chapter 5) that large, internally heterogeneous electoral constituencies would help keep partial, local interests out of the national legislature, were overly optomistic, but not because his theory of electoral dynamics was wrong. Rather, its necessary conditions for success – such as the inability of local groups to coordinate with each other – were not met.[62] The largeness of the congressional district may well have foiled smaller partisan groups from joining together and electing a representative closely allied to them if not for the emergence of political parties. Political parties allowed even large groups to solve the communication and coordination problems whose rectification were at the heart of Madison's hopes.

Manipulation of the election laws and systems for party gain emerged in the early 1790s, just as political parties were becoming entrenched. In Pennsylvania, for example, the legislature proposed electing its congressional delegation by statewide vote. Madison, in a letter to Jefferson that year, seemed intrigued by the possibilities of using states as laboratories for democratic institutions. But those who proposed the delegation had more self-serving plans. They understood that the population was not distributed equally between farming and mercantile interests, the latter being concentrated around Philadelphia. Since the majority of Pennsylvanians lived around Philadelphia, if the state were to elect its entire statewide delegation by simple majority rule rather than dividing the state into territorial constituencies, the entire delegation would be members of the new Federalist Party. As other historians have documented, this pattern repeatedly plagued the early republic.[63]

Even in those states that used districting to allocate their representatives, gross manipulation regularly occurred. The term "gerrymander" – the practice of manipulating district lines to maximize the number of representatives a given party sends to Congress – dates from this period.[64] In 1812, Massachusettes Governor Elbridge Gerry approved the districting map proposed by the Republican state legislature that secured greater support for his Republican Party over the Federalists. A local political cartoonist satirized one of the resulting districts, which looked oddly like a salamander, and labeled it "gerry-mander." Other cases were common.

In response to electing delegations by majority statewide vote (rather than holding several elections in each district in the state), Congress repeatedly

---

[62] Madison's theory may have been wrong also, but its failure is attributable to the rise of unforeseen causes, namely political parties.

[63] For the history of districting during the early republic, see, Richard C. Cortner, *The Apportionment Cases* (Knoxville, TN: University of Tennessee Press, 1970); Robert G. Dixon, Jr., *Democratic Representation: Reapportionment in Law and Politics* (New York: Oxford University Press, 1968); Andrew Hacker, *Congressional Districting: The Issue of Equal Representation* (Washington, DC: Brookings Institution Press, 1963); McKitrich, *The Age of Federalism*; Rosemarie Zagarri *The Politics of Size Representation in the United States 1776–1850* (Ithaca, NY, and London: Cornell University Press, 1987).

[64] In America, the practice of drawing district lines for partisan advantage predated the term by about one hundred years and was used sporadically during the American colonial period. In England, rottenboroughs could be thought of as a "desuetudinal gerrymander" – the manipulation of representation by self-consciously leaving the established district lines as they were.

attempted to pass laws to force states to divide their delegations into as many separate districts as they had representatives. In 1842 they finally succeeded, and the law has been repeatedly passed and rescinded through the years since.[65] The most recent law requiring the single-member district in every state was passed in 1967, and the bill proposed by Representative Melvin Watts (D-NC) in 1999 allowing multimember districts would take its place had it passed.[66]

Since 1842, districting and apportionment have been dynamic and controversial issues and have been treated by a vast amount of scholarship. For reasons discussed in section 3.3, I will not spend much time detailing this material here except to note that the use of territory to define districts was never seriously questioned. A brief review of the two of the most salient events of this period will help illustrate the habit of mind that territorial districts have become. First, I will take up the urban and rural districting controversies that animated the first half of the twentieth century. Second, I will briefly review the voting rights acts of the middle 1960s that led to the racial redistricting controversies of the last decades of the twentieth century. Out of these cases, I conclude this historical section with a possible explanation for why territory itself was never seriously raised as an issue.

By the early decades of the twentieth century, industrialization drew people into cities and caused massive population redistributions. After World War I, for the first time in U.S. history, more adults lived in urban areas than on the farm. During this time, Congressional district lines remained rather stagnant so that districts that had been roughly equal prior to population shifts now had wildly disproportionate numbers people in each. In some states, population disparities between Congressional districts approached a hundredfold – some congressional districts numbering close to one million people, others in the tens of thousands. The disparity mapped out exactly along rural and urban lines – urban districts contained vastly more people than did rural districts, simply because people moved into the cities, and legislatures did not redraw district lines to reflect these changes in population density. The rotten borough of seventeenth century England had emerged again on the other side of the Atlantic.[67]

The situation in some states – Illinois and Tennessee in particular – remained unremedied for over fifty years, as state legislatures refused to change district lines. And the federal government had its hands tied: While the U.S.

---

[65] 5 Stat. 491. Despite being on and off the books throughout the years, the vast majority of all Congressional districts have been single-member districts. For the history of this period, see Dixon, *Democratic Representation*; Hacker, *Congressional Districting*; Zagarri, *The Politics of Size*.

[66] See section 3.1.

[67] The term "rottenborough" is an anachronism here, as it dates only to the nineteenth century. But it describes a practice that had been well-known for hundreds of years and so seems appropriately descriptive. See, for example, John Locke's discussion of the issue in section 157 of his "Second Treatise of Government," in *Two Treatise of Government*, ed. Peter Laslety, Cambridge Texts in the History of Political Thought (Cambridge, UK: Cambridge University Press, 1988 [1690]). I thank Martin Battle for this clarification.

Constitution mandated that each state receive an equal number of delegates relative to its statewide population, the apportionment of these representatives to districts within the state was left to its own legislatures. Even though Congress passed a law that required single-member districts, the relative size of those districts had not been specified; districts could be drawn with vastly different populations. Further complicating this was the stipulation in Section 2 of the fourteenth Amendment, which explicitly provided a remedy for laws that effectively denied groups of citizens their equal voting power. That clause was added during the deliberations over the fourteenth Amendment in 1866. The clear intent of those who wrote and ratified that amendment was to extend equal protections of all laws to all its citizens (Section 1) but to provide states the explicit right (with a penalty) of denying groups the right to vote (Section 2).[68]

Because of these facts, the Supreme Court did not view the population inequalities between electoral districts to be a violation of the Constitution, even if they were an affront to political equality. The Constitution does not embody every abstract idea of political justice, and indeed in 1946 the Supreme Court explicitly declined to hear a case raised by this problem on the basis that it was a political question for the state of Illinois to address.[69] Over the following fifteen years, repeated attempts for judicial relief were consistently denied. In 1962, after over fifty years of various litigation, the Supreme Court finally agreed, in *Baker v. Carr*, that the issue was judiciable. But the nation would have to wait until 1964 for specific relief. In *Reynolds v. Sims*, the Court established the one-person, one-vote standard that mandated strict population equality for all districts within each state (and thus close population equality between state districts).

From our standpoint, the most striking fact about these developments was that the question of territorial districts never arose in the arguments raised in court or, as far as I have been able to tell, in advocacy statements prepared for these cases.[70] Even when urban/rural was the relevant distinction,

---

[68] See William E. Nelson, *The Fourteenth Amendment: From Political Principle to Judicial Doctrine* (Cambridge, MA: Harvard University Press, 1988). This argument constitutes Felix Frankfurter's later opinions in *Colegrove v. Green* and *Baker v. Carr*, and is taken up by Justice John M. Harlan in *Baker* and again in *Reynolds v. Sims*. Frankfurter and Harlan appear to be on strong historical grounds that the fourteenth Amendment permitted states to exclude groups of citizens from voting. Indeed, the debate separating voting rights from the equal protection clause illustrates the self-consciousness of its writers on exactly this point: Worried that without the exemption of voting rights the fourteenth Amendment would fail, its supporters agreed to the compromise. A remedy for this abuse is also explicitly provided in the fourteenth Amendment. None of this justifies the exclusion of groups of citizens. Rather, it is to say that history supports Frankfurter's argument about intent even if justice or the equal protection clause supported the one-person, one-vote ruling.

[69] The case was *Colegrove v. Green*. For a compelling and entertaining account, full of intrigue and murder, see Cortner, *The Apportionment Cases*.

[70] See Andrew Rehfeld, "Silence of the Land," Ph.D. Dissertation, University of Chicago, 2000, Chapter 6.

the territoriality of the electoral constituency appears not to have been noticed.

The fact that the early apportionment cases were primarily about an urban/rural issue has been obscured over the last thirty-five years by the passage of the Voting Rights Act in 1965, and the subsequent districting that the act brought about from the 1970s to the 1990s.[71] These latter developments have transformed the districting debate into one of ensuring group representation, particularly that of blacks, Hispanics, and minority language groups. Now, gerrymandering refers to the practice of creating districts that are "majority-minority," even if such districts also secure party success in elections.[72]

In both the debates over rural and urban representation and more recently in the case of minority representation, the focus first on population equality and then racial equity goes a long way to explain why territory as such was never much noticed for subsequent generations of Americans. Further, the political stakes in each of these debates also offers a plausible hypothesis for why the concept of constituency was also not noticed as such.

The historical section of this book began in Chapter 3 by outlining the substantive and methodological issues of historical justification for American territorial constituencies. In Chapter 4, I argued that the origins of the territorial constituency go back to a time when the representative district and the local community were coextensive. I argued that even at the founding of the United States, House electoral districts transcended local borders. In Chapter 5, I reviewed and rejected four plausible justifications for territory: Territorial constituencies were not meant to represent communities of interest; they were not expected to foster attachment to the national government; they did not serve to protect property; and they did not enable consent to the choice of constituency by enabling citizens to "choose" in which constituency they would live. However, the fifth justification – a set of three features of democratic representation that territorial constituencies enabled – was more promising. I thus argued in this chapter that territorial constituencies facilitated the communication of information to the national legislature. Second, they promoted deliberation among citizens for the dual purpose of electing more virtuous candidates and cultivating citizenship skills. Finally, by defining constituency territorially, elections could become tangible moments of consent. The territorial nature of electoral

---

[71] For two accounts among many, see Grofman, Handley, and Niemi, *Minority Representation and the Quest for Voting Equality*; Abigail M. Thernstrom, *Whose Votes Count? Affirmative Action and Minority Voting Rights* (Cambridge, MA: Harvard University Press, 1987).

[72] Until recently, most majority-minority districts were Democratic and thus the racial politics breathed new life into the very old practice of gerrymandering. In any event, the motivation was to secure minority districts for the purposes of race and the reason it was so broadly used was surely in part because these districts mapped so well onto party affiliations. I will discuss these issues as they relate to contemporary justifications for territorial districts in Chapter 7.

constituencies in the United States has never seriously been reconsidered, but simply subsumed under other more pressing debates of political and racial equality.

Are large territorial constituencies defensible today? If not, what alternative should we endorse, and upon what normative principles should we base this endorsement? I take up these questions of normative institutional design as we move into Part III.

NORMATIVE APPLICATIONS

On Legitimate Representation and Institutional Design

7

Territory Reconsidered

In the end, though, Mr. Clinton's success in twisting arms had little to do with the bill's economic merits [of granting permanent normal trade status to China]. He won over the undecided using a bit of Lyndon Johnson–style vote-buying – one congressman got a zip code for a small town, and two others got a natural gas pipeline near El Paso.

– David Sanger[1]

Life in any large nation in the twenty-first century is, in most ways, different from life in the late eighteenth century. Yet the places people live still seem to define who they are, and constitute a seemingly "natural" way of organizing electoral constituencies. In the words of Tip O'Neill, former speaker of the U.S. House of Representatives, "All politics is local." But, as I argued in Chapter 1, politics is local largely because territorially bound constituencies create incentives for politicians to deal with local issues in their compaigns. Put differently, if constituencies were defined by profession, then all politics would be vocational. The question remains whether, in the twenty-first century, we can justify defining extremely large electoral constituencies for representation in a national legislature by territory.

On the face of it, territory seems just as good or better than most constituency definitions. After all, physical proximity allows constituents to interact with each other and allows their representatives to have easy access to them. We tend to spend a good deal of time in and around these places, even if we often work outside them and even if we have interests that transcend local communities. Territorial lines also allow the possibility for fair play; the Supreme Court's standard that districts should be drawn only with the considerations of equality of population and geographical compactness conforms to our sense of fairness. The fact that some state legislatures approve plans that are explicitly

[1] David E. Sanger, "Rounding Out a Clear Clinton Legacy," *New York Times*, 25 May 2000, p. A10.

partisan and designed to maximize electoral outcomes justifies reform; it does not necessarily justify full-scale change. Alternatively, some people would even say that such partisan districting just *is* fair play.

One problem is that whenever *electoral* constituencies are defined by a certain quality – be it territory, profession, race, religion, gender, ideology, party ID, or so on – the defining quality introduces a de facto interest into the legislature even as it defines the nature of political representation within the polis. By appearing "natural," territory hides the fact that it puts national legislation at its service, no more or less than if constituencies were defined by wealth (religion, race, and so on). It does so because of the incentive effects of any electoral constituency. One question we will revisit in sustained terms in this chapter is why we would want to structure political constituencies for *national* representative government so that they can represent local interests rather than some other particular interests.

Yet, the force of the argument in Part II of this book, and particularly in Chapter 5, was that territorial constituencies have always been too large to represent any community interest. How can it be that territorial constituencies simultaneously do and do not represent communities of interest? Which is it, do they or do they not?

The answer has to do with parsing the source and direction of different kinds of interests. The interests that influence a *representative* (and thus influence the national legislature) emerge not only from those that "naturally" exist among her constituents, but also from those goods and services that the representative can deliver back to her constituents. These incentives produce legislative be- havior that is not necessarily coincidental with the national interest. By having to appeal to their local constituents political representatives must not only con- vey their constituents' "voice" into the legislature, they have incentives to steer budget and other legislation back to the citizens of their own districts. So even if there is no coherent sense of "community of interest" within an immensely large territorial constituency as long as political constituencies are defined by *any* particular dimension that can be serviced in this way, this influence will affect them.

Consider an example. After the U.S. Defense Department awarded the lu- crative Joint Strike Fighter (JSF) project to Lockheed Martin in October 2001, U.S. Representative Richard Gephardt (D-MO) expressed regret using terms that made him sound like an expert in the field: "Boeing produced an excellent prototype for the JSF and it is unfortunate that the Department of Defense did not choose Boeing as the lead contractor for this award.... I am confi- dent that Boeing's superiority in many aspects of fighter aircraft design, pro- duction and management will lead to its continued participation in the JSF program."[2]

---

[2] Richard Gephardt, press release, 26 October 2001. Retrieved from http://dickgephardt.house. gov/info/press_release/index.asp?ID=55.

Gephardt had never distinguished himself as an expert on aeronautical design, so his evaluation of the merits of Boeing's proposal is surprising. More likely, of course, it was a trumped-up claim (whether or not true) made because the company is located near St. Louis, Missouri, within a few miles of Gephardt's electoral constituents. Had the project been awarded to Boeing, the whole region would have benefited in jobs and related economic spending. It is thus not surprising that all congressional delegations from eastern Missouri and southwestern Illinois – an area known more for its expertise in agriculture than aeronautics – joined in support of the project. The project would have meant billions of dollars spent on their constituents.[3] It is, perhaps, more surprising that any representative from the region argued in terms of the public interest at all – the fact that Boeing would make a better product was purportedly not just good for their constituents, or that it was good for the nation to have better fighter jets. While all Americans want their representatives to "bring home the bacon," they nevertheless like their bacon wrapped in a flag.[4]

Because the definition of electoral constituencies determines the kinds of goods and policies for which representatives advocate, we need an argument that *this definition* but not *that* one is likely to produce better outcomes. And to make this determination, we will need to know in reference to what are these outcomes purportedly better. But to repeat a point made in Chapter 1, the practice of logrolling (you vote for my bill, I'll vote for yours) will yield dramatically different outcomes depending on how constituencies are defined. We cannot simply say that logrolling ensures the national good without considering what kinds of logs are being rolled.

Apart from issues of interest representation, how should we evaluate the attachment, property, consent, and enabling justifications that I laid out in Chapter 3? Do they aim at normative goals that we should endorse? And are territorial constituencies the best way to achieve them? These are the questions to which we must now turn.

With this informal discussion, we begin the third section of the book, in which our analysis turns from the historical to the normative, from questions of the origins of past institutions, to questions of justification for their present and future design. Over the next three chapters, I ask whether territorial constituencies are justified today (Chapter 7); argue for a default position of involuntary, permanent electoral constituencies that look like the nation they collectively represent (Chapter 8); and spell out how these electoral constituencies might look in practice (Chapter 9).

---

[3] Lockheed had its own territorial fangs in the administration. It is located in Texas, home of then president (and former Texas governor), George W. Bush.

[4] The fact that Gephardt was preparing for his own run for the presidency may also explain why he framed the contract not in terms of loss of jobs but in terms of benefits to the nation.

7.1 INTRODUCTION: ON THE FUNCTION OF
POLITICAL REPRESENTATION

Let me begin more formally by asking whether territorial constituencies are justified today. The answer depends on context and function; I will explain each in turn. By context, I simply mean that before asking whether *any* institution is justifiable, we need to know something about the surrounding culture and history of the people who will be using the proposed institution. For example, defining constituencies based on race will probably not be justified in Iceland. They may be justified in the United States or South Africa. The point here is that context matters, and our decisions about whether institutions are justifiable depend on the context in which they are operating. For this reason, I will focus on the case of the United States and whether it is justifiable to define electoral constituencies by where people live in this case. However, context can also distract from the broader point. So I emphasize again that much of the argument that follows is relevant to any large nation in which enormous electoral constituencies are used.

Context is not all that matters. Perhaps most importantly, before we can determine whether territory (or any other definition) is justified, we must consider the function of the particular representative body for which electoral constituencies are used. Put another way, political representation is not had for its own sake.[5] Rather, representation is created through a set of institutions or rules for a very particular purpose or set of purposes and we can call this purpose its "function." It is then only by reference to this purpose or function that we can evaluate whether or not a proposed definition of electoral constituency is justified (or even justifiable).

To give one example, a representational body created to write a professional policy statement for physicians has a different function than a national legislature, and this fact will be reflected in its institutional design. For such a case, there are plausible reasons to define electoral constituencies by medical specialty, having neurosurgeons, pediatricians, and psychiatrists each elect their own representative. But defining constituencies here by specialty may be less justifiable if the function of this representational body is to design a "doctors only" retirement plan. In this case, having constituencies defined by age cohorts may be beneficial so that the interests of doctors nearing retirement can be weighed against those who are just beginning their careers. It is thus only by reference to the function of a representational body that we can think about how its institutions ought to be designed.

Let me then suggest that the function of any large nation's national legislature is to pursue its national interest. That is, the very reason that a legislature is established is to pursue the good of the whole, and it is by reference to that function that we must evaluate its underlying supporting institutions such as the electoral constituency. Of course, this begs one of the most important

---

[5] I am grateful to Marion Smiley for emphasizing the importance of this point.

questions in the political theorist's proverbial book: What exactly do I mean by the national interest, or the good of all? Perhaps unfortunately, I will not attempt to defend a substantive view of what the "nation's interest" amounts to (though I will offer a conceptual definition of "interest" in section 7.2). Thus I leave open any conception of the national good for further debate. The national interest may be identical to the narrow interests of the majority of the nation. It may be determined by the deliberative or aggregative result of particular interests voicing and voting in the legislature and limited by the protection of individual rights. Or we might best achieve the national interest by pursuing world peace and justice, which will demand material sacrifice from the very nation that promotes them. (To forestall an early objection, I take it as consistent and coherent to speak of moral obligations to others as part of what constitutes acting in our interest.)

The point, then, is not to defend a substantive account of the national interest here. Rather, it is the prior theoretical point: There is simply no plausible justification for establishing a national representative legislature *without* some reference to the resulting good of all, whatever the good of all may turn out to entail. Put differently, the proper function of any national legislature is to pass laws in the nation's interests *whatever that means* rather than laws that serve "Joe's interests" or "the interests of Chicago," even if it turns out that either one of these is exactly the same as the national interest. So the justification of territory or some other constituency definition must be put in reference to an account that it aids or hinders a nation's ability to achieve its own collective good. As we will see in section 7.2, one of the first problems with justifying territorial constituencies as representing "communities of interest" is that this formulation smuggles in a normative view of the collective good that weakens the territorial claim: If subnational interests ought to be represented in the national legislature, nonterritorially based interests have a much greater justification for being present than do territorial communities of interest.

Given the context of the United States, and that the function of a national legislature is to pursue the nation's collective good, are territorial constituencies justifiable for the House of Representatives? To answer this question, I use the indirect method discussed in section 3.3 prospectively to test the five plausible justifications that animated my earlier discussion[6]: Are the aims of a particular justification normatively endorsable and is it reasonable to expect that territorial constituencies will achieve these normative ends? Because we are thinking now about contemporary practice and possible future reform, we add a third dimension: Even if territorial constituencies could empirically achieve a purported normative goal, is territory a reasonably efficient way to achieve that goal, relative to other alternatives? In what follows, I argue that each

---

[6] See section 3.3. On the similarity to Claus Offe's "dual nature of institutions," see footnote 20 of Chapter 3.

justification fails (or is surprisingly weak) in contemporary America for one of these three reasons:

- The justification fails for *normative reasons*: The normative aims of the justification should not be endorsed.
- The justification fails for *empirical reasons*: Territory cannot reasonably be expected to achieve the normative aim of the justification.
- The justification fails for *efficiency reasons*: Even if territory *could* achieve the normative aim, it fails by comparison to other nonterritorial definitions that more efficiently achieve the purported normative aim.

Note that the efficiency claim is a subset of the empirical claim: A justification cannot be an efficient means to an end if it is not in fact a means to that end. The argument presented in this chapter is not that territory is an altogether bad way of defining national constituencies but it fails and succeeds in often surprising and unexpected ways.

Of the five justifications I discussed in section 3.2, I will not take up the property justification here. The property justification reflected the intuition that especially in the eighteenth century there might be an important connection between landed property and political life. In the United States today, this justification is simply not persuasive, for two reasons. First, property is even less land-based today than it was at the founding. If we wanted to define constituencies in order to protect or advance property interests, it is not clear why we would single out real estate over more liquid, nonterritorial assets. More importantly, the normative claim seems as objectionable as any justification we might think of. Even if we thought that defining constituencies around levels or types of property ownership was a good way of encouraging capitalist activity and ensuring representation was influenced only by those with a stake in society, why should this be limited to territorially based property? For historical reasons, it was useful to consider the role of property in constituency definition. For contemporary society, however, it seems sufficient to reject this out of hand.

Before starting, it will help to keep one central fact about the size of electoral constituencies in mind. In large nations, electoral constituencies are enormous, and many of the arguments in this chapter assume that constituencies consist of at least one hundred thousand people. In the United States, the case I take up repeatedly, electoral constituencies for the House of Representatives are over six times that size. So, for example, if we are going to claim that territorial districts form "communities of interest," we have to explain how it is that a community of that size forms a coherent "community of interest." More often than not, I argue our intuitions about the benefits of "local" representation apply to much smaller groups, such as a neighborhood or town. This was the reason that Nancy Schwartz's praise of territorial districting to foster citizenship was more appropriate for local governance than for national representation.[7]

---

[7] See section 2.1 for a discussion of Nancy L. Schwartz, *The Blue Guitar: Political Representation and Community* (Chicago: University of Chicago Press, 1988).

The chapter precedes over six more sections. In sections 7.2–7.6, I consider the four remaining justifications separately: communities of interest, attachment, enabling consent to a constituency, and enabling democratic values within a constituency. In section 7.7, I offer a summary and synthesis of the discussion, which is summarized in Table 7.1 at the end of the chapter.

7.2 COMMUNITIES OF INTEREST AND INCENTIVE EFFECTS

For everyman seeth that some laws are addressed to all the subjects in general, some to particular provinces, some to particular vocations, and some to particular men, and are therefore laws to every of those to whom the command is directed, and to none else.

– Thomas Hobbes[8]

The most persistent argument for territorial electoral constituencies is that they allow the interests of local communities to be represented at the national level. This in turn depends on two subordinate claims: first that electoral constituencies ought to be defined around interest groups at all, and second that "local communities" are the particular interest around which electoral constituencies should be defined. In this section, I argue that the strongest argument for defining electoral constituencies around interest groups in general is to link these interest groups to the proper function of the representative body that they will constitute. In short, any interest group will have a stronger claim to form its own electoral constituency the more relevant its interests are to the function of the representational body. Workers, for example, have a strong claim to form an electoral constituency for a labor relations board because their interests are relevant to the proper function of that representational body. Since the proper function of a *national* legislature is to pursue the nation's interest (see section 7.1), the communities of interest justification for territory emerges hobbled because local interests are not the most relevant to this function, even though they are not wholly irrelevant to it. If we think that constituencies ought to be defined around "communities of interest," then interests other than territorial ones are more directly relevant to the proper aims of national representation.

I develop this by explaining the relationship between constituency definition and interest representation (section 7.2.1); reframe the justification into its three components (section 7.2.2); and then take up each of these components in order (sections 7.2.3–7.2.5).

7.2.1 Incentive Effects and Communities of Interests

The communities of interest justification reflected the intuition that people should be represented by where they live because people purportedly live in "communities of interest" that are relevant to national political representation. As I will argue below, the communities of interest justification depends upon

---

[8] Thomas Hobbes, *Leviathan* (Indianapolis, IN: Hackett, 1994), 26.4, p. 173.

a view that representatives should be advocates for the interests of their constituents. But before I take up this advocacy argument in section 7.2.2, I want to clarify how interests of a community are translated into advocacy through the incentives that any constituency definition creates.

"Incentive effects" explain how a community's interests are likely to get represented at all: The prospect of reelection increases the probability that representatives will pursue the interests of their electoral constituents in Congress. But if the desire for reelection explains *why* a representative does what she does, the way a constituency is defined explains what kinds of issues and projects she will pursue. When constituencies are defined by "where people live," representatives have incentives to maximize territorially defined resource distributions and advance territorially specific interests. If, by contrast, constituencies were defined by religion, for example, representatives might pursue "faith-based" initiatives (church–state constitutional limits notwithstanding). The practice of securing funding for "local projects" is thus underdetermined by a desire for reelection. To put it another way, *territorial* constituencies explain *local* pork.

To create incentives that representatives can act on, electoral constituencies must be serviceable in some way by legislation.[9] The easiest way to be a serviceable constituency is to be highly homogeneous around some interest.[10] For example, when constituencies are defined by political party, legislation may be directed toward the explicit satisfaction of the the party platform. But constituencies need not be homogeneous to create incentives for representatives: As long as they are serviceable by national legislation, they can create their own incentives for representatives. This is precisely the case with territorial constituencies: Even though they can be more heterogeneous than other kinds of constituencies because of their enormous size, they create incentives for representatives to pursue territorially defined goods (local pork) because subgroups within them can be serviced by these spending projects.

Taking account of how particular incentives get defined is an important addition to normative accounts of electoral dynamics that often equate the public good with acting on incentives for reelection. Usually this is tied to a straightforward notion of accountability – the public good is said to be achieved when representatives are advocates of their constituents' interests within the legislature. A representative's desire for reelection thus leads to her making trade-offs in the national legislature to secure these local goods, a practice that overall it is held leads to the public good. In these pluralist accounts of democratic trade-offs, logrolling is not so much *against* the national interest as it just *is* the national interest.[11]

---

[9] I will take up other kinds of constituent service – such as helping navigate the federal bureaucracy – later in this chapter.

[10] See Chapter 2 for the discussion of homogeneity.

[11] By "pluralist accounts" or "pluralism," I mean a view of politics in which the national good emerges from a battle of competing interests within the legislature. There are variations within the pluralist view, including one in which representatives are impartial judges who adjudicate between competing interest groups who come before them or one in which representatives are themselves advocates for a partial interest. The classic statements of pluralism are found

Yet logrolling vastly underdetermines the national interest because legislators would roll very different logs if their electoral constituencies were defined differently. As I mentioned previously, if constituencies were defined by religion rather than by territory, we might see the legislature pass more "faith-based initiatives" than they do now despite the fact that the nation in both cases is exactly the same, and thus presumably has exactly the same "national interest." So instead of defining the public good as simply what emerges from the give and take of advocacy representation, we need an argument that the advocacy of and trade-offs between these interests but not those is what will most likely produce outcomes that aim at the national interest. We cannot simply say that logrolling ensures the national good without considering what kinds of logs are being rolled.

When we ask whether *this* community of interest should receive representation rather than *that* one, we must also include a judgment about how to structure the incentives of political representatives relative to the national good. Why, then, do we think that territorially defined constituencies would promote the national good rather than some other kinds of interests? We now can approach the communities of interest justification in its prospective form.

7.2.2 Recasting the Justification

The communities of interest justification for territorial constituencies can be broadened, then, from the narrow one we used for historical purposes to these claims:

Normative claim: Local communities of interest ought to be represented in the House of Representatives because of their relevance to national political representation.

Empirical claim: Territorial Congressional districts are coterminous with local communities of interests.

Efficiency claim: Territorial electoral constituencies are the most efficient way to represent local communities of interests.

The communities of interest justification for territorial constituencies or any other constituency definition conditionally assumes that political representatives ought to be advocates for the interests of their electoral constituencies. It assumes, that is, the basic position of pluralist political theory: Constituencies should be defined in order for their interests to be promoted, secured, and

in Robert A. Dahl, *A Preface to Democratic Theory* (Chicago: University of Chicago Press, 1956); idem, *Polyarchy: Participation and Opposition* (Chelsea, MI: Yale University Press, 1971); David Truman, *The Govermental Process: Political Interests and Public Opinion* (New York: Knopf, 1953). For a good contemporary summary of pluralism and its critics, see David Held, *Models of Democracy*, 2nd ed. (Stanford, CA: Stanford University Press, 1996), pp. 201–13. For a recent statement of political representation as advocacy, see Nadia Urbinati, *Mill on Democracy: From the Athenian Polis to Representative Government* (Chicago: University of Chicago Press, 2002), pp. 81–8. For an alternate view, see Cass Sunstein, "Preferences and Politics," *Philosophy and Public Affairs*, 20, no. 1, Winter 1991: 3–34.

protected within the legislature because this is what is meant by the national good. We, however, are not endorsing this particular view of political representation (or the national good), but rather acknowledge that if territorial representation is justified based on its ability to define a particular community of interest, it rests on the prior claim that the purpose of political representation is to represent communities of interest. The question this normative justification answers, then, is which interests should define the electoral constituency. What follows is a conditional account under which we may appeal to forming a community of interest for the purpose of representation. To the extent that the community's interests are relevant to the proper functioning of a legislature, it has a stronger claim.

7.2.3 The Normative Claim

Because the normative claim assumes that representatives ought to pursue the interests of their constituents, it may be unpacked as follows:

> **Revised normative claim**: Local political interests ought to be represented in the House of Representatives because
>
> a) "where people live" is relevant to the proper function of the House of Representatives.
> b) Electoral constituencies ought to be defined based on the relevance of communities of interest to the function of a particular representative institution.

This account depends a great deal on what we mean by "communities of interests," "relevance," and "proper functioning," so I begin by defining these terms.

A "community of interest" is a community of individuals who share a particular set of interests. The term "interest," while widely used, is not often defined.[12] Interests are sometimes defined as individual preferences about outcomes that benefit those who have them. So if John prefers to have a turkey sandwich for lunch, one interest of his would be to get that turkey sandwich for lunch. But interests are not simply what one prefers; one often seeks to find those outcomes that would benefit her or be in her interest before

---

[12] Those who use the term "interest" use it for very specific reasons and thus have no need to formulate a comprehensive account. For example, Sunstein, "Preference and Politics," uses "interest" to differentiate public and private reasons; Kristen Renwick Monroe, *The Heart of Altruism: Perceptions of a Common Humanity* (Princeton, NJ: Princeton University Press, 1996), uses the term to develop theories of altruism; Russell Hardin, *Morality within the Limits of Reason* (Chicago: University of Chicago Press, 1988), pp. 11, 42, passim, uses the term to achieve a combination of both ends. A careful discussion of interest in this context is found in Brian Barry, *Political Argument: A Reissue with a New Introduction* (Berkeley, CA: University of California Press, 1990), pp. 173–86. See also Pitkin, *The Concept of Representation*, pp. 156–62.

preferring them.[13] Sometimes it will be in a person's interests *not* to achieve her preferences, for a person can prefer things that bring her harm. Importantly, current interests are always future-regarding – one cannot coherently have an interest in things past. One might have an interest in "coming to know about past events," or an interest in "using past events for future gain." But in these cases, it is the "coming to know" and the "using" that constitute a person's interest, not, strictly speaking, the past event itself.[14] Finally, an interest is always connected in some way to the interest holder's good.

Acknowledging the complexity of what follows, we will use the following definition of "interest"[15]:

> Interest = df. A set of future states of affairs that aim at a good to which a person or group is related because of self-referential, duty, or rights-based reasons.

The definition accounts for the fact that interests can be true or false. A "true" interest is just an interest that aims at a real (not merely purported) good; the "truth" referred to is that the interest really is a good one. The definition also explains how some particular individual or group (rather than some other individual or group) comes to have them – that is, why the particular interest is "Carla's interest" and not "Lori's interest." An interest attaches to some particular person or group through self-referential, duty, or rights-based reasons, as the definition describes.

When we speak of communities of interest, then, we mean those people for whom some future state of affairs is good, even if in each case their interest in that future state of affairs derives from very different sources. Thus, a parent and child may have the same set of "true interests" in the child's education, even though the child's interests derive from self-referential consequences and the parents from meeting duty-based obligations (and a different set of self-referential reasons).[16] A community that shares a particular set of future states of affairs in this way defines a community of interests.

The fact that interests are future-regarding leads us to the concept of relevance. The "relevance" of an interest to the proper function of an institution describes the closeness of fit between a particular interest and the institution

---

[13] Barry, *Political Argument*, pp. 180–1.

[14] I am grateful to Suzanne Dovi for helping me clarify this point.

[15] This is an admittedly abbreviated account of a very complex topic. For more, see the previous citations and Andrew Rehfeld, "Silence of the Land: An Historical and Normative Analysis of Territorial Representation in the United States," Ph.D. Dissertation, University of Chicago, 2000, pp. 480–93. My definition diverges from Barry's, particularly regarding duties and obligations.

[16] The claim that one's interests may arise out of one's duties is controversial; the reader need not accept this assertion. Even if interests arise only from self-referential benefits (and not from duties and obligations), interests can still overlap because the same future states of affairs can benefit people for different reasons. "Eating a sundae" and "watching a person eat a sundae" both involve pleasure derived from similar if not precisely the same future state of affairs ("that person eating a sundae"). Watchers and eaters both share an interest in having the eater eat ice cream even though the reason it is in their interest is different.

through which its corresponding future state of affairs is obtained. In the case of political representation, a group's interests are relevant to a particular institution to the degree to which that institution can secure them and, given its proper functioning, ought to secure them. This entails the following:

i) The representative body has the *power* to secure, protect, or advance the interests of the relevant community.
ii) The *proper function* of the representative body is to secure, protect, or advance the interests of the relevant community.

I will treat each of these entailments in turn.

The first clause (i) can be called the "power clause": A community of interest can be relevant to a representative body only when that representative body has the power to secure the future state of affairs at which that community's interests aim. Toxic-waste workers and nuclear plant operators form two communities of interest relevant to a representative group that has the power to negotiate a labor contract for waste removal from that plant.[17] If the representative group does not have the appropriate power to write and enforce a contract, then these interests are not relevant to it. Similarly, in this case, wine connoisseurs would not be a relevant community of interest to the toxic-waste group (unless, of course, the waste removed is spoiled Chianti).

This first "power clause" is not enough because many representative bodies have the power to secure a set of interests for some group but doing so would violate a normative rule that properly limits the representative body. For example, most national legislatures are perfectly able to secure immense riches and honors for a sporting club without violating their legal or constitutional limits. If it is in the club's interests to be wildly rich and honorable, then given only the "power clause," that interest would be relevant to the legislature and, under the communities of interest justification, the sporting club should now form an electoral constituency. Yet, such an allocation would presumably violate any reasonable account of what the legislature ought to be doing.[18] The "proper functioning" clause (ii) explains why even under the communities of interest justification not all interests potentially affected by legislation should be treated as relevant to that representative body. "Proper functioning," then, describes the legitimate limits of a representative body's exercise of power.

We can see now why the claim that constituencies ought to represent territorial communities of interests entails the kind of revisions I suggested at the start of this subsection. A claim that territorial communities of interest ought

---

[17] We assume here that the only question is who gets the contract and does not include larger policy issues like through whose communities should the waste be removed, or even more basic, whether we should be generating any toxic waste. If the representative body must develop an answer to those questions, then the relevant groups will be much larger than what I am arguing for here.

[18] Such an allocation is possibly endorsable, but not merely on the basis that the club desired the allocation. Rather, the allocation might be endorsable if it leads to the satisfaction of other interests, or one collective interest of the whole.

to receive representation assumes that pluralistic models of the national good are endorsable. It also presumes that territorial communities of interest are the kinds of interests relevant to the achievement of the national good, and that other kinds of interests are not as compelling.

To endorse the normative claim associated with the communities of interest justification thus requires not simply an up or down judgment about territorial representation. It requires us to give an up or down judgment of what kind of representation will constitute the national good, a project that others have explored, if not necessarily in these terms.[19] As promised in section 7.1, though, because it is a much larger and different project, I will not take up such a judgment here. Instead, I will argue that even if we accept this view of what political representation entails, territorial representation is not particularly compelling on its own terms.

7.2.4 The Empirical Claim: Does Territory Define Interests?

For the moment, we thus assume the second part of the normative claim is true: By hypothesis, electoral constituencies ought to be defined to maximize "relevant" political interests. The justification then hinges on whether local communities are, in fact, relevant to the proper functioning of the House of Representatives. This claim is not implausible but it is rather weak.[20] Even more so, if constituencies really ought to be defined by interests that are relevant to national politics, other kinds of interests – communities of interests – are more relevant to its proper functioning.

What are territorial interests in the first place? First, let us parse "territorial facts" into two sorts, ones that are *essentially* tied to territory – such as land and roads – and others that are *incidentally* about territory – such as demographic patterns. Any "interests" that arise from territory may entail both: Where a school is built, for example, and the quality of its program depend on essential and incidental facts about territory. We need things "on the ground" to build a school (land, roads, electricity, and so on). But the need for the school, its curriculum, resources available to it, and such will all be influenced by incidental facts about territory – the people who live near it and use the school. This is true for the vast array of public and private social services – hospitals, police and fire departments, retail space, and zoning regulations. If territorial communities have interests that are inherent to them, these are the kinds of things that are affected by who lives where, but are nevertheless territorial issues.

---

[19] For some recent examples, see Jane Mansbridge, "Rethinking Representation," *American Political Science Review*, 97, no. 4, November 2003: 515–28; Henry Richardson, *Democratic Autonomy: Public Reasoning about the Ends of Policy* (New York: Oxford University Press, 2002), pp. 193–202; Iris Marion Young, *Inclusion and Democracy* (Oxford, UK, and New York: Oxford University Press, 2000), pp. 121–53.

[20] Of course, if territorial constituencies are used for national representation, then they are relevant to national politics because they are used. But our question is one of justification: Apart from the fact that they are used, why should they be used?

These kinds of issues are primarily (not exclusively) ones of state and local concern, though this admittedly assumes a substantive view about federalism and the proper role of national legislatures to determine local policy. Regardless of one's view about federalism, a stronger argument for territorially based constituencies can be made in the case of local city government, whose proper function is limited to *local* resource allocations in which territorial groupings are just what we mean by (or are likely to be the most important) "relevant political interests."[21] In such a case – where the scope of the government was limited and the numbers of citizens were both compact and in a small enough geographical context – territory would be justified as the most relevant interest worth representing. But given the multifaceted functions of national representation, territory ranks low as a strongly relevant interest, and seems hardly justifiable even as a weak one.

A more promising argument rests not on the essential facts of territory, but rather on the observation that territory serves as a reasonably good proxy for communities of interest that happen to be territorially segregated. Here, we still accept the normative claim as true ex hypothesi (electoral constituencies ought to be defined by communities of interests), but the "relevant political interests" are not territorial per se, they just happen to be territorially contiguous. For example, communities may be concentrated by race or ethnicity, and using territory as a proxy for these interests is an efficient way of turning those racial and ethnic communities into an electoral constituency. Similarly, people who value nature are likely to live near one another, as are people who value symphonies and art museums. If we choose where to live based on a host of interests that happen to be territorial, then using territorial constituencies as proxies may well be endorsable.

Using territory as a proxy for these other communities of interest may be the strongest argument for using territorial constituencies, but it raises two important problems. First, when territory becomes a proxy for some other community of interest, the "communities of interest" justification no longer justifies the use of territory per se. Rather, territory is justified as a means to represent the other interests for which it serves as a proxy. But then we need an argument that electoral constituencies should be defined by the specific interest for which territory serves as its proxy – race, ethnicity, social class, and so on. Perhaps we should define electoral constituencies by race, class, ethnicity, or an interest in arts or rural life – but that is another matter.

Were we to take this road of justifying territory as a proxy for other communities of interest, we then run into a second, more important, problem: Territory

---

[21] Whether territory is the most relevant interest to be represented in city government will depend. In large, heterogeneous cities, territory may be less relevant than other interests; in smaller, homogeneous environments, territory will be more important. Thus in a rural community in central Iowa, territorial interests are likely to be more relevant than they may be in Los Angeles. In both cases, however, resource allocation *to* local territories and particular local problems form the central function of government. The larger the polis, the less true this will be and thus the less relevant territoriality will be.

can serve as a proxy only for interests that are territorially contiguous, and there is no reason to think that only territorially contiguous interests are the most relevant to national politics.[22] For example, as long as men and women live together, and as long as lawyers, doctors, firefighters, and teachers like to live near where they work, we could not define electoral constituencies by gender or profession. Once we endorse defining constituencies by communities of interest, there seems no good reason to restrict those communities to territorially bound ones, a fact that moves us to consider the efficiency of using territory, given our normative aims.

7.2.5 Efficiency Claims

The empirical argument admittedly bleeds into the efficiency claim: If territory does not capture relevant interests, then tautologically it cannot be an efficient way to capture them. But we can take a more nuanced approach to the empirical claim: Even though territory may not do a good job representing the interests most relevant to national politics, it may represent interests that are not wholly irrelevant. Further, it is this moderation that should recommend territory to our reflective judgments. Interest group politics enables more "relevant" interests to organize and lobby representatives when the need arises in ways that are less readily available to large territorial communities. So perhaps all things considered territory is the most efficient way to represent interests precisely because they are not likely to be represented by other means.

There is certainly strong prima facie support for this claim. Some political issues do arise locally and themselves form particular interests relevant to national representation, interests that are unlikely to be represented by other voluntary interest groups. In the United States, we can point to the Hoover Dam, the Tennessee Valley Authority, or the interstate highway system, to say nothing of redistribution policies that will treat urban poverty differently than rural poverty, and the issues of small farmers – a particularly local and territorial interest – as distinct from these others. Territory allows local issues to be represented in Congress even if the territorial constituency does not neatly map onto them, or in some cases extends into multiple districts that share the same set of interests with each other (think "Nebraska" or "New York City").

I do not want to reject this benefit of using territorial constituencies, but neither do I want to overstate the claim. The argument may be particularly good for nations whose main government is national and that do not have any strong checks on federal power. But in the United States, local and state governments check federal authority and provide a source of advocacy and information into the national government. Furthermore, in the United States, the Senate already represents the state as a corporate entity. There is thus an

[22] See a related point by Melissa S. Williams, *Voice, Trust, and Memory* (Princeton, NJ: Princeton University Press, 1998), p. 206.

institutional outlet for local information and advocacy already available in Congress. To the extent local concerns form relevant political interests, they are readily expressed elsewhere in the system.

This last efficiency claim returns us to the normative claim. Are territorially defined interests relevant to national legislation or not? Indeed, many interests are territorially bound – one has to build a dam or highway *somewhere*, and the residents of that area stand to benefit or be harmed more than others. Furthermore, it is in the nation's interest to build defense bases with geography in mind; it won't do much good to build ships on the Great Salt Lake (a land-locked lake in Utah). We could name others, but the point is that there are many territorially bound interests about which the national legislature has the right to legislate.

The argument then amounts to a tepid endorsement (or perhaps a mild re-jection) of territory on the basis of communities of interest. It is not so much that territorial constituencies are wholly irrelevant to the national good. Rather, once we allow constituencies to be drawn for the purpose of interest representa-tion, territorial interests seem not particularly important compared to the many other kinds that might be represented.

7.3 ATTACHMENT

A statesman or patriot, who serves our own country, in our own time, has always a more passionate regard paid to him, than one whose beneficial influence operated on distant ages or remote nations; where the good, resulting from his generous humanity, being less connected with us, seems more obscure, and affects us with a less lively sympathy.... The same object, at a double distance, really throws on the eye a picture of but half the bulk; yet we imagine that it appears of the same size in both situations; because we know, that, on our approach to it, its image would expand on the eye and that the difference consists not in the object itself, but in our position with regard to it.

– David Hume[23]

7.3.1 Recasting the Justification

The attachment justification for territory begins from this observation: It is hard for citizens within large, representative governments to form "strong chords of sympathy" toward their national government. Organizing into local constituent groups may help them build these chords. The following restates the justification and adds an efficiency claim:

  Empirical claim: Territorial constituencies facilitate local attachment to the national government.
  Efficiency claim: Territorial constituencies are the most efficient way to fa-cilitate local attachment.

[23] David Hume, *Enquiry Concerning the Principles of Morals*, ed. J. B. Schneewind (Indianapolis, IN: Hackett, 1983), p. 48.

Normative claim: Constituencies ought to be defined based on their ability to facilitate local attachment to the national government.

I will treat these in order.

7.3.2 The Empirical and Efficiency Claims

Do territorial constituencies facilitate the attachments of citizens to their national government? I know of no studies that have tested precisely this question.[24] Instead, we might get at the answer by reframing the issue in terms of governmental responsiveness. Attachment to national government might be facilitated by electoral constituencies that enabled representatives to attend to their constituents personally. Defining constituencies by territory enables this interaction because, by definition, citizens are territorially proximate to each other. There is data to support this reframed attachment claim at least tentatively: Constituents *are* consistently satisfied by their representative's services to them.[25]

---

[24] An empirical test might be done by comparing levels of "trust" between electoral districts of different territorial size. The null hypothesis would be "citizens in districts of smaller territorial size will tend to trust the national government more than citizens in larger districts." A similar test might be done using "patriotism" or other variables. Further, a comparative study between states might prove fruitful because state districts vary also by population. To the best of my knowledge, the current data on these affective qualities among American citizens could not be used because of the problems of disaggregation. It also seems difficult to test, because geographically large congressional districts are more rural (Montana as the extreme case) and small ones are more urban. The effects of rural versus urban living, education, and so on, upon "trust" and its related independent variables would thus be hard to disentangle. Further, except for the concentrated density of urban districts, most other districts have a good deal of population density variance within them, so more disentangling would follow. All of which is to mention briefly how one might test whether the hypothesis that living near one another in order to form a constituency affects attachment to the national government.

[25] Bruce Cain, John Ferejohn, and Morris Fiorina, *The Personal Vote: Constituency Service and Electoral Independence* (Cambridge, MA: Harvard University Press, 1987). Early data on the effects of constituent service on electoral success (indirectly related to the attachment issue) came up with the surprising findings that there was no relation between the two. That is, research seemed to show that nothing legislators did affected voters. For example, see Richard Fenno, *Home Style: House Members and Their Districts* (Boston: Little, Brown, 1978); Gary Jacobson, *Money in Congressional Elections* (New Haven, CT: Yale University Press, 1980). See also the truly surprising findings that casework, representative activities, and campaign spending do not affect elections in John R. Johannes and John C. McAdams, "The Congressional Incumbency Effect: Is It Casework, Policy Compatibility, or Something Else?: An Examination of the 1978 Election," *American Journal of Political Science*, 25, August 1981: 512–32. A review of this literature may be found throughout Cain et al., *The Personal Vote*, especially at pp. 122–3. Cain et al. overturned this research showing there was such an effect. Referring to Imre Lakatos and Karl R. Popper, they point out, "When research results conflict with theory, commonsense, or even political folklore, scholars should entertain the possibility that something could be wrong with the research." Cain et al., *The Personal Vote*, p. 123; Imre Lakatos, "Falsification and the Methodology of Scientific Research Programs," in *Criticism and the Growth of Knowledge*, eds. Imre Lakatos and Alan Musgrave (Cambridge, UK: Cambridge University Press, 1970); Karl R. Popper, *The Logic of Scientific Discovery* (New York: Basic Books, 1959).

Is this satisfaction with representative service due to territorially defined electoral constituencies? A better explanation for good constituent service depends not on territorial proximity, but again on the electoral incentives that representatives have to serve their constituents no matter how constituencies are defined. Citizen attachment (that is, constituent satisfaction) would thus arise in *any* system in which representatives stand for reelection. But there may be a stronger argument in favor of territorially proximate constituents because a representative's reputation is often fostered by word of mouth – an extremely likely and documented phenomenon.[26] So a representative is likely to provide a constituent with good service (and thus, presumably, foster attachment) first because it increases the probability that that particular constituent will vote for her, and second because that constituent is likely to publicize that service to other constituents nearby. Since people who live near each other are more likely to talk to each other about these things, territorial constituencies will likely magnify the effects of constituency service on the representative's chance of reelection. If constituents did not communicate with each other and publicize the representative's actions, the representative would have less of an incentive to serve that constituent. So if territorial districts amplify the benefits to a representative of constituent service, it likely increases that service and increases attachment. The corollary to this is that any plan that would undermine this amplification effect would decrease the likelihood of constituent service and thus possibly undermine the attachment of individuals to their national government.[27]

Assuming that constituent service is desirable, any electoral constituency plan that structures the incentives of representatives to provide such services is, on the face of it, better than one that does not. But notice two things about this observation. First, *any* system in which publicity is readily available through reputable sources will be as good as any other, so that modern communication over the Internet may serve as an alternative to territorial proximity.[28] Second, and more to the point, the argument is limited because constituent service fosters attachment less to the "system" than to the representative himself. So if this is a compelling account, such interaction would also undermine attachment to the system if a constituent receives bad service. Territory might facilitate publicity about the representative's action, but in terms of attachment to the system, it seems unlikely.

In contrast to "electoral constituencies," local, nested governments may be extremely useful in fostering attachment to the state. Both Edmund Burke, in his observations of the revolution in France, and Alexis de Tocqueville, in his chronicle of Jacksonian America in the 1830s, emphasized the attachment that arises from local citizen participation, as distinct from the responsiveness of

---

[26] Cain et al. *The Personal Vote*; Fenno, *Home Style.*

[27] Of course, if a representative were nonresponsive to his constituents, this would breach many other norms of representative government than merely that they failed to foster "attachment."

[28] I will deal with problems of non-universal access to the Internet in Chapter 9.

government to the citizen.[29] For Burke, the reason not to substitute geometrical districts for longstanding provincial government was that it would undo the bonds that individuals had to these already extant structures of local governance. Similarly, Tocqueville was impressed not by the local attachment of citizens to the ballot box but by their ability to participate actively in local government and local civic associations. These local connections – especially to a town council – where citizens actively engaged in and contributed to political life more plausibly increase attachment to the larger system.[30]

These local activities, nested within larger county, state, and national systems, should not be confused with electoral constituencies because the latter are too large to speak coherently of fostering citizen engagement, and the role of the citizen as constituent is rather limited and does not extend to governance. The vast majority of local governments in the United States are divided into wards that dwarf the size of the national constituency. In 1997, for example, there were over 87,000 local government units (an average of about one for every 2,800 people).[31] The point is that where local units allow individuals to act and where individual effort is likely to be felt and realized, a strong case for attachment might be made, but this is not the case with electoral constituencies of 600,000 people.

If attachment requires citizen activity and for the moment we endorse the normative claim, then we should radically decrease the size of electoral constituencies so that local neighborhoods can be represented and these local communities could be locations of democratic activity. Communities could hold neighborhood meetings filled with hours of deliberation and consideration of who should represent them. Such a change, however, would entail an increase in the size of the House of Representatives so that, among other things, districts could be smaller.

The thought of enlarging the House to promote civic engagement is hardly original. As Arendt Lijphart recently restated Rein Taagepera's observation, "the size of a country's national assembly tends to approximate the cube root of its population size," and "the exact cube root of 270 million [the approximate population of the United States] is 646." The upshot is a proposal for a House of 650 members. One reason for his advocacy of the plan is directly connected

---

[29] Tocqueville would make the case for nested political jurisdictions for similar reasons. His description, though, emphasized the educative value of local activity, rather than the chords of sympathy toward the larger polis likely to emerge from such activity. For Tocqueville, local governance (that is, political association) provided civic education first and foremost. Alexis de Tocqueville, *Democracy in America* (New York: Harper Perennial, 1988), 1.2.4, 2.2.5, pp. 189–95, 513–17.

[30] Ibid. On the importance of local involvement to civic life and its connection to trust, see Robert D. Putnam, *Bowling Alone: The Collapse and Revival of American Community* (New York: Simon and Schuster, 2000), pp. 31–180.

[31] *Statistical Abstract of the United States: 1998* (Washington, DC: U.S. Bureau of the Census, 1998), Table 496. Local governments include "county," "municipal," "township and town," "school district," and "special district."

to the attachment concerns I am discussing: "First, increasing the membership of the House by about 50% entails a decrease in the population size of the average congressional district by about 50%, which would lessen the distance between voters and their legislators."[32]

Although the math is not quite right,[33] the point is well taken: An increase in the size of the legislature would entail a shrinking of the electoral constituency. But it is doubtful that decreasing the size of a constituency from six hundred thousand to three hundred thousand would change much about the "distance" one feels from one's representative.[34] By contrast, if we imagine a constituency small enough to engage citizens, such as one of about ten thousand people, we would need a House that numbered over twenty-five thousand members. Even if constituencies were reduced "only" to one-tenth their current size to about sixty thousand, the House would have to have about five thousand members. At its current size of 435, the House suffers from deliberative imperfections. It is not hard to imagine what a House of five thousand members might look (and sound) like.

More important, such proposals for increasing the size of the House are temporary ones that completely ignore population growth. The reason the size of the House was fixed at 435 in the first place was because it was threatening to become too large.[35] For issues of attachment to local constituencies, it is extremely unlikely that any reasonable increase in the size of the House would result in tangible connections between citizens and their national government, and if they did they would ultimately be temporary fixes. So the argument here is one of likelihood: It is extremely unlikely that there is any added attachment value of territorial constituencies once the number is extremely large.

7.3.3 Attachment's Normative Claim

The preceding empirical argument is indirect and is mostly impressionistic, supported by scant empirical data. So let us now assume it is mistaken. Let us assume that territorial constituencies of even extremely large dimensions really do foster attachment in one way or another – either through constituent/representative interaction or through the bonds of sympathy that arise when you know that you live within some boundary on a map. What follows from this fact? Is the normative claim worth pursuing? Should we define constituencies in order to generate attachment to the system?

---

[32] Rein Taagepera, "The Size of National Assemblies," *Social Science Research* 1, no. 4, 1972: 385–401. Quoted in Arend Lijphart, "Reforming the House: Three Moderately Radical Proposals," *PS: Political Science & Politics*, 31, no. 1, March 1998: 10–13.

[33] A 50 percent increase in the House size would result in a 33 percent decrease in the size of constituencies. To cut the size of each constituency in half, one would have to double the size of the House of Representatives to 870.

[34] Since constituencies were once that size, this forms a testable hypothesis.

[35] To be charitable, advocates such as Lijphart who seek a larger House want the larger body for purposes of making proportional representation even more useful; a modest increase of House size, regardless of the constituency size, would be beneficial for that purpose.

Let me propose that we care (and ought to care) about attachment because it strengthens the bonds by which individuals are more likely to obey and feel close connection to some other thing. So I am attached to some person, just in case I am loyal to him, willing to do what he asks and the like. At a personal level – attachment between two people – we are most likely to see reciprocity at work. My children are attached to me both out of love and necessity, and I am attached to my family for similar reasons. At this close level, attachment may not only be an important good, it may even be necessary for human development. But as we expand the spheres, the role of attachment becomes less a reciprocal arrangement between people and simply a way to ensure obedience. Why do we think fostering attachment is good itself, except because it fosters compliance with law and generates patriotism more generally? And here, to restate the Federalist position, the object deserving our obedience is not a particular person or system, but the just (or good) laws that the system produces. We should not promote something as a means of attachment itself, unless it is, independently, a good, just thing. So as a means to an end, territorial constituencies look highly suspect: They rely on fellow-feeling to foster attachment.

If this is so, then even if very large districts foster attachment, this is not a good reason to endorse them. Rather, good laws and consensual institutions ought to be the ends. If it turns out that one of these consensual institutions is territorial constituencies, then it is the fact of consent to the system rather than territory that would be doing the work of attachment. Of course, we should not endorse plans that would needlessly undermine attachment of citizens to their nation. But the normative premise concerning attachment is a positive requirement and here it seems unpersuasive.

7.4 ENABLING PERSONAL CONSENT TO ONE'S CONSTITUENCY

7.4.1 Recasting the Justification

The consent justification can be reframed as the following:

Empirical claim: Territorial districts allow citizens to consent to their particular electoral constituency.

Efficiency claim: Territorial districts are the most efficient way to provide citizen consent to electoral constituencies.

Normative claim: Constituencies ought to be defined such that they allow citizens to consent to them.

What then do we make of these particular claims?

The normative claim is presumptively true: All things considered, the institutions that govern us should allow for the broadest possible consent from those they govern. I will argue in Chapter 8 that, while true, this presumption turns out to be remarkably weak. But for the purpose of evaluating this justification for territorial constituencies, we presume that the normative claim is true and see what follows from it.

The empirical claim is true for any society in which citizens have the freedom to choose where they live. After territorial lines are drawn, people can move from one district to another. This is why I claimed territorial constituencies are more voluntary than other kinds of constituency plans.[36] Yet there are two objections. First, the empirical claim in practice treats households, rather than individuals, as the locus of consent. Second, the efficiency claim is simply false by a large margin. If constituencies ought to be defined to maximize (or even allow) meaningful consent, many other options would be preferable. I will treat each of these separately.

7.4.2 Treating Households as the Source of Consent

It would be a mistake to argue that territorial constituencies allow individuals to choose their electoral constituency because territorial constituencies define domiciles, which in the United States (and the world) most often include more than one adult. For example, in 1997 at least 58 percent of all households included more than one adult over eighteen (53 percent were married couples).[37] Of the remainder, 25 percent were single adults living by themselves, another 17 percent were parents with children under eighteen and "no spouse present." Although these figures hide some important information ("no spouse present" apparently means the head of the household is not married but does not preclude other nontraditional partnerships[38]), the point still applies. About 75 percent of all adults in the United States live with another adult.[39] Any institutional scheme that treats groups of adults (presumably families) as a unit of consent does not give these individuals the opportunity to choose separately from their partners.[40]

---

[36] See Chapter 2.

[37] All population figures come from *Statistical Abstract*, Table 71.

[38] *Statistical Abstract*, pp. 1–6.

[39] The figure is likely greater than 75 percent. If 58 percent of all households had only two adults in them, then 73.4 percent of all adults would live in such arrangements. But the 58 percent figure includes households with more than two adults and thus the total percentage of adults living with at least one other adult is likely to be significantly larger than 73.4 percent. (For the calculation assuming that only two adults live in each joint household, let "J" = % of joint households, and let "I" = percent of single-member households. To calculate the percentage of individuals living in joint households, let: $[\frac{2J}{2J+I} = \frac{2(58)}{2(58)+42} = 73.4\%]$.

[40] Given the numbers, "only" about 37.5 percent of the population would be unable to consent. Assume that in each household one individual determines its fate. Call that adult the "house dictator." Assume now that 75 percent of all adults live with one other adult, with the remaining 25 percent living by themselves. With these assumptions, only those living with the "house dictator" but not the dictator himself – about 37.5 percent of all adults – lose their ability to consent. The number may be higher since some households have more than two adults in them. But it may be significantly smaller because in perhaps most cases, all adult members would agree about residency, just as most couples tend to support the same political party and candidate. Nevertheless, the fact that we would find such an arrangement objectionable at the level of voting (see the discussion in this section) leads me to the conclusion we ought to feel the same way about choice of constituency definition, no matter how small the actual violation turns out to be.

But the fact that adults give up their effective ability to consent individually to where they live may not be objectionable, assuming the choice to enter and exit a particular household is a voluntary one itself. After all, any decision within a family, including the choice of where one lives itself, is not a matter of individual consent, but some agreement between adults. The decision to live together entails giving up certain spheres of autonomy, including the choice of where to live, the pursuit of career opportunities, and more trivially, what foods to eat, what art to hang on the walls, and so on. We are not troubled by adults who give up these spheres of autonomy in exchange for the benefits of a healthy relationship. The present question, though, does not deal with these broader issues internal to the relationships of the adults living under one roof. Rather, it asks whether or not political institutions ought to treat citizens as individuals or as they collect themselves into households.

It is hard to see a persuasive argument in support of treating households, rather than citizens, as the loci of consent. Indeed, if households should be treated as political units, why not give every household a single vote to cast in elections? Such an arrangement could even be made consistent with voting equality by weighting the ballot based on the number of adults present in the house. While each ballot would be capable of expressing only one choice for each office, each would be weighed differently. The Rodney household's ballot would be worth two votes because two adults live there, but the Dawna household's ballot would be worth one vote because only one adult lives there.

We should not endorse such a scheme because of our commitments to autonomy: Political institutions ought to treat individuals and not households as the proper source of consent. The fact that territory allows consensual expressions only within the context of the household undermines the claim that it provides an outlet for consent at all.[41]

7.4.3 The Inefficiency of Territorial Consent and Voluntary Constituencies

Let us again assume that my first argument is wrong and that it is perfectly reasonable for the state to treat domestic partnerships as the unit of consent; the

---

[41] For an excellent and much broader treatment of justice applied within the family, see Susan Moller Okin, *Justice, Gender and the Family* (New York: Basic Books, 1989). It is instructive to note that religious organizations sometimes treat family units (whether single, married, or with children) as the relevant object of their governance. For example, the Union for Reform Judaism (the organization of Reform Jewish Congregations in North America) treats the family as its "member unit." The reason is that the URJ does not wish to encourage the affiliation of one spouse without the other. As an historical matter, it is odd that Reform Judaism treats "the family" as member units because the organization derived from the German Enlightenment, and the Kantian ideal of the individual still remains as the (purported) source of moral authority. For an excellent discussion of these issues, see Arnold M. Eisen, *Rethinking Modern Judaism: Ritual, Commandment, Community* (Chicago: University of Chicago Press, 1998); Martha Nussbaum, "Judaism and the Love of Reason," in *Philosophy, Feminism, and Faith*, eds. Ruth Groenhout and Marya Bower (Bloomington, IN: Indiana University Press, 2003).

choice to live with someone else entails political consequences along with other lifestyle limits, and the state does not oblige individuals to live together. Even if territorial constituencies offered citizens as households a meaningful outlet for consent, moving residences is extremely costly to individuals and partnerships. If so, the normative aim of allowing greater consent to the institutions that govern us can be achieved with much greater efficiency by using other methods of constituency definition.

First, costs of moving are tremendously high, and the very small added value of being in a particular district will be dominated by the economic and psychological costs of the move.[42] To maintain political equality, we would have to keep district populations roughly equal and thus regularly change district lines to reflect population shifts within each district. This imposes additional incentives for moving (and thus more people facing the cost) because everyone will live in a partially reconstituted district every ten years or so.[43] So even if territorial lines allow individuals to choose a particular electoral constituency, such consent comes at too high a cost to realize.[44]

We might reduce the uncertainty of redistricting by keeping district lines set for much longer than a decade, or even make them permanent. We could achieve this without violating political equality by using weighted voting within the legislature. Weighted voting would allow each representative to have a vote weight commensurate with the population of the district he or she represents; a representative from an electoral constituency with a million residents would have twice as many votes in the legislature as a representative from a constituency

---

[42] Further, as Lani Guinier writes, "... voters do not move to an election district; they move to a neighborhood community." Lani Guinier, *The Tyranny of the Majority: Fundamental Fairness in Representative Democracy* (New York: Free Press, 1994), p. 129.

[43] The particular benefits of living in this, rather than that, constituency change for all members of the constituency whether or not their particular residence is in the same district or a different one after redistricting. Any time anyone moves in or out of a district, whether by moving, coming of age, or dying, the district's composition changes. Thus, even without a change of boundaries, the constituency will change over time.

[44] We might push this further, along the lines of Tiebout, and treat political representation as a local public good – like schools and fire protection services – and see whether people are likely to move to a community that has representation more to their liking. Here the local public good of political representation would be of two kinds. First, it would be the pride (or embarrassment) one feels to be a member of a particular constituency that regularly and reliably votes in one way or for a particular person. Second, it would be the tangible benefits (or harms) that membership in the district would provide in terms of constituent service. I think this is a promising way to think about political representation at a theoretical level. As a practical matter, it is not likely to go very far because the value of membership in a particular district is going to be extremely low relative to the cost of a move. People are not likely to move to *this* district (rather than *that* one) because of the political representation they are likely to receive. Rather, the local public goods distribution of a local community, along with job opportunities and so on, are likely to factor into the costs of a move and, along with those costs, dominate any good or harm that one receives from living in any particular district. See Charles M. Tiebout, "A Pure Theory of Local Expenditure," *Journal of Political Economy*, 64, No. 5, October 1956: 16–24. I am indebted to Jim Fearon for a discussion about this topic.

with half that population.⁴⁵ Weighted voting is how publicly held corporations allocate vote shares. Each investor gets as many votes as he or she has shares, even as each has a right to attend meetings and speak out on issues. Such voting would allow territorial districts much longer stability without compromising the standard of electoral equality.

The U.S. Constitution does not prohibit the use of weighted voting in the House of Representatives. While the Constitution restricts senators to one vote each,⁴⁶ no similar rule applies to members of the House. So there is extremely strong prima facie evidence that vote weighting in the House is not only constitutional but perhaps implicitly allowed by the absence of a similar clause applied to the House.⁴⁷

Returning to the main issue, if consent is the normative goal of a constituency definition, many other constituency plans do not pose the kinds of problems that territorial constituencies do. These other constituency plans fall into two types. The first are plans similar to territorial constituencies in which a constituency is formed prior to the act of voting. The second, more familiar plan of voluntary constituencies – proportional representation – is one in which the electoral constituency is formed simultaneously as the vote is cast.

In a completely voluntary constituency, citizens define themselves, choosing to opt into this or that electoral constituency, or even start a new one for the purpose of electing political representatives and being represented in Congress. It would, in short, be the idea of free civic (or interest group) associations transformed through institutional rules into electoral constituencies themselves. So perhaps Rosi cares about theatrical stage design and decides that is how she wants to be represented. Raffi wants to be represented as a chess-playing Rastafarian, and Zoe by her commitment to economic justice. Putting aside the consequences of such an institution, could we devise a system to accommodate these different groupings?

In fact the procedures would be rather straightforward: Along with registering to vote, individuals would either check off a preset list of possible affiliations or list their own as the way they wished to be represented.⁴⁸ If each constituency had to have equal numbers, each category would constitute a constituency just

---

⁴⁵ For a good discussion of the mechanics of weighted voting, see Thomas Pogge, "Self-Constituting Constituencies to Enhance Freedom, Equality, and Participation in Democratic Procedures," *Theoria*, June 2002: 26–54.

⁴⁶ "[E]ach Senator shall have one vote." (U.S. Constitution, Seventeenth Amendment). The clause was repeated from the original document, at Article I, Section 3.

⁴⁷ The lack of symmetry on this issue between the House and Senate is striking. The clause was inserted in Section 3 concerning the Senate to reassure the smaller states that their senators would be treated equally compared to those from larger states, rather than because the framers consciously permitted vote weighting in the House. However, Madison supported the inclusion of this clause in Section 3, "as there might be other modes proposed...." See Madison's Notes, 9 August 1787, in *The Founder's Constitution*, ed. Philip B. Kurland and Ralph Lerner, Vol. 1, Article 3, Clause 2, no. 2, p. 208.

⁴⁸ For a particularly good development of this process, see Pogge, "Self-Constituting Constituencies to Enhance Freedom, Equality, and Participation in Democratic Procedures," pp. 26–54.

in case it reached a certain number, such as four hundred thousand people. The remainders might be grouped in a new related constituency that was approved by the citizen herself. So a grade school teacher might want to be represented as a grade school teacher and list that on her ballot. She would hope that enough grade school teachers would do the same so that they could form an electoral constituency. But she might also be required to list other more general categories that she would find acceptable in case the group did not meet the cutoff – "teacher," perhaps. Then, once constituted, this group would form an electoral constituency and elect a member (who may or may not have to be a member of the constituency).

There are three important differences between voluntary constituencies, as we have described them, and proportional representation, where voters can vote for many different candidates or parties, whose success is then pinned to the proportion of the vote they receive. First, under the voluntary plan, citizens opt into an electoral constituency *before* voting for a party or a candidate. Second, voluntary electoral constituencies could be far more stable, because we could require that citizens define themselves according to a stable feature of themselves (race, ideology, and so on) and not move around from election to election. (Why permanent, stable constituencies are endorseable will be taken up in Chapter 8.) Finally, voluntary constituencies allow for a greater possibility of citizen definition that is not limited to political parties that are already formed. If enough people want to be represented as teachers, lawyers, Presbyterians, Chicagoans, and so on, then they will check off that box (or write it in) and they will be able to vote collectively for a candidate or party in the subsequent election. To state again a point from Chapter 2, one benefit of separating constituency definition from the act of voting is that we see how we could have voluntary constituencies that do not change over time.

In sum, there are ways of maximizing voluntary consent to constituencies that are more efficient and less costly than territorial constituencies. Territory thus does not fare well on the empirical and efficiency claims we have detailed because it treats families and domestic partnerships rather than individuals as the object of consent, it is costly, and finally, it can be achieved far more efficiently in other ways.

7.5 ENABLING DEMOCRATIC VALUES WITHIN THE CONSTITUENCY

7.5.1 Recasting the Justification

This justification can be recast as follows:

> **Empirical claim:** Defining constituencies by territory enables representative government to function properly, by allowing deliberation among constituents and forming a tangible if symbolic moment of consent.
>
> **Efficiency claim:** Territorial districts are the most efficient way to provide these logistical benefits.

Normative claim: Constituencies ought to be defined such that they enable these values among citizens.

In this section, I will assume the normative claim without argument. I take it that we should approve of electoral institutions that enable the democratic values previously listed, for reasons well described by others, particularly well described in the recent literature on deliberative democracy.[49] So in this section I will look only at the empirical and efficiency claims: Do territorial constituencies enable these democratic values? And if so, are territorial constituencies the most efficient way to enable them?

7.5.2 The Problem of Large Size

Any contemporary claim that territorial districts foster democratic, deliberative virtues must confront the fact that the size of electoral constituencies in the United States is over a half-million people.[50] Individuals tend not to know that many people, let alone discuss matters with them, let alone gather on election day to give their "huzzahs" to their representative as a good soul who ought to represent them. Any logistical benefit to accrue from physical proximity in contemporary America or any large nation must, then, apply at a local level, for example, at the level of the neighborhood or the voting precinct. Of course, these physical demarcations do not form fixed walls. The people whom Hoben knows and interacts with "locally" know a set of different people who in turn may or may not live "outside" the boundaries of that which constitutes "local" for Hoben. These people in turn will know people who know people who live outside their local boundaries, and so on. The result is a likely overlapping map of "local" social networks that extend quite far. In other words, the people who constitute *my* local community have a set of people comprising *their* local community who will likely be outside of the territorial boundaries of my community. Territory – any territorial line – would likely include some and exclude others in a way that 250 years ago would not have been true because individuals tended to live far more geographically limited lives.[51]

---

[49] For a particularly insightful development, see Michael James, *Deliberative Democracy and the Plural Polity* (Lawrence, KS: University of Kansas Press, 2004).

[50] As a reminder, I use a "half-million people" for rhetorical purposes. Only adults vote, and in the 1996 congressional elections, only two hundred thousand adults on average voted in each district. But there were approximately four hundred thousand adults per district, the more important number. Because the order of magnitude is the same, and population is increasing in the United States, the argument applies just as well whether we speak of two hundred thousand, four hundred thousand, or a "half-million" voters.

[51] See Chapter 4. An enormous literature on social networks and social network theory grew out of the disenchantment with treating communities as geographically "local." If we think social networks ought to be the basis of political representation, it would be useful to know whether or not our social networks are geographically bounded; this is closely aligned with the communities of interest justification. The present discussion frames the different question of whether territorially bounded communities could serve to increase deliberation between people, whether or not these people are connected in a social network. I am indebted to Robert Chaskin

The critical point is that if territory is "useful" because it facilitates "constituent deliberation," the useful boundaries will be much smaller than required for a contemporary congressional district. And these boundaries will differ depending on population density: The right size may be one city block in Manhattan or one square mile in a neighborhood on the southside of Chicago. The area may comprise one thousand people or fifty thousand people. I am less concerned with pinning down a precise number than to note the central feature: The only plausible territorial benefit comes from a grouping of people that is dramatically smaller than the contemporary congressional district. Thus, even if territory facilitates these deliberative benefits, it does so in a way that requires only recombination of smaller groups.

If the purported logistical benefits of territorial constituencies arise only in the smaller context of what I am calling the "neighborhood," recombination of different neighborhoods might be possible, giving rise to new alternatives for constituency definition. For example, fifty neighborhoods of ten thousand people each from around the country might together form one electoral constituency, with citizens in each of these neighborhoods using the same ballot for election. In each neighborhood, we might see real deliberation about candidates and policies. And indeed today many citizens attend candidate meetings that are held nearby and discuss politics with their neighbors. But suppose we separate the benefits of deliberation within a much smaller neighborhood from a justification for territorial contiguity, the project of constituency definition starts afresh, and justifications would be needed for any particular grouping of neighborhoods. For example, should groups of ten thousand (or two thousand, or fifty thousand) be combined in a territorially contiguous manner? Or should they be combined in a way that maximizes the subdistricts' consent (for example, each subdistrict could voluntarily decide how it wanted to be represented – by racial composition, socioeconomic class, major employer for that district, and so on). Perhaps they should be combined so that a common "community of interest" is formed between these smaller subunits (one possible example is a community or urban neighborhood with a major research university in it – perhaps the communities of Hyde Park, Illinois (University of Chicago); Berkeley, California (UC–Berkeley); West Philadelphia, Pennsylvania (University of Pennsylvania); and Morningside Heights, New York (Columbia University) should form a single electoral constituency). The bottom line is that because of the large size of the district, logistical deliberative benefits themselves at best form a reason for small territorial subdistricts. They do not serve to justify the large territorially contiguous district.

7.5.3 Symbolic Consent and Information

In addition to the deliberative benefits between constituents that territorial constituencies purportedly enabled, there were two other sorts of benefits: First,

and John Dilts of the Chapin Hall Center for Children in Chicago for extended conversations on the subject and to Jon Padgett for a brief but useful discussion.

they enable election days to become tangible moments of consent; second, they enable local facts, what I previously call hard knowledge, to get into the legislature. I will take each in turn.

Do territorial constituencies enable election days to become "tangible moments of consent"? Maybe in theory, but certainly not the way current elections are held. Voters line up at a local election precinct along with a few dozen people (sometimes more, often many less) and wait to step into an isolation chamber (that is, a voting booth) to cast their vote privately. If this forms a "tangible moment of consent," territoriality has little to do with it; the act of voting rather than the communal nature of the event ties the activity to any notion of consent.

But let me push this issue further. The private ballot essentially separated the act of voting from any value of a community gathering to vote. We can thus value the communal act of going to the polls together on the same date, of meeting our neighbors at the precinct, of standing in line shoulder to shoulder with our fellow citizens without requiring that we all are in the same constituency. The goods that derive from territorial voting (as compared to voting via the Internet or by mail) accrue from gathering to vote and do not require that we all receive the same ballot. Thus, the private, secret ballot actually allows nonterritorial constituencies to function without giving up the communal benefits of voting day. As long as ballots are privately cast, territorial constituencies per se do not foster tangible moments of consent.

Do territorial constituencies enable the transmission of local facts to the national legislature? First, summarizing the previous argument, this is not a necessary requirement for House constituencies given the plethora of other avenues of local information. Local governments form their own lobbying groups, and the Senate itself is set up to be a representative of a local unit, the state. More to the point, what local information is there that organizing by territorial constituencies makes possible? The founding example is useful. As Madison argued in *Federalist 56*, the kind of information needed at the national level concerns the laws and geographical facts of the nation, something readily available today to anyone with Internet access.[52] Further, with the rise of communications technology, territorial groupings are not necessary to "make one's voice heard" to the representative; any constituency definition would allow citizens to lobby their representative about issues of concern. To get information into the legislature, territorial constituencies seem to offer little added value over other forms of constituency definition.

In sum, the size of modern constituencies undermines the particular benefits that territorial constituencies may have enabled at the founding. Territory of the size of contemporary electoral districts does not facilitate local deliberation, nor is it necessary for the communication of local needs into the national legislature. In this case, some other kind of constituency definition would more likely achieve these aims.

---

[52] Madison, *Federalist 56*, pp. 378–83.

7.5.4 Enabling Political Organizing

There is one last feature of democratic government that the territorial district arguably enables, one that did not apply during the founding era, and indeed was anathema to the goals of the founders: Territorial constituencies might enable political organizing and campaigning. In this section, I will distinguish this argument from the deliberation arguments already discussed, and show why political organizing forms the strongest contemporary enabling justification, even though it turns out to be much weaker than we might expect.

The logistical benefits of territorial constituencies lie in their ability to facilitate and foster constituent-representative communication. In particular, territorial proximity between constituents allows a representative to meet and greet her constituents. She can stand in front of a supermarket in her neighborhood and talk to citizens who are in her district. Another can organize a town hall meeting and have a group of constituents attend. Again, remember that only a very small subcommunity within the large district that is really being served in this way – a representative does not meet and greet her entire constituency at any one time. But by being territorially proximate, a representative can easily access her constituents physically in a manner that would not be possible were they scattered around the country. More importantly, because of territorial proximity, broadcast media can be used for political communication in a more efficient and less costly way than if the constituency were territorially dispersed. Nonterritorial constituencies would make physical meetings and communication via media difficult if not impossible. This, then, forms a strong justification for local constituencies: They enable political campaigning, and the transferal of information between the candidates and their voters.

This argument becomes particularly strong when we think of political opponents organizing in opposition to a sitting candidate. Territorial proximity reduces the costs involved in door-to-door campaigning that has been the hallmark of local political organization, particularly for unknown insurgent candidates. Individual citizens have a chance to participate and mount a campaign by getting out to "meet and greet" the same voters the sitting representative is meeting. Local associations regularly form the backbone of such campaigns. So any nonterritorial constituency will lose this benefit, and perhaps give even greater power to incumbents, power that may well undermine democratic ends. Territorial constituencies allow upstarts some chance of success to become known to their constituency by pounding the pavement and organizing local networks and associations.

Both of these arguments are strong ones in favor of territorial constituencies but are weakened somewhat by the development of communications technologies in the last decade. Broadcast media (that is, radio and television that are literally cast out broadly to whomever is close enough to receive their signal) are fast becoming a thing of the past being replaced by direct media – whether through the Internet, cable, or satellite feed. Communication to a dispersed group scattered across the nation is readily becoming as easy (and by definition,

TABLE 7.1. *Summary of Case for Territorial Constituencies*

Justification Particular reason for (or goal of) using territory (chapter section listed in parenthesis).	Empirical Claim Do territorial constituencies achieve the goal?	Efficiency Claim Do territorial constituencies efficiently achieve the goal?	Normative Claim Should electoral constituencies be defined to achieve the goal?
Communities of interest (7.2)	No[a]	No	Maybe Relies on a particular version of the pluralist model applied to electoral and non-electoral constituencies
Attachment (7.3)	No	No	No
Property (7.1)	No	No	No
Enabling consent to the electoral constituency (7.4)	No High costs of moving and treating households rather than individuals as the objects of consent temper its success.	No	Yes
Enabling other democratic values within the constituency (7.5)	Maybe On a scale much smaller than the congressional district, "yes." Too large for the whole district to provide benefits.	Maybe Other technologies may provide a better (or as good) an option.	Yes

Note: [a] "Yes," "No," and "Maybe" indicate whether the particular claim for the justification was successful. Comments are brief summaries of the main points but do not exhaust the reasons given in the text.

more efficient and direct) as buying ads in a local media market. These changes make it easier to target your communication and ads to individual households and increasingly to individuals, whether they live next to each other or thousands of miles apart. At present, these technologies do not allow the kind of "meet-and-greet" local outreach of a visit to the local supermarket. Further, the use of these media is very costly, and candidates who have time but not money would stand to lose. However, this is a function of campaign laws, and is meant only to show the possibilities of political organizing without using territorial constituencies. The point here is that because of advances in technology, territorial proximity is becoming less and less critical to getting out one's message. (The ramifications of this will be treated in greater detail in Chapter 9.)

7.6 SUMMARY AND CONCLUSION

On the whole, the arguments of this chapter have raised doubts about the use of territorial constituencies by comparing them to a series of reasonable and promising justifications for their use (see Table 7.1). Yet representative government needs representatives, and any representational system will entail the creation of at least a single national electoral constituency, and most probably the creation of many electoral constituencies within the whole. One cannot simply "reject" one plan without offering something better in its place. Nor should we hope for an ideal system. The questions now arise, what might an alternative look like and upon what basis should we evaluate it?

Even though territory may not fare well as an ideal constituency, it now has the benefit of a long history and precedent. Although "use" does not form a justification internal to the territorial constituency, in the United States territorial constituencies are familiar by virtue of history. Any change will entail costs and a new system that is unfamiliar to citizens.[53] Before we simply "reject" territory, we need to have a superior plan that either fixes its particular deficiencies or at least offers some prospect of being better overall. In the next chapter, I begin to set out the contours of such a plan.

---

[53] This brief historical justification is, of course, reminiscent of Burke's critique of the new French system that defined precincts by laying a grid on a map, thereby obliterating political boundaries that had been in long use. See the discussion above in section 5.2.2. Edmund Burke, *Reflections on the Revolution in France*, ed. J. G. A. Pocock (Indianapolis, IN: Hackett, 1987), pp. 152–67, 173. As I argued in Chapter 3, history does not form a justification for an institution at the moment of a founding, though "long use" may justify any institution once it has been used for any length of time.

8

Legitimate Representation and Institutional Design

For Permanent, Involuntary, Heterogeneous Constituencies

8.1 INTRODUCTION

If territorial constituencies face the kinds of problems we outlined in the previous chapter, we need to ask, "what's the alternative?" In the next chapter, I will argue that randomized, national, permanent constituencies offer a promising one. Their promise rests upon the implications of some minimal aims of legitimate political representation, the subject of this chapter.

I begin the analysis by ignoring the costs of change and assume that we could redefine constituencies in any manner we wanted. If we were to build a large nation's electoral institutions from scratch, how should we think about constituency definition? Can there be a universal starting position, a baseline from which deviations must be justified? If so, what would that position be?

In this chapter, I argue that all things considered, electoral constituencies should be heterogeneous, stable, and involuntary,[1] and they should create incentives for representatives to pursue the public good. These features form a default position derived from the limiting conditions of any plausible theory of legitimate political representation – conditions as noncontroversial as "representatives should be accountable to those they represent." As a default position, these features of heterogeneity, stability, and involuntariness may be overridden by other more pressing values. But because they form a default position, the burden of justification will rest upon others who want homogeneous, unstable, or voluntary constituencies, including advocates of group representation or proportional systems. The burden of justification will also rest upon those who want constituencies to provide incentives for group advocacy absent some explanation of how the advocacy of their particular group is likely to serve the public good.[2]

---

[1] See Chapter 2 for a discussion of these terms.
[2] See section 7.1.

The actual choice of a constituency plan will depend, of course, upon the particular context. As I noted in Chapter 2, there may be compelling reasons to define constituencies in other ways, whether to build the capabilities of citizens or to promote the voice of oppressed groups. But we are aiming at foundations here, asking, "what are the minimums of a legitimate system?" rather than "what can be done to make things more fair?" Indeed, the kinds of remedies that are often sought through institutional design are ones that require the pursuit of justice, not institutional design, a point to which I will return in section 8.5.1.[3]

After a brief note about institutional default positions, I consider the limiting conditions of legitimate political representation (section 8.2). In sections 8.3–8.5, I argue that these conditions respectively entail constituencies that are heterogeneous, stable, and voluntary. However, for reasons I explain, this triad is inconsistent. Because "voluntariness" is the least important of the three features (for reasons I discuss in section 8.4), I argue that constituencies ought to be stable, heterogeneous, and involuntary. Section 8.6 concludes with a brief reconsideration of territorial constituencies in light of these baselines.

8.1.1 A Note on Institutional Default Positions

The strength of our conclusions, but not the conclusions themselves, depends upon a notion of an institutional default position. Before proceeding, let me briefly explain what I mean by it.

An institutional default position (IDP) is the normative baseline or starting point for institutional design, from which deviations must be justified. IDPs are derived from the normative ends at which any institution aims.[4] Although they are not easily determined and are often contested, many IDPs are readily endorsable and appealed to in the context of institutional analysis. For example, the "one person, one vote" standard is a democratic IDP: One rightly assumes that where democracy is endorsed, all citizens should receive equal vote shares unless there is some other compelling reason to deviate from this default position.

Most norms are complex and often conflict with other compelling norms. IDPs are thus not necessary entailments of norms, as if "democracy" just meant "one person, one vote," but starting positions that must be weighed against other competing claims. A good historical illustration in this case is John Stuart Mill's argument that university graduates and others of the "liberal professions"

---

[3] Or as Joshua Cohen has written, "we cannot expect outcomes that advance the common good unless people are looking for them." Quoted in David Estlund, "The Democracy/Contractualism Analogy." *Philosophy and Public Affairs*, 31, no. 4, Fall 2003: 387–412.

[4] On the normative aims of an institution, see sections 3.3 and 7.1, and Claus Offe, "Designing Institutions in East European Transitions," in *The Theory of Institutional Design*, ed. Robert E. Goodin (Cambridge, UK: Cambridge University Press, 1996), pp. 199–207.

should be given two votes in elections.[5] Mill thought that because educated people were likely to make better voting choices than uneducated people, the overall influence of giving them double votes would be beneficial to the whole. Mill also supported the innovation because distributing votes equally without reference to educational achievement seemed to devalue education: "It is not useful, but hurtful, that the constitution of the country should declare ignorance to be entitled to as much political power as knowledge."[6] And by explicitly rejecting property qualifications and considering it "an absolutely necessary part of the plurality scheme, that it can be open to the poorest individual in the community to claim its privileges," Mill's is an elite view of representation in only the strictest of senses – it gives benefits to an exclusive group, but encourages all citizens to enter.[7] In this case, the deviation from the democratic IDP of "equal vote shares" was plausibly justified by an appeal to another norm.[8]

Because IDPs are conceptual entailments of normative positions, they are universal, applicable to *all* systems anywhere in the world. Thus, "one person, one vote" is a democratic IDP for any nation that purports to be democratic, whether India, Brazil, Iceland, or the United States, because equal vote shares are an IDP of democracy. Context *becomes* critical in the process of institutional design and reform. In the United States, for example, the historical oppression of African Americans and other races may justify a deviation from certain democratic IDPs in order to correct that oppression, while in Montenegro other arguments might apply. Context does not create normative standards for institutions; it spells out their design implications given a background standard.[9]

In the end, IDPs operate as prima facie assumptions about how institutions should be designed given their own normative aims, aims that will have to be justified on their own strengths. IDPs thus operationalize normative positions of the institutions designed to express them prior to confrontation with other values and contexts with which those positions may conflict.[10]

---

[5] John Stuart Mill, *Considerations on Representative Government* (Amherst, NY: Prometheus 1991 [1861]), Chapter VIII.

[6] Ibid., p. 340.

[7] For a recent alternative view that Mill simply wanted to stack the political deck rather than encourage education, see Lynn Sanders, "Against Deliberation," *Political Theory*, 25, no. 3, June 1897: 347–76.

[8] See also Dennis F. Thompson, *John Stuart Mill and Representative Government* (Princeton, NJ: Princeton University Press, 1976), Chapter 3; John Rawls, *Theory of Justice* (Cambridge, MA: Harvard University Press, 1971), pp. 232–3.

[9] For a broader view on the development of formal and informal institutions in analytical and historical contexts, see Jack Knight, *Institutions and Social Conflict* (New York: Cambridge University Press, 1992); Douglass C. North, *Structure and Change in Economic History* (New York: Norton, 1990).

[10] I thank Jack Knight for discussion about this section.

This is an admittedly brief pass through controversial terrain. As I claimed previously, only the strength of this chapter's conclusions depends on the notion of an IDP. The substantive conclusions of this chapter still stand: Basic norms of any plausible theory of legitimate political representation generate prima facie claims in favor of stable, heterogeneous, and involuntary constituencies. The arguments that follow are, at their weakest, a set of prima facie normative claims to be balanced against other political values. At their strongest, the arguments demonstrate that norms entail specific institutional designs. In either case, while there may still be good reasons to deviate from this position, it forms a strong starting point.

8.2 THE LIMITING CONDITIONS FOR LEGITIMATE POLITICAL REPRESENTATION

In this section, I will argue that there are five uncontroversial limiting conditions for any plausible theory of legitimate political representation (section 8.2.1). I then explain how this modifies Hanna Pitkin's seminal account (section 8.2.2). In section 8.2.3, I link these conditions to structural features of electoral constituencies.

8.2.1 Five Limiting Conditions

In section 1.2, I argued that a comprehensive account of political legitimacy would specify the conditions under which a government has the right to make and enforce laws over a given group of people. To repeat my one assumption: It is a necessary condition of any legitimate representative government that its political representatives themselves be legitimate. A comprehensive account of political legitimacy would specify the necessary and sufficient conditions for legitimate political representation and would enable us to tell whether these representatives (but not those) were legitimate.[11] Since I am not offering a comprehensive account of political legitimacy, I proceed more cautiously from what I assume any plausible account of legitimate political representation will include, a position that will generate the broadest conditions and, I hope, will permit widespread agreement.

I identify four procedural limiting conditions and one substantive limiting condition within which we can presume a theory of legitimate political representation to operate. (I phrase them here in the negative because they are limits.) A political representative will presumably *fail* to be legitimate – she will fail to have the authority by right to make law – when:

- The representative was selected via "inappropriate" *decision rules*.
- The decision rules used to select her employed "inappropriate" *vote weights*.
- She does not represent those who *authorized* her to act.

---

[11] The statement assumes there can be "illegitimate" political representatives and thus poses a problem for Pitkin's account, which I take up in this section.

- Those who hold the representative *accountable* are not those whom she represented.
- She has *inappropriate aims* in executing the duties of her job.

These limits are closely connected to prominent features of Piktin's account of political representation,[12] a point to which I will return in the next section.

Framed in the positive, these five conditions mean that legitimate representatives must, first, be selected and limited by the right sort of decision rules (presumably "unanimity" or "majority rule") rather than the wrong sort of decision rules (ones like "Joe decides" or "the candidate with the least votes wins").[13] Second, legitimate representatives must be elected by voters each of whom have an appropriately weighted vote (usually, but not necessarily, equal shares).[14] Third, legitimate representatives need to be authorized by all or some of those who will be represented by them rather than authorized by those who will not be represented by them.[15] For example, if I am a citizen of the United States, my representative in Congress should not be chosen by Canadians. Fourth, legitimate representatives should be held to account by the people to whom they were accountable during their term of office. A member of the U.S. Congress from the Fifth District of Illinois thus should not be held accountable by members of the Seventh District of New York. Finally, in executing her duties, a legitimate political representative must have proper aims, rather than improper ones. Proper aims may include "the nation's good" or "my constituents' interests." Absent some compelling argument to the contrary, legitimate representatives may not, for example, aim at the good of some other nation, nor may they aim at their own personal enrichment.

[12] Hanna Fenichel Pitkin, *The Concept of Representation* (Berkeley, CA: University of California Press, 1967).

[13] An account of legitimacy would stipulate what a "right" decision rule is. There may be times when "Joe decides" or "least votes wins" is the right kind of decision rule. Maybe we all trust Joe and give him the authority to decide. Or maybe we agree with our grade school experience that elections are just "popularity contests" and the loser is actually the best one for the job. The point here is that a right decision rule, whatever it is, is needed to legitimize a political representative. I thank Emma Greenberg Rehfeld for reminding me of the popularity dimensions of grade school elections.

[14] See section 8.1.1 for Mill's argument that some voters should receive double votes. Vote shares and decision rules are two distinguishable parts of this analysis. A decision rule translates votes into a decisive outcome regardless of how many votes each voter has. For example, we can use majority rule as our decision rule, even in cases where I have forty-five votes and everyone else has one. Public corporations do this regularly, using "majority rule" and assigning vote weights to people depending on the number of shares of stock they have.

[15] The condition leaves open the question whether a representative must be authorized by all, most, or some of those whom he represents. The condition is meant only to exclude "outsiders" from authorizing a representative who does not represent them. In most presumably legitimate cases, many of a representative's electoral constituents do not actually authorize him either because they are ineligible (children), because they voted for someone else (in single-member districts), or because they chose not to vote at all. Again, a full account of legitimate political representation would specify these details. Here we are simply drawing the limit: To retain his legitimacy, a representative must *not* be authorized by a third party.

TABLE 8.1. *Limiting Conditions for Legitimate Political Representation, with Examples*

Condition	Description	Plausible Examples
Appropriate Decision Rules	The decision rule used by the selection agents is an appropriate one.	Majority vote; the Hare system; super-majorities; other forms of proportional representation.
Appropriate Vote Weights	Votes have appropriate weights	"One person, one vote."
Proper Authorization	The representative must be authorized to act by some or all of those he represents.[1]	Elections in which a representative is elected by the voting citizens of his district.
Proper Accountability	The representative must be accountable to some or all of those he represents.[2]	A representative of Uttar Pradesh explains his vote to the citizens of Uttar Pradesh; a representative of the labor party is returned to office by voting members of the labor party.
Appropriate Substantive Aims	The representative must act in accordance with appropriate aims.	Representatives who advocate for their constituents' interests; representatives who advocate on behalf of the common good.

Notes: [1] This *only* excludes those not represented by him, but it does not imply that he necessarily was selected by all of those he represents. See footnote 15.

[2] See note 1.

Table 8.1 lists the conditions for legitimate political representation and provides plausible examples of them in practice. Table 8.2 lists cases in which these conditions fail to be met to demonstrate the necessity of their inclusion in any plausible account of legitimate political representation.

These conditions should seem almost trivial, perhaps even simply conceptual extensions of what must be meant by legitimate political representation. How, for example, could a woman elected by the people of Ghana have the right to be a member of the U.S. Congress, representing the people of northern Florida? The point, then, is to see what follows from these trivial assumptions about what any account of legitimate political representation will flesh out.

This raises a question: If these are trivial entailments of a theory of legitimate political representation, why do I call them "limiting conditions"? By using the term "limiting conditions," I emphasize that they are firm guideposts for which any theory of legitimate political representation will have to account. But there may be exceptions at exceptional moments, moments that a more comprehensive theory of legitimacy would specify. For example, when a representative

TABLE 8.2. *Presumed Violations of the Limiting Conditions for Legitimate Political Representation, with Examples*

Condition	Description of the Failure	Plausible Examples[1]
Improper Decision Rule	The decision rule used by the selection agents is **improper**.	"The candidate with the biggest shoe size is the winner."
Improper Vote Weights	Votes have **unequal** weights	"This person, one vote; that person, 3,000 votes."
Improper Authorization	The representative is authorized by those he does not represent.	The representative for Normandy is selected by the residents of Bordeaux.
Improper Accountability	The representative is accountable to those he does not represent.	The representative of London explains his actions to the residents of Bristol; meanwhile, in the next election, citizens of Liverpool vote whether to return him to parliament.
Inappropriate Substantive Aims	The representative has inappropriate aims.	The representative supports legislation based on whether it he will personally benefit from it.

Note: [1] As with all of these examples, we could imagine possible ways in which they illustrate "proper" or "appropriate" standards. However, any plausible theory of legitimate political representation will have to explain how these could be plausible.

unexpectedly leaves office in the middle of his term but prior to the date of an election, a governor of a state (or the head of a party) may have to appoint a replacement to serve in his place. This violates the condition of authorization – the representative in this example has been authorized to act by the governor, a person whom he does not represent. A full-blown theory of political legitimacy would account for this, explaining why (or possibly why not) this is a permissible response to an emergency vacancy. The point here is not to work out that detail but to say that any theory would have to explain such a violation.[16]

8.2.2 Hanna Pitkin's *The Concept of Representation*

I said previously that these limiting conditions are closely related to Pitkin's account in her seminal *The Concept of Representation*.[17] In her conceptual and historical account of the concept of political representation, political

[16] This is also why these are "limiting" rather than "necessary" conditions for legitimate political representation.

[17] Pitkin, *The Concept of Representation*.

representatives are authorized and held accountable by those they represent, and they act in a way that substantively pursues the interests of either their constituents or the greater good of the whole. That is, the conditions by which Pitkin evaluates whether a person is a representative are what I am treating as the limiting conditions of legitimate political representation.[18] This distinction – between the conditions that render a representative legitimate versus the conditions that render a person a representative at all – is an important if overlooked one.

By the account presented here, a person who fails to meet one of the limiting conditions – such as someone who has inappropriate substantive aims and acts only for personal gain – will fail to be legitimate even though she may still be a political representative. Imagine an elected representative who uses his influence only for personal gain: He never shows up for a vote and uses taxpayer money to take a vacation. It may be reasonable for us to say that that person is not a legitimate representative of the people who elected him, for he is failing to perform his responsibilities. But it would be a mistake to say he is not the representative of those who elected him. If we asked his constituents who their representative is, they would rightly point to him. Of course, such dereliction of duty may well lead to his being impeached or removed from office, in which case he would fail to be a representative at all. But so long as he remains in office, he would remain the political representatives of a particular group, even if he failed some very minimal test or normative legitimacy.

Pitkin apparently disagrees, arguing that these conditions are limits on the concept of representation itself: Violating one of these conditions, a person fails to be a representative at all. The best example of this comes in her discussion of "formalistic" views of representation – views advanced by Max Weber and Eric Vogelin in particular – in which representation purportedly arises by the mere act of authorization without any structures of accountability.[19] Pitkin rejects formalistic views as not representation at all. Hobbes's sovereign is her clearest example: Despite Hobbes's claims to the contrary, the sovereign in *Leviathan* is not, by Pitkin's account, a representative of the people because he lacks substantive limits on what he can do, and there are no procedures of accountability to remove him from power.[20] "Most modern readers of the *Leviathan* ... suddenly want to say, 'Oh, well, call the sovereign a representative

---

[18] Ibid., pp. 209–40. I take up Pitkin's account despite its age because of its influence since it was published. I do not dispute her historical account, or its conceptual usefulness in framing the debates that followed. As I will show, I think she mistook features of political legitimacy for features of political representation. The challenge to Pitkin's rejection of "Symbolic representation" by difference theorists is illustrative of my point, since I think we should understand this challenge as one of legitimacy: Symbolic representation can be a legitimate political form.

[19] See Pitkin, *The Concept of Representation*, pp. 38–59.

[20] In Chapter 16 of *Leviathan*, Hobbes defines a representative as someone who has been authorized by someone else, with no limits on the purported representative's activities once authorized. Thomas Hobbes, *Leviathan* (Indianapolis, IN: Hackett, 1994), Chapter 16.

if you like, but it's sheer hypocrisy. He doesn't really represent the people at all.'"[21]

My claim is that it is not hypocrisy to call Hobbes's sovereign a (political) representative.[22] But you should not call him a legitimate representative because inter alia there are no limits to what he is authorized to do and an account of legitimacy would properly limit the scope of his activity. Our account thus reframes Pitkin's historical and conceptual analysis: Political representation may take many forms, but the legitimacy of a particular case depends upon the procedural conditions out of which it arises, and the substantive conditions by which and toward which it aims.[23]

These five conditions set the limits on a plausible account of legitimate political representation; they set the categories that any account of legitimate political representation will have to fill, or explain why they can be overridden. The conditions correspond to features not only of Pitkin's analysis but of the history of purportedly legitimate political representation.[24] Even though the substance of these conditions has been intensely controversial, categorically they appear to describe features of a broad range of accounts. Thus we proceed assuming that some account of these conditions is necessary for representation to be legitimate whatever one's account of the substance of these conditions is.

---

[21] Pitkin, *The Concept of Representation*, p. 35.

[22] Would he not rightly be accepted as a representative of his nation by anyone with whom he enters into negotiation? Should we look to my Uncle Eddy or Aunt Vicki as representatives instead, or deny that illegitimate regimes can ever have political representatives? Admittedly, these questions are not an argument, but form the intuitions out of which an alternative view arises.

[23] Instead, I believe representation is simply audience-dependent – a representative is someone who is accepted by a relevant audience as being a representative. For an unpolished alternative account of the concept of political representation, see Andrew Rehfeld, "Silence of the Land: An Historical and Normative Analysis of Territorial Representation in the United States," Ph.D. Dissertation, University of Chicago, Chapter 7. See D. A. Lloyd Thomas, "The Concept of Representation, Book Review," *Philosophical Quarterly*, 19, no. 75, April 1969: 186–7, a review of Pitkin that, in passing, saw the paradox of assuming a normative judgment as part of the concept of representation itself. F. R. Ankersmit's recent work distinguishes between political representation and legitimate political representation, although in ultimately unpromising ways. See F. R. Ankersmit, *Political Representation* (Stanford, CA: Stanford University Press, 2002); Andrew Rehfeld, Book review of *Political Representation*, by F. R. Ankersmit, *Ethics*, 113, no. 4, July 2003: 865–8.

[24] For a variety of historical accounts see Robert G. Dixon, Jr., *Democratic Representation: Reapportionment in Law and Politics* (New York: Oxford University Press, 1968); Constantin Fasolt, "Quod Omnes Tangit Ab Omnibus Approbari Debet: The Words and the Meaning," in *In Iure Veritas: Studies in Canon Law in Memory of Schaefer Williams*, eds. Steven B. Bowman and Blanch E. Cody (Cincinnati, OH: University of Cincinnati College of Law, 1991), pp. 21–55. Bernard Manin, *The Principles of Representative Government* (New York: Cambridge University Press, 1997); Pitkin, *The Concept of Representation*; J. R. Pole, *Political Representation in England and the Origins of the American Republic* (New York: St. Martin's Press, 1966); John Philip Reid, *The Concept of Representation in the Age of the American Revolution* (Chicago: University of Chicago Press, 1989).

8.2.3 Limiting Conditions and Constituency Definition

I draw upon these five conditions of legitimate political representation to develop an institutional default position for electoral constituencies. To summarize the conclusions that will follow in sections 8.3–8.5, we arrive first at stable, voluntary, and heterogeneous constituencies:

- Stable or permanent constituencies (section 8.3): Authorization and accountability assume a stable population that authorizes a representative at one point in time, and then later holds him to account for his job at another point in time. This presumes stable constituencies.
- Voluntary constituencies (section 8.4): Appropriate decision rules and vote weights are intimately tied to a theory of consent and individual equality; this creates an assumption in favor of voluntariness through the political system.
- Heterogeneous constituencies (section 8.5): A representative can pursue appropriate aims by direct or indirect means (as in "republicanism" and the advocacy of the public good, or through "pluralism" and the advocacy of some partial good). Only heterogeneous constituencies are consistent with both pluralist and republican models of "proper substantive aims," and thus heterogeneity constitutes a default position for electoral constituencies.

For reasons we discussed in Chapter 2, the triad of stable, heterogeneous, and voluntary constituencies is not a practicable option; as a practical matter, voluntary constituencies are likely to be extremely homogeneous, perhaps perfectly so. We will thus have to keep two and reject one of these three features. As it turns out, the argument for voluntary constituencies is surprisingly weak because the argument for individual political equality that grounds a preference for voluntary consent is a trivial one (see section 8.4). Thus, we keep the more important conditions of stability and heterogeneity, and assume as a default that electoral constituencies should be involuntary and defined at the constitutional level.

8.3 MAKING SENSE OF "SELF-RULE": PERMANENT CONSTITUENCIES, ACCOUNTABILITY, AND AUTHORIZATION

Electoral constituencies mediate the relationship between "the people" and their government,[25] specifying who it is that authorizes the representative and to whom the representative must account for his performance. As I argued in Chapter 2, stability measures how constant the constituency's membership remains over time. Because accountability and authorization are closely related – representatives should presumably be accountable to those who authorized

---

[25] Compare Melissa S. Williams, *Voice, Trust and Memory* (Princeton, NJ: Princeton University Press, 1998), Chapter 1. Williams, and Dahl before her, rightly emphasizes the additional importance of non-electoral constituencies.

them to act and for that which they were authorized to do – this creates an IDP for extremely stable constituencies. Put differently, the reason a representative is accountable to *this* group (but not *that* one) is that *this* group authorized him to act in the first place. The relationship between authorization and accountability generates a prima facie claim that electoral constituencies should be permanent and unchanging so that the group who authorized the representative is in fact the same as the group to whom the representative is accountable.

"Accountability" and "authorization" complement each other in substantive and procedural ways. Substantively, as Mark Warren has observed, the terms upon which a person is authorized to do some act "may also serve as standards of accountability."[26] Procedurally, the person or group who has the authority to authorize an agent may also serve as the one to whom that agent must account for her actions. These may not be necessary conditions and there are possible exceptions: A last will and testament may authorize a particular person to spend the deceased's money with no directives at all as to how to spend it, nor with any accountability structure involved (the recipient might blow the money on a bet at a casino without violating that which he was authorized to do). But in most cases, when Ruth authorizes Rex to "do X," she creates standards by which Rex will be held to account ("doing X"), and specifies to whom Rex is accountable (Ruth, or someone she appoints). Again, these observations demonstrate the close linkage between accountability and authorization rather than establish a necessary connection between the two.[27] And, in any particular context where accountability and authorization operate (employment, law enforcement, representative government, and so on), the contours of their relationship may be different.

In the context of legitimate representative government, the substantive connection between authority and accountability will range between highly specific

---

[26] Mark E. Warren, "Deliberative Democracy and Authority," *American Political Science Review*, 90, no. 1, March 1996: 46–60. Warren argued for "authority" in the context of a deliberative democracy, dependent in part upon citizens being able to hold authorities accountable for their actions. Elsewhere, James Fearon argues that accountability involves an "understanding that *A* is obliged to act in some way on behalf of *B*," a fact with which I agree, although I differ in that this obligation is not a condition of accountability as Fearon has made it. James D. Fearon, "Electoral Accountability and the Control of Politicians: Selecting Good Types versus Sanctioning Poor Performance," in *Democracy, Accountability, and Representation*, eds. Adam Przeworski, Susan C. Stokes, and Bernard Manin, Cambridge Studies in the Theory of Democracy (New York: Cambridge University Press, 1996), p. 55.

[27] I think there is a necessary connection between accountability and authorization that would emerge from properly locating "authority." In most cases of third-party accountability, it only appears that the principle does not specify who should hold the agent to account. In fact, the "authority" is actually not the principle but some fourth person or thing (a set of rules, a constitution) that by virtue of its authority sets the standards and specifies who will hold the agent accountable. This view would require an extended argument tangential to the present discussion. The critical question before us now depends only on the relationship between accountability and authorization in the context of democratic self-government, and need not rely on a full-blown conceptual analysis.

and nonspecific (that is, general) versions, depending, among other things, upon one's account of legitimacy. At a minimum, any account of legitimate representation will specify that the representative has the right (by virtue of authorization) to participate in the process of legislation for the whole. This is the "general" version because it sets a single, nonspecific standard for which the representative is accountable ("participate in legislation"). It does not specify what it means to "participate" – whether, for example, the representative should aim at the public interest or his constituents' needs. Nor does it tell him whether he should consult his constituents as their delegate, or act as a trustee making decisions by his own lights.[28] At the other extreme, of specific authorization, very exacting standards are specified beyond the general right to participate in legislation. These standards may influence how the representative should vote on a particular measure or tell him when he should follow the experts. Specific authorization should not, however, be confused with the "delegate" model of representation. An electoral constituency may very specifically authorize the representative to act in the public good but leave the determination of the public good up to the representative. The fact that this very specific standard of action creates a huge practical problem of accountability ("did she really believe *that* was in the nation's interest?") is a conceptually distinct issue.[29]

In usual practice, the level of specificity will range between the "general" and "specific" versions of authorization, much of it emerging from what a candidate promises ("If I am elected I will ..."). When candidates or parties run for reelection, they are quick to remind voters that they did what they said they were going to do. And when they fail to meet their promises, they are often called to account for this failure (whether or not they are returned to office). This is well known to any casual observer of politics; I merely point it out to show that the reason these promises count as the standard by which representatives are held to account is because they were specified in the authorization that purportedly made them legitimate representatives in the first place.

While the substantive standards of accountability may range broadly (and a theory of legitimacy might explain what the right level of specificity should be), the procedural connection between accountability and authorization will always be very close: The reason a representative is accountable to this group (rather than that one) is that she was authorized by this group (and not that one) to act. And the reason she was authorized to act by them (and not by a third party) gets to the very heart of self-government. If we chose representatives for other groups and others chose representatives for us, it is hard to imagine that would even count as self-government.

---

[28] The distinction between "trustee" and "delegate" models of representation is historical and well developed in Pitkin, *The Concept of Representation*, pp. 112–43.

[29] See section 8.5.2 for a continued discussion of this point.

Notice that "accountability" in ordinary language incorporates two distinct, if related dimensions.[30] When we say, "Noah is accountable to Evie," we usually mean two things:

- *Deliberative dimension*: Noah has a responsibility to account for his actions to Evie.
- *Sanctioning dimension*: Evie has the power to sanction Noah for a failure to complete those actions.

This maps onto the sense in which political representatives are "called to account" for their actions, such as, in a town hall meeting where they are asked to explain why they supported a particular piece of legislation (the deliberative sense), and are later "held to account" by, for example, being defeated or reelected at the next election (the sanctioning sense).

I assume that "sanctioning" will be incorporated into any reasonable account of legitimate political representation. It is unlikely that a system would be legitimate in which representatives were required merely to give an account of their actions without any risk of sanction (reward or penalty); in fact, such a system may fail to have accountability built in at all. Imagine a representative, operating in a system where voters had no ability to sanction or reward him, claiming she is fully accountable to her constituents because she regularly deliberates with them (with full publicity and honesty) about her policy positions. "Why, just last night," Beverly might say to us, "I patiently explained to my constituents why I voted to confiscate the contents of their bank accounts for my own personal use. You see, I really needed a new car." Without their ability to sanction her (at least by voting her out of office), we should not find plausible Beverly's claim that, having met the deliberative dimension, she was in fact accountable to her constituents.

---

[30] In the empirical literature, "accountability" usually measures "policy congruence" between voters and their representatives. This assumes a plausible, if simplistic, normative assumption that representatives ought to act according to the policy preferences of their constituents. See, for example, Eric M. Uslaner, and Ronald E. Weber, "Policy Congruence and American State Elites: Descriptive Representation Versus Electoral Accountability," *Journal of Politics*, 45, no. 1, February 1983: 183–96. Such a standard would have to explain *when* the congruence has to happen for it to count as "accountability," since a representative can often take an unpopular position and change his constituents' minds without failing to be accountable to them. In their otherwise terrific recent volume, Adam Przeworski et al. do not provide a coherent description of what "accountability" qua accountability entails. *Democracy, Accountability, and Representation*, eds. Adam Przeworski, Susan C. Stokes, and Bernard Manin, Cambridge Studies in the Theory of Democracy (New York: Cambridge University Press, 1999). The closest I could find was Jon Elster's description, "an agent A is accountable *to* a principle B *for* an action X." Jon Elster, "Accountability in Athenian Politics," in Przeworski et al., *Democracy, Accountability, and Representation*, p. 255. Elster adds, "We need to define the idea of 'holding accountable.'" Ibid., p. 255. Elster's discussion is more nuanced than most, but nevertheless leads one back to the question: What is the activity called accountability? Here we find it means to be responsible to give an account and to be sanctioned for one's actions. I owe to Sue Stokes the observation that the triad still provides no description of accountability as an activity.

I expect that the deliberative dimension of accountability will also figure in a more complete account of legitimate political representation; but I do not here presume its necessity.[31] A system in which representatives did not deliberatively account for their actions but nevertheless stood for regular reelection would be minimally "accountable" in a way that incorporating only the deliberative dimension would fail to be accountability at all. But note that if a theory of legitimacy required the deliberative dimension (as in Amy Gutmann and Dennis Thompson's argument), this would strengthen our argument for very stable constituencies. If a representative is required to give an account of his actions (not merely be sanctioned for them), he is required to give that account to those who voted for him rather than to those who did not.

Even if accountability entails only its sanctioning dimension, the very idea of self-government explains why electoral constituencies should remain stable between elections. Imagine a situation in which constituency A elected a representative who served in office for one term and then stood for election before some other constituency, B (and membership in A was exclusive of the membership in B). Members of B might conceivably hold the representative to account for her job in office as a representative of A based on the substantive standard of activity for which A authorized her. But the fact that the members of B were sanctioning A's representative simply undermines the claim that this arrangement would be one of self-government. For if self-government is required by a theory of legitimacy (and I assume that it is), then it is hard to conceive of a plausible version in which some third party (B in our example) would have the right to sanction a representative for her service to her electoral constituents (A in our example).

Yet, from the argument so far, it only follows that changing the membership of an electoral constituency *in its entirety* between elections is an assault on the very concept of democratic self-rule. However, it is much less clear that, for example, switching one member of the constituency between elections constitutes that much of an assault. For example, if an electoral constituency has ten voters when it elects a representative, and then at reelection time one of those voters is different, we would still want to call this "self-rule." When the numbers in large democratic governments that use territorial constituencies are in the tens and hundreds of thousands, the fact that one of them is different between elections should be of little real concern. But that begs the standard setting question: If a change of one member is not enough to pass the self-rule threshold, but an entire change of membership violates it, what constitutes too much instability?

---

[31] I thus agree with Amy Gutmann and Dennis Thompson, who argue that accountability entails more than just trying to win election. Amy Gutmann and Dennis Thompson, *Democracy and Disagreement* (Cambridge, MA: Belknap Press, 1996), pp. 129, 144–51. As they rightly emphasize, this requirement emerges out of a theory of deliberative legitimacy rather than simply from the condition of accountability itself.

I am not going to propose a precise answer to this problem except to say that as an IDP, electoral constituencies should be as stable as possible because the greater the continuity of membership between elections, the more plausible it is that self-rule is coherently being realized. And the best way of making an electoral constituency stable is to have its membership permanent: After joining a constituency, a citizen *never* leaves. One way of making constituency membership permanent is to let voters choose how they wish to be represented (as a member of the labor party, by where they live, by their cultural or ethnic origins, and so on) and then never permit any changes to their membership. A much different way is for the government to assign voters to electoral constituencies in which they remain for the rest of their lives.

Because people die, come of age, or lose their voting rights, the idea of a perfectly stable electoral constituency is unlikely to be achieved even if constituency membership were permanent. But again, we are looking for the IDP given that the very notion of self-rule leads us to a close connection between accountability and authorization. As I said previous, there may be other reasons for an IDP to deviate from this default, but for the reasons just developed, permanence should be the starting point against which others must argue, because it comes the closest to ensuring perfect stability between elections and thus the best chance to make sense of self-rule.

I close this section with a related note on prospective and retrospective voting that begins with Pitkin's observation that voting simultaneously authorizes representatives and holds them to account for their actions once in office.[32] We want to draw our attention to the fact that in most elections voters only get one vote in which to both hold a representative accountable for his past service and authorize him (or a replacement) for future service. The fact that voting collapses the institution of accountability with authorization ("simultaneously") is precisely why scholars wonder whether they vote "prospectively" (to authorize a representative) or "retrospectively" (to hold a representative to account for his past activity).[33] But if every elected official had to survive two votes – an "accountability vote" based on past performance and then an "authorization vote" in the form of a regular election – this problem

---

[32] Pitkin, *Concept of Representation*, p. 43. For a restatement, see Iris Marion Young, "Deferring Group Representation" in *Nomos XXXIX: Ethnicity and Group Rights*, eds. Ian Shapiro and Will Kymlicka (New York and London: New York University Press, 1997). Voting need not simultaneously authorize and sanction a representative, but most contemporary elections simultaneously authorize and hold to account. See the discussion later in this chapter.

[33] Pitkin's discussion is the source. Young's recent argument again puts accountability in a central location. Ibid. Both appear to be a combination of normative and descriptive arguments, yet neither offers any evidence that elections actually do hold representatives accountable for any particular action. In fairness, Young merely argues that elections "can" hold representatives to account for some action. Ibid., pp. 360–1. For an excellent collection of formal and empirical studies of whether elections in fact hold officials accountable, and exactly what it is they hold them accountable for, see Przeworski et al., *Democracy, Accountability, and Representation*.

would be transformed.[34] The simultaneity of "authorizing" and "sanctioning," however, is a contingent fact about how most elections are run, and should not change our judgment about the importance of the stability of an electoral constituency.[35]

8.4 VOLUNTARY CONSTITUENCIES: WHY "ONE PERSON, ONE VOTE" IS A TRIVIAL STANDARD

We hold that . . . one man's vote in a congressional election is to be worth as much as another's.

– Justice Hugo Black, writing for the majority, 1964[36]

The limiting conditions of "vote weights" and "decision rules" pointed only to "appropriate" ones, leaving the substance of that judgment for a theory of political legitimacy to flesh out. But I presume that any plausible theory will begin with an assumption in favor of "one person, one vote" and "major-ity rule" as the respective "vote weights" and "decision rule" largely because they correspond to the two defining features of democratic self-government: political equality and self-rule. Following from this, voluntary constituencies have a strong claim as an IDP, because allowing individual voters to decide for themselves how to be represented would help equalize their voting power, and increase their opportunities for consent.[37]

Indeed, among the most significant problems of implementing the current system of territorial districts in the United States is its obscene violation of voter consent. Mandated under court order to equalize populations every ten years, redistricting is frequently dominated by partisan politicians drawing lines for their own political gain. Voter consent is no more achieved in those states in which independent or bipartisan districting commissions draw the lines, though the outcomes may be more just. But, instead of leaving it to third parties to

---

[34] The problem would not necessarily be solved, because strategic considerations might lead some voters to vote prospectively when being asked to take a first vote on a candidate's record.

[35] The recall vote of California Governor Grey Davis in the fall of 2003 is an important exception to the rule, and provides a possible way to separate holding to account from authorizing. In the recall ballot, voters were asked two questions: First, should Davis be recalled? Second, which of a list of candidates should replace him if he is recalled? The first question allows voters to sanction (pro or con) Davis for his performance in office; the second question allows voters to authorize a replacement should the sanction be a negative one. By not moving to the second question if the first one is answered positively, the ballot also illustrates that a positive sanction for past activity can be equivalent to an authorization for future representation.

[36] *Wesberry v. Sanders*, 376 U.S. 1, 1964 FindLaw, at 1–52.

[37] See Chapter 2 for details. To understand why voluntary constituencies would maximize the power of a vote, and to read about a terrific development, see Thomas Pogge, "Self-Constituting Constituencies to Enhance Freedom, Equality, and Participation in Democratic Procedures," *Theoria*, June 2002: 26–54. On the connection between voluntariness and political equality, see Thomas Christiano, *The Rule of the Many: Fundamental Issues in Democratic Theory* (Boulder, CO: Westview Press, 1996), pp. 219–24.

decide which voters go where, voluntary constituencies would allow individuals to be represented for themselves as they wish.[38]

I assume, then, that an endorsement of political equality and consent leads to an IDP of voluntary constituencies because it maximizes voter equality and allows an additional point of consent into the system. The problem, however, is that voluntary electoral constituencies will tend to be homogeneous, and we will have to decide how committed we should be to these positions. Here, I will argue that our preference for voluntary constituencies is remarkably weak because the appeal to "make votes count" (that is, equalizing the effective power of every voter's vote) is an almost trivial aim and obscures the fact that the very electoral arrangements that purportedly "make votes count" actually make "groups" and "political parties" count for much more.[39] The argument behind "making votes count," then, should be based exclusively on the well-observed disparate aggregative effects on election results of different voting systems and constituency definitions rather than upon a trivial appeal to equal voting power. Similarly, in terms of consent, it matters much more that voters consent to the institutions that govern them than it does that every institution once established be consensual – we do not, for example, think that every citizen must consent to every law passed, but rather that they consent to the system of lawmaking that governs them. Thus it matters far more that a nation consents at the constitutional level to whatever definition is used for its electoral constituencies, because this definition – whether by territory, race, or votes – is far more important than is the enabling of citizens to choose for themselves how they are represented during each election.

The point here, again, is not to argue that voluntary constituencies are not preferable – they are. Rather, it is to show that this preference is a weak one, in anticipation of the fact that voluntary constituencies conflict with permanent, heterogeneous constituencies. Thus, the endorsement of involuntary constituencies will be premised on the admittedly harder argument that voluntariness as a desideratum of constituency design is a weak goal, which is the purpose of this section.

8.4.1 On Political Equality

Most accounts of political equality start with the assumption (or fully stated argument) that the state should treat individuals as if they were morally equal,

---

[38] By contrast to territorial districts, most forms of proportional representation involve voluntary constituencies; voters can choose to be represented as a member of the Labor Party by voting for the Labor Party. But as I noted in Chapter 2, the concept of constituency need not be collapsed with voting; constituencies may be completely voluntary and independent of the act of voting. Indeed, given our discussion about the need for stability between elections, there is good reason to prefer the formation of constituencies prior to elections, with voters only then voting on a particular candidate or party once the constituency is formed.

[39] For a treatment of electoral rule effects on voting outcomes, see Gary W. Cox, *Making Votes Count* (New York: Cambridge University Press, 1997).

either because they really are morally equal[40] or for other reasons (such as efficiency, utility, or stability).[41] This leads to the claim that barring some other compelling reason, citizens should share equally in the state's political power, the basic unit of which is the vote. Thus from the standard of "one person, one vote" emerges the concern with equalizing and maximizing the expression of those votes.

A standard of "equal voting power" begs the question, how does one measure that power in order to equalize it? Since there are no markets in votes to set a financial amount to them, the power of a single vote has been cast by both normative and empirical authors as its probability of affecting the outcome of an election.[42] Thus, various voting systems might be valued based on how valuable the system makes all votes (that is, how likely it is that an individual vote will be decisive in the outcome of an election). This formulation of equal voting power is explicit in the literature on voting systems where "wasted votes" – votes cast that do not contribute to a candidate's success[43] – have become a pox on the house of democracy.[44] The aversion to "wasted votes" is likely explained by a

---

[40] As Jeremy Waldron notes, most contemporary writers focusing on equality look toward its implications rather than presenting any complete argument about the foundations of this equality. Jeremy Waldron, *God, Locke, and Equality: Christian Foundations in Locke's Political Thought* (Cambridge, UK: Cambridge University Press, 2002), pp. 1–4. I suspect this is only in part because foundational equality of individuals has become a commonplace, and a philosopher would have to pretend to be a "weirdo" (to use Waldron's technical term) not to accept it. Another reason, indicated previously, is that an endorsement of the implications of equality need not presume that people really are morally equal, it need only treat them *as if* they were. Thus, a focus on policy outcomes can simply assert the position of moral equality without argument because the argument may not be critical. Of course, this is just conjecture here and would require far more evidence.

[41] See, for example, Isaiah Berlin's claim that "One can perfectly well conceive of a society organized on Benthamite or Hobbesian line … in which the principle of 'every man to count for one' was rigorously applied for utilitarian reasons." Isaiah Berlin, *Concepts and Categories*, ed. Henry Hardy (Princeton, NJ: Princeton University Press, 1999), p. 81, quoted in Waldron *God, Locke, and Equality*, p. 14. Contra Waldron, this is not "hopelessly confused," nor does it derive utilitarianism from the principle of "every man to count for one." Utilitarianism counts every man for one because that is a useful way of counting – other ways would lead to worse outcomes. Rather, it is a statement that *even if* there are no deeper arguments for the principle of equality, a society may nevertheless treat its members in a way that appears to reflect some foundational basis for the principle of equality despite there being none.

[42] See Robert A. Dahl, *A Preface to Democratic Theory* (Chicago: University of Chicago Press, 1956); Rawls, *A Theory of Justice*, p. 223. Dahl applies the equal power standard more generally to collective decisions taken.

[43] The literature on voting systems generally treats wasted votes only as "losing votes." However, the reason they are "wasted votes" according to the definition given in this literature is that they did not contribute to the success of a candidate. By that standard, we should count losing votes plus those cast for a winner in excess of what was necessary to win as wasted. Cox rightly notes this conceptual point and treats it accordingly. Cox, *Making Votes Count*. Notice, though, that in single-member districts, since only one vote is ever necessary to elect a candidate, all votes but one are wasted.

[44] Most prominent supporters of proportional systems extol as its virtue the fact that it will reduce wasted votes. Formal theorists, such as Cox, assume this also to be the case. For a small sample, see Douglass Amy, *Real Voices New Choices* (New York: Columbia University Press, 1993);

deep commitment to political equality and consent: Voters whose votes are not cast for winners (or in excess of what the winner needed to win) did not have equal vote shares, and political representation that lacks full consent may not be legitimate (or fair).

Normative theorists are generally more nuanced in their treatment of political equality, noticing that, depending on what one means by "political equality," very different outcomes and institutional arrangements will emerge. In his sustained treatment of the topic, Charles Beitz more usefully distinguishes between three kinds of equality, each of which may conflict with the other: equal political power (one person, one vote); equal opportunity of electoral success; and equal opportunity of legislative success. For example, while it is true that individual African Americans have no less power at the voting booth than individual whites anywhere in the United States, the effects of voting equality are substantially altered if they are grouped such that they will never elect a candidate of their own choosing.[45] More recently, Ronald Dworkin has similarly appreciated the nuance of the concept of political equality, arguing *against* the principle of political equality as equal voting power.[46] Falling under what he calls a "detached conception of democracy," the principle must be rejected, but only because of other more important "dependent" kinds of equality.[47] Even where it is rejected in favor of other conceptions of equality, equal voting power is treated as an important value not to be easily rejected.

By contrast, I suggest that in large constituencies, equal voting power is virtually unimportant, because the very power that is said to be equalized – the likelihood of affecting the outcome of an election – is infinitesimally small. And generally, the importance of equal distribution of any power or good is directly proportional to the value of that power itself.

Before illustrating this, I want to emphasize that there are other reasons to favor the distributions of vote shares, reasons that are not captured by the mantra "make votes count." There are important symbolic effects of the state extending "equal vote shares" to all adults as a reflection of the equal respect with which it and the community should hold every citizen. Nor does the present argument deny that in the aggregate, different vote weights will matter quite a bit (an unoriginal point to which we will return later). The argument that advocates promote to "make votes count," however, is not based on either of these arguments; it is supported instead by the claim that more voluntary electoral choices give individuals a greater (and thus more equal) voice in the political process. It is this last, consequentialist justification for equal voting shares that I think is trivial.

Cox, *Making Votes Count*; Lani Guinier, *The Tyranny of the Majority: Fundamental Fairness in Representative Democracy* (New York: Free Press, 1994).

[45] Charles Beitz, *Political Equality* (Princeton, NJ: Princeton University Press, 1989), p. 8.

[46] Ronald Dworkin, *Sovereign Virtue* (Cambridge, MA: Harvard University Press, 2000), Chapter 4, "Political Equality."

[47] Dworkin argues against a more nuanced version of the condition stated here, extending into equality of political influence. But the condition of political equality as stated here captures the essence if not the complexity of his argument. It is importantly similar to that of Beitz.

To make this argument, let me begin with an analogy. Imagine tomorrow the government announces a cash distribution program in which some of its citizens will receive a payment of some fixed amount and others will receive one hundred times that amount. (We can stipulate that the government will arbitrarily assign who gets which amount.) We can assert that it really was an unjustified, unequal distribution of income. How important would this violation of equality (and by assertion justice) be?

The answer would depend almost exclusively on how much money was actually allocated.[48] If, for example, the government's plan were to distribute $10,000 to some individuals, but $1,000,000 to others, then we would very likely raise this objection: The distribution is unfair because it gives some individuals unequal financial power for no good reason. It is a violation of a standard of equal treatment.

Now consider what our objection would be were the government to give one-one hundredth of a cent to some and a penny to others. Proportionally, the situation is exactly the same in terms the equal distribution of shares: Some individuals are being given one hundred times (gasp!) the financial power of others. But the claim that the plan was objectionable *because* it gave individuals "unequal financial shares" is ridiculous. It would remain an objectionable distribution plan because it violates a standard of equality; it just would not be *that* objectionable on any claim tied to a need for equal financial power.

In large elections, even where proportional representation is used, the parallel between the financial and political case is very close: The likelihood that a voter's vote will ever affect the outcome of an election – the standard upon which the "one person, one vote" standard is based – is infinitesimally small.[49] How important, then, is a violation of equality in which I have a .00001 chance of deciding the outcome of an election but another voter has a .001 chance?[50] In theory, this constitutes a huge violation – that another citizen has one hundred times the political power I do. But a hundred times nothing (or almost nothing) is also nothing (or very close to it). Put differently, before we try to "make votes count," we ought to remember that they don't count for much in the first place.[51]

---

[48] We will return to this condition later.

[49] It won't even help to revise this usual account away from a likelihood of deciding the outcome to the desire that we should all contribute equally – or in Dahl's formulation, "the preference of each member is assigned an equal value." For if I am one of three hundred thousand voters even in a very close ten-way race, my vote will not amount to more than one-thirty-thousandth of the decision and probably less. Nothing in the decision would have changed had I not voted at all.

[50] The fact that people vote at all given the very low value of actually voting is a problem that has resisted solving unless one turns to other kinds of motivations than the value of an actual vote. For one example, see Howard Margolis, *Selfishness, Altruism and Rationality: A Theory of Social Choice* (Chicago: University of Chicago Press, 1984). My question comes directly out of that literature – if a single vote has no effective power, why exactly is it so important to equalize?

[51] As with the financial example, if you distributed vote shares such that some individuals had a real chance to determine the outcome of an election but others did not, that would constitute a violation of this norm. In small constituencies, this is more likely the case if vote shares

Finally, the notion that we should value our ability to "make our vote count" in terms of increasing the likelihood that our individual vote would actually be decisive in an election is an oddly undemocratic virtue. Why should we design systems whose value is to increase the likelihood that everyone can be a dictator over a communal choice? The standard is indeed odd.

From the standpoint of "making votes count," a standpoint purportedly emerging from one norm of political equality, voluntary constituencies form an IDP but one that is particularly weak and unimportant *as long as no vote is likely to affect the outcome of an election*. While allowing voters to choose how they are represented for the purpose of political representation would help equalize the weight of all votes, it is a trivial aim given the insignificance of the equalized good.

8.4.2 Consenting to the System Rather Than Within It

Previously I stated that the importance of the violation would depend almost exclusively on how much money was actually allocated. Why else might we object to the distribution of unequal shares? The answer, both obvious and unoriginal, is that a harm may arise in the aggregate were the state to allocate those small amounts in a way that amounted to real power to one group over another. Returning to the financial claim, if 200 million Sneetches received one penny each but one million Loraxes received only one-one hundredth of a cent, the Sneetches' collective buying power would be increased by $2 million, while the Loraxes increased their collective buying power by only $100.[52] In the political case, using the example from the early U.S. apportionment cases, if rural voters have a twenty-five times greater chance than urban voters to affect the outcome of an election, then, proportionally, "rural" interests will get twenty-five times more weight in the legislature thanks to a definition of constituency that was fixed and unchanged.

The real problem, to continue this unoriginal point, comes from aggregating these insignificant amounts together. If they are aggregated such that distinct groups benefit and others suffer, then the effect of aggregation and not individual inequality itself would be the relevant issue of political power. Thus, the relevant objection to unequal voting power does not apply at the level of the individual, but rather at the level of the group. The questions to be asked are, who gets to determine how votes are aggregated and correspondingly, what groups will benefit from this aggregation. This is just another way of asking who gets to define how electoral constituencies are defined and which voting rules are established once constituencies are defined. This is why the concern

---

are unequal; thus did I condition the argument on applying only in large constituencies and stipulated the real-world conditions that all votes are extraordinarily unlikely to affect the outcome of an election.

[52] The reference is to Dr. Seuss, *Sneetches and Other Stories* (New York: Random House, 1989). I thank Hoben Greenberg Rehfeld for help with this example.

for "making votes count" is simply a call to "make parties count," begging the question, "which parties?" For these reasons, it matters far more that citizens collectively agree to the way that they are defined for representation than it does that constituencies themselves be voluntary.

There are two points at which consent can enter into the question of constituency definition: when a nation determines how to structure its electoral system; or when building into the system more places for ongoing consent. In general, I take it to be a commonplace that if consent theory legitimizes states, it must do so at least at the level of consenting to the institutional design whether or not it includes ongoing points of consent. Compare one case in which a thoughtful citizenry deliberates and decides to use territorial constituencies for representation with a second, in which a crafty dictator (or partisan legislature) dictates that individuals will be allowed to decide voluntarily how to be represented. It seems rather clear that the first case is very much a candidate for being legitimate; the second probably not despite the fact that it has more internal institutions that embody consent.

Two points follow from this discussion of consent. First, as a principle for constituency definition, we should reject constituency plans whereby a few people decide how votes are aggregated, because this decision effectively gives those few people nontrivially greater voting power than other citizens. This means establishing constituency definitions at the level of the constitutional order. Second, as a desideratum of constituency design, voluntary constituencies are one of many that, while marginally preferable because they allow greater individual consent, may very easily be rejected if other plans are more compelling.

From the preceding discussion, we can summarize the important points about vote equality and vote aggregation. First, where the actual value of a vote is extremely small, nonbiased distribution of votes is more important than vote equality. If biased distribution of unequal votes is unjust, it is for either of two reasons, neither of which is due to inequalities of individual voting power. First, if the distribution of votes maps onto voting patterns, bias skews voting decisions. But unbiased distribution of infinitesimally small voting power can also have citizenship or prejudicial effects even when it has no political consequences. Arguments for equal vote shares are thus comprehensible only from these two familiar considerations of group aggregation and what have been called "citizenship effects" but not because people should have equal power to affect outcomes. When the good to be equalized is infinitesimally small, it is an almost meaningless consideration.

Vote aggregation thus becomes the more important issue, and involves not only electoral rules but an explicit definition of constituency. Because these are more fundamental concerns than should be governed by ordinary legislation, we should conclude that any plan of constituency definition ought to be made constitutional, that is, requiring a higher level of acceptance by a polity and then governing the representative institutions that are created. Legitimate representation thus requires citizen consent to whatever method of constituency definition is to govern vote aggregation within a polity.

As a principle for constituency definition, we should reject constituency plans whereby a few people decide how votes are aggregated because this effectively gives those people greater voting power. Instead, constituency plans should allow either a nonbiased (in reference to outcomes) aggregation rule, or full voter autonomy to decide where the vote is aggregated. Alternatively, as I have said, it should allow citizens to alienate this right only at a fundamental level of political society. In terms of an IDP, we can say then that while voluntary constituencies are in fact an IDP, they are easily trumped by appeals to other values of political equality and by the placement of the definition of constituency at the level of the constitutional order.[53]

The upshot of all this is to undermine the strength of arguments that certain electoral systems should be chosen in order to avoid wasting individual votes. If there were no institutional costs to be paid, we could certainly choose a system in which we each select our own electoral constituency, either by our own choice or using some form of proportional representation (PR). But there are institutional costs to be paid because voluntary constituencies are inconsistent with permanent, heterogeneous ones, for reasons discussed in Chapter 2 a point to which we will return at the close of this chapter.

8.5 HETEROGENEOUS CONSTITUENCIES: PLURALISM, REPUBLICANISM, AND THE ASSUMPTION OF SOCIAL COOPERATION

The final limiting condition of legitimate political representation presumed that legitimate political representatives should act in accordance with "proper" substantive aims. They should not, for example, act "improperly." This sounds trivial as stated. But even without an agreed-upon account of legitimate political representation that would define what counted as "proper" activity, we can say more than this, based on two plausible claims about what "proper" might mean in this context.

First, I presume that any activity will be deemed "proper" largely, if not exclusively, by reference to whether it furthers the aim or function of the particular representative body in which the representative is acting.[54] Given our focus on a national legislature, this means that the "properness" of a representative's activity will be based on how well or poorly it achieves the aims of a national representative body, and thus, as I argued in Chapter 7, how well or poorly the activity promotes the national good. Second, given the historical debates on

---

[53] See Rawls, *A Theory of Justice*, p. 223, where he argues for the establishment of unbiased districting rules at the level of the constitutional order. Rawls assumes that constituencies will be territorial.

[54] For more on "function" and political representation, see section 7.1.1.

political representation, there are broadly two different ways a representative might plausibly act to pursue this good: either as an advocate for the representative's constituents' particular interests or as an impartial deliberator to discover the national good. From these two observations, I argue, emerges an IDP of constituencies that look like the nation they collectively represent because only then can a representative act in pursuit of both goals simultaneously.

8.5.1 The Assumption of Social Cooperation and a Public Good

Political representation is a weak public good that assumes a fair amount of social cooperation among the collective for which it is enacted. The existence of representative institutions for any length of time indicates that there is enough stability for elections to be held, meeting rooms to be secured, and, more generally, a legislature that creates law that a society actually follows. When social cooperation does not underlie representative institutions, political institutions either cease to function (for example, the U.S. government during its Civil War or, arguably, the Continental Congress under the Articles of Confederation), or are simply ineffective because they are ignored (for example, arguably the United Nations). Thus, to speak of functioning representative government is to presume a fair amount of underlying social cooperation.

In addition to indicating a fair amount of social cooperation, functioning institutions of representation indicate a collective purpose – a shared aim, even if that shared aim is extremely narrow. For example, consider labor negotiations in which representatives from union and management meet to negotiate a contract. The existence of the meeting is evidence that there is a fair amount of social cooperation between the groups, enough so that they are not on strike or refusing to negotiate. Similarly, even though each side may have contrasting particular aims (increase wages versus reduce costs), the existence of the meeting is evidence that there is at least one collective aim: getting a job contract signed. Indeed, getting the contract signed was the function of this case of representation. The same goes for any case of functioning representative government: There is a fair amount of social cooperation and a common purpose toward which that cooperation aims, even if individuals and groups, like parties to the labor contract, have very different and conflicting aims.

The underlying social cooperation and unity of purpose is, however, merely a descriptive fact about representative government, but does not assume that this cooperation was brought about properly or that the shared purpose is a good one. The government of South Africa under Apartheid was highly functioning and relatively longstanding but bought at a price of injustice and violence. And even where social cooperation is very high, the aims may be deplorable, as in Nazi Germany. But this example demonstrates that the mere existence of representative institutions is evidence of a fair amount of underlying social cooperation – however achieved – and a common purpose – whether noble or ignoble – toward which that cooperation aims.

8.5.2 Pluralism and Republicanism

Since the function of a representative body comprises the collective efforts of the individual representatives, any account of what constitutes their "proper" activity must, then, justify that activity based on its contribution to the shared purpose or common good of the institution. No one reasonably argues otherwise that the role of representative institutions is to harm the collective of which it is a part. Even the argument that representatives ought to be fierce advocates for their own constituencies is justified only by reference to the collective good; the public good, so some forms of "pluralism" have it, emerges collectively out of such partisan clashes within the legislature, a point we will develop momentarily.

In conceptual terms, a representative will fall between two poles: On one side, she may be a completely partisan advocate of her constituents' interests; on the other side, she may advocate for the greater good without special preference for what will make her constituents' better off.[55] In more contemporary terms, the contrast between these two poles is represented by the pluralist and republican models of politics applied to political representation. Pluralism claims that the public good emerges from trade-offs made in the legislature between representatives advocating on behalf of their constituents' interests, a model best articulated by David Truman and Robert Dahl that arguably fits with parts of John Stuart Mill's theory of representative government.[56] By contrast, the republican model of politics emphasizes the role of the representative as deliberator within the national representative assembly, a position that has been taken up by a number of recent authors, perhaps most clearly by Philip Pettit and Cass Sunstein.[57] The republican position links back to the thought of Edmund Burke and James Madison.[58] The public good emerges from deliberation of representatives who bring to the table information and perspectives (or in the

---

[55] These are not mutually exclusive, as when, for example, a representative's constituents are interested in the general good.

[56] Dahl, *A Preface to Democratic Theory*; David Truman, *The Govermental Process: Political Interests and Public Opinion* (New York: Knopf, 1953); John Stuart Mill, *Considerations on Representative Government* (Amherst, NY: Prometheus, 1991 [1861]). For an account of Mill as an advocacy theorist, see Nadia Urbinati, *Mill on Democracy: From the Athenian Polis to Representative Government* (Chicago: University of Chicago Press, 2002).

[57] Philip Pettit, *Republicanism: A Theory of Freedom and Government* (New York: Oxford University Press, 1997); Cass Sunstein, "Preferences and Politics," *Philosophy and Public Affairs*, 20, no. 1, Winter 1991: 3–34.

[58] Edmund Burke, *Reflections on the Revolution in France*, ed. J. G. A. Pocock (Indianapolis, IN: Hackett, 1987); James Madison, *The Federalist*, ed. Jacob E. Cooke, Essay 10 (Middletown, CT: Wesleyan University Press, 1961 [1787–8]). The claim that Madison is a republican seems widely accepted by historians who have long ago rejected Dahl's reading of him in 1956. Within political science, however, Madison is regularly and mistakenly portrayed as an originator of pluralism, thus perpetuating Dahl's mistake (based as it was on Charles Beard's resurrection of the essay after 125 years of neglect). For more, see the discussion of Madison in Chapter 1.

terms discussed previously, "hard" and "soft" knowledge) of their particular constituency but are free enough to change their positions based on the result of deliberation. The constituency thus may be a source of information, but also provides a check on representative's activity through the prospect of reelection – a point we will return to in a moment.

I should deviate briefly from the present discussion to distinguish the pluralist/republican distinction from another familiar distinction: whether representatives should be delegates or trustees of their constituencies, a distinction that speaks to how independent from (trustee) or how bound to (delegate) the opinions and dictates of his constituents a representative must be. I want to differentiate clearly this delegate/trustee distinction as a second, epistemic one different from the pluralist/republican distinction, because whether a representative pursues the public good independently (republican) or advocates for his constituents' interests (pluralist) is conceptually distinct from the source of his knowledge about what the common good or his constituents' interests entail. A representative committed to the "republican" pursuit of the national interest may act very closely to what his constituents take to be the national interest.[59] Similarly, a representative acting under the "pluralist" model, may completely ignore what his constituents think is in their best interest, independently advocating for legislation that he believes is in their true interests (but not necessarily the collective's).

The result is that any representative's activity may be defined on a two-dimensional space that places him in terms of his republican/pluralist proclivities, on the one hand, and on the extent to which he takes his constituents as the source of his information or not. The four quadrants of this space and examples are listed in Table 8.3.

The upper-left and bottom-right cells in the table are perhaps the most familiar examples. When representation is seen as advocacy for constituent interests (that is, pluralism), the relationship is most often framed in terms of delegation – representatives should advocate the interests of their constituents *as their constituents define them*. Similarly, when representation is seen as deliberation about the public good (that is, republicanism), the relationship between representatives and their constituents is most often framed in terms of trusteeship – representatives should be freed from constituent demands in order to deliberate about the public good. But as the table illustrates, we can well imagine representatives as trustee pluralists (lower-left cell) who believe they should advocate for their constituents' interests *as the representatives view those interests*. Similarly, we can imagine delegate republicans (upper-right cell) who believe they

---

59 It might seem that because the republican view includes deliberation as part of it, the representative will require a higher level of independence. But this is not quite right: We could imagine the representative deliberating in good faith as he believes his constituents' would, rather than as he believes he should. They may change their minds for different reasons than he, and thus we could imagine the mandated deliberator fully capable of meeting the republican standards of activity.

TABLE 8.3. *The Distinction between "Pluralist/Republican" Views of Representation and "Delegate/Trustee" Views of Representative Responsibility*

	Pluralist Activity: Aiming at the Partial Interests of One's Constituents		Republican Activity: Aiming at the Common Good	
	Conceptual Description	Example	Conceptual Description	Example
Representatives as Delegates: bound closely to the dictates of one's constituents.	A representative who advocates for the narrow interests of her constituency, *as her constituents define it.*	A representative pushes to increase public spending in her district because *that's what her constituents believe would be beneficial to them.*	A representative who aims at the public good *as her constituents define it.*	A representative advocates for increased spending on emergency relief that will primarily aid nonconstituent members, because *that's what her constituents believe would be best for the nation.*
Representatives as Trustees: acting based on the representative's own independent assessment of what is best.	A representative who advocates for the narrow interests of her constituency, *as the representative defines it.*	A representative pushes to increase public spending in her district because *that's what the representative believes would be best for her constituency.*	A representative who aims at the public good *as the representative defines it.*	A representative advocates for increased spending on emergency relief that will primarily aid nonconstituent members of the public, *because that's what the representative believes would be best for the nation.*

should deliberate about the public good *as their constituents' instructed them to do so.*

Although the labels of "delegate" and "trustee" are conceptually different, and any complete account of legitimate political representation will quite plausibly argue for one side or the other, neither will have any effect on whether a constituency ought to be more or less heterogeneous.

Returning then to the salient pluralist/republican issue, any theory of legitimate political representation will specify where on the continuum between pluralism and republicanism a representative should be, thus specifying whether "proper activity" involves "constituent advocacy," "advocacy for the public good," or some position in between the two. Second, the justification for any particular point on the continuum will be in reference to how it helps promote the common good. We can now propose that only constituencies that look like the nation they collectively represent would provide the right kind of incentives or otherwise enhance a representative's ability to act toward the public good, no matter which side of the republican/pluralist continuum emerges as the legitimate one. Because of this congruence, high heterogeneity emerges as an IDP: The electoral constituency should be demographically identical to the nation it constitutes.

Why does high heterogeneity – or looking like the nation it represents – emerge from the pluralist/republican dichotomy? Let's consider how political representatives under both pluralist and republican models would act if they were elected from constituencies that looked like the nation as a whole. First, under the pluralist model, when a representative advocated for the good of his constituency he would, by definition, be advocating for the good of the whole. Consistent with the pluralist model, he serves as an advocate for the interests of his constituents, but now his constituents are not easily defined by any particularity except that they share the common fate of the nation in which they all live. This IDP thus forces any pluralist who thinks that the public good will emerge from a battle of interest group advocacy in the legislature – whether territorial, economic, racial, or party ID – to justify a move to whatever particularity he thinks would more reliably enhance public welfare. It will force him to give an account that moves beyond the paean to advocacy representation, and more clearly to what interests should be advocated. And it will help make clear that representative advocacy need not assume interest groups united around any similarity beyond being members of the same nation.

Now consider that under the republican model, representatives who served constituencies that looked like the nation they collectively represented would face the right kinds of electoral incentives for a republican to deliberate freely about the public good. The most effective way of providing electoral incentives to work for the public good is to have those who hold the representative to account for his actions be the very collective toward whose good he purportedly aims. Thus with a heterogeneous constituency, the republican model would depend even less on there being "virtuous" representatives to deliberate on behalf of the common good. Heterogeneous constituencies instead structure electoral incentives so that representatives get a greater benefit from acting as if they are really concerned with the public good, whether or not they really are. It is a tactic taken directly from Madison's theory of political representation.[60]

How exactly would these incentives work? Facing any constituency, whether or not heterogeneous, a representative would always be constrained by how deep (strength of feeling) and broad (numbers who hold a view) her constituency's views on a particular topic were. In cases where the majority is wide but not deep, she may be able to shift constituents' opinion by providing them reasons to support what she believes would be in their collective good. Furthermore, she will be mightily constrained not to act upon positions that her constituency widely and deeply holds. That does not mean she cannot go against them, but it means that going against them increases the risk of electoral failure.

When constituencies look like the nation as a whole, it is hard to see why these kinds of incentives are not exactly the right kinds of incentives for her – or pluralist representatives – to have. Admittedly, this will enhance the power of majorities within the legislature: If a nation has a strong and clear position on some issue, legislation would reflect this fact. But if one is committed to democratic self-rule, it is unclear what good reasons there can ever be for allowing minority views to be adopted or granted authority in the legislature simply on the basis that they are minority views. Indeed, the best reason for going with what a minority wants may again be epistemic. In a particular case, they may be better suited to know what's best for them or the collective. But such a position is not a plea for minority rights. It is rather evidence that the majority is uneducated and might not be suited for democratic rule.

Even other plausibly good reasons for letting minorities win fail. Consider a concern for stability: Unless a permanent minority gets its way now and then, society will be terribly destabilized. To which we can say, if the majority finds this to be a compelling reason for supporting their legislation, then, the minority, having persuaded the majority, should get its way. Of course, minority rights are, as a matter of justice, in need of safeguards. But, as Jeremy Waldron has well argued, someone will have to determine what these rights consist in prior to their being protected.[61] And it seems more plausible in terms of legitimacy that majorities should specify these minority rights. This means, of course, that the trampling of minority rights is a fundamental risk of democratic government (a point perhaps even more unoriginal than the earlier ones about political equality).

In Chapter 9, I consider other problems that attend to enhancing the power of majorities within democratic societies, including the important problem that such majority-controlled constituencies would create legislatures that lack any meaningful voice for minorities. But as a theoretical matter, it extends Waldron's call to appreciate the virtue of majority rule, and more broadly the "dignity

---

[60] See Chapters 2 and 5.

[61] Jeremy Waldron, "Precommitment and Disagreement," in *Constitutionalism: Philosophical Foundations*, ed. Larry Alexander (Cambridge, UK: Cambridge University Press, 1998), pp. 271–99.

of legislation,"[62] something that seems of late to have been lost in critically important concerns for group and cultural rights. Indeed, the great fear of uncontrolled majority tyranny has left us perhaps too sensitive to the idea that a national will ought to be somewhere, somehow, formally expressed within the legislature. If the legislature ought to represent the people as a nation, it ought to represent them as a collective, with their majorities formed and unformed as they are.

This is not to defend the unbridled use of majority rule as a just or unproblematic institution. The point, again, is to outline a default position against which the relaxing of majority rule must be argued. The endorsement of constituencies that are highly heterogeneous, looking like the nation they collectively represent, emerges as a default position. It depends on not taking a substantive position on the pluralist/republican debate. But even if one takes a position of advocacy of particular interests within the nation as a way to get at the common good, one must justify this move to particularity against the IDP of heterogeneous constituencies.

8.6 CONCLUSION

The argument of this chapter was that the IDP for electoral constituencies in legitimate political systems should be permanent, heterogeneous, and voluntary. Of the three, the strongest claim was for permanence, since permanent constituencies make the most sense toward achieving the end of self-rule. Heterogeneity was preferred because it, rather than homogeneity, was the only constituency definition consistent with both pluralist and republican models of how political representatives should act. But it was less strong a default position than that of permanence, because, presumably, a theory of legitimacy, justice, or context will dictate both how a representative should act and what kinds of particularity (if any) he should pursue. And while we endorsed a default position in favor of voluntariness, it was of trivial importance for reasons connected to the trivial power of any single vote.

I conclude here by repeating the problem first noted in Chapter 2: Any constituency that is in fact voluntary (defined by individual voters who choose how they will be represented) is likely to change over time and is unlikely to be heterogeneous. Thus I conclude that a coherent default position for electoral constituencies would be one that was permanent, heterogeneous, and involuntary, though approved of at the constitutional level.

In more familiar terms, a heterogeneous, permanent, involuntary constituency is one into which voters are placed according to a constitutionally written definition, for their entire lives, such that each individual constituency looks like the nation it collectively represents. In the next chapter, we will discuss how to construct such an electoral constituency and speculate about what politics might look like under such an arrangement.

---

[62] Jeremy Waldron, *The Dignity of Legislation* (New York: Cambridge University Press, 1999).

8.7 CODA: TERRITORY REVISITED

In Chapter 7, I raised questions about using territorial constituencies. Given the IDP developed here, how well does territory fare?

8.7.1 Stability

Our default position favored electoral constituencies that remained stable in order to make democratic self-rule coherent. As such, territorial constituencies fare better than some other arrangements, but with their decennial line changes, and the fact that moving out of a constituency undoes its permanence, territorial constituencies may be too unstable to make coherent the virtues of democratic self-rule.

8.7.2 Voluntariness

By the very weak standard of political equality and consent, we said that constituencies ought to be more voluntary than less. Territory is more voluntary than some other plans because people can theoretically move, but, as we noted in Chapter 7, the costs to individuals are too high to make this a truly consensual constituency plan, and households rather than individuals are treated as the unit of consent. Furthermore, because third parties change territorial lines every ten years, the value of voluntariness within territorial systems is minimized further: I can move into one district this year, only to find myself in a different district after apportionment. Given that other constituency plans – such as those of proportional representation – involve regular consenting to how a vote is counted, territorial representation faces a strike against it in the absence of some other justifying action.

But voluntariness also described whether the plan had been endorsed at a constitutional level. Given the particular case of the United States, the use of territorial constituencies is not particularly compelling because of the silence with which territoriality has been treated at the level of the constitutional order. There simply has been no real debate that territorial constituencies are the proper way to define constituencies, and the regular wrangling of state legislatures around this issue shows the need for standards at the constitutional level. The idea again is that for political representation itself to be legitimate, the manner in which votes are counted must be agreed to by citizens or at least be a known part of the law because it defines the terms by which citizens are represented and thus they – and not third parties, let alone third parties with vested interests – should decide how their votes should be aggregated.

8.7.3 Homogeneity

Territorial constituencies can be more or less homogenous depending on how interests are defined and how territorially segregated these interests are. We observed in Chapters 2 and 7 that territory may be a good proxy for nonterritorial interest representation only when nonterritorial interests are spatially concentrated. At the one extreme, "gender interests" simply cannot practically be separated by territorial lines. At the other, "neighbor interests" simply cannot be avoided by territorial lines, just in case "neighbor" means "live next to one another"; such interests are definable, and the line can be as thin as a single row of homes.

Against the IDP of heterogeneity, territory fares better in some cases and worse in others depending on the context. But in general terms, harkening back to Madison's argument in *Federalist 10*,[63] the larger the territorial district, the more likely it is to be heterogeneous around any descriptive feature, and the greater incentives representatives will have to frame their activity away from any partial view and toward the good of all.

[63] See Chapter 1.

9

Random Constituencies

9.1 INTRODUCTION AND CHAPTER OVERVIEW

A legislature, John Adams argued in 1776, "should be an exact portrait, in miniature, of the people at large, as it should think, feel, reason and act like them."[1] Over two centuries later, this call for "mirror representation" works most effectively as a critique: How can a legislature of mostly white men, for example, possibly represent the wide interests and perspectives of a diverse population? Of course, it is more problematic to specify which other features of the whole ought to be added. As Pitkin noted, few would want a legislature that looked like a nation in terms of reflecting, for example, its average "intelligence, public spiritedness, and experience."[2] Still, the concern for mirror representation has led to legislatures that are more deliberatively heterogeneous in ways that seem reasonable, even necessary to the proper function of representative bodies. In the United States, for example, territorial districts are drawn or gerrymandered to ensure the election of minorities and political parties into the legislature. In France, throughout Latin America, and most recently in Afghanistan, democracies are experimenting with gender quota laws that would increase the number of women in the candidate pool and legislature. And the move to proportional representation has been justified by its ability to elect a legislature that is a clearer reflection of the nation's underlying ideological and political views. In short, the "politics of presence," as Anne Phillips has called it, is gaining traction as an endorsed principle of institutional design.[3]

---

[1] John Adams, "Thoughts on Government," in *American Political Writing during the Founding Era: 1760–1805*, vol. 1, eds. Charles S. Hyneman and Donald S. Lutz (Indianapolis, IN: Liberty Press, 1776), pp. 401–9.

[2] Hanna Fenichel Pitkin, *The Concept of Representation* (Berkeley, CA: University of California Press, 1967), p. 76.

[3] "Politics of presence" is from Anne Phillips, *The Politics of Presence* (New York: Oxford University Press, 1995). For a subtle development, see Robert E. Goodin, "Representing Diversity," *British Journal of Political Science* 34, no. 3, July 2004: 453–68.

Whether for or against, the debate about mirror or descriptive representation has focused on the benefits of creating a *legislature* that shares certain features of the nation it represents. In this chapter, I consider instead what would happen were national electoral constituencies defined to look like the nation they collectively represented. This inquiry emerges directly from the discussion of Chapter 8, where I argued that legitimate political representation created a default position in favor of heterogeneous, permanent constituencies that were publicly known and constitutionally ratified. To create these electoral constituencies, we would randomly divide the population into separate electoral constituencies, thus creating demographically identical electoral constituencies from which representatives to the legislature would be elected. Inverting the tradition of mirror representation, electoral constituencies would thus each look like the nation they collectively represented.

In this chapter, I take a step forward and present a speculative discussion of what politics might look like were these constituencies to replace the territorial districts now used for representation in the U.S. House of Representatives. Far from being merely a default position – as we described it in Chapter 8 – there are good reasons to prefer this plan, reasons that apply to any large, diverse nation. These reasons cast serious justificatory barriers for any electoral plan that involves homogeneous and impermanent constituencies, first among them most systems of proportional and group representation.[4]

The surest and least biased way to create electoral constituencies that look like the nation they collectively represent is to assign each citizen randomly to a separate electoral constituency. These assignments would be permanent (for reasons discussed in section 8.3), changing only as members gained or lost their citizenship rights when they came of age, died, emigrated, immigrated, and so on. These constituencies would be national, and in no way based on where a person lived. Finally, for reasons to be explained momentarily, I assume that each constituency sends one representative to the legislature.[5]

For ease of discussion, in the remainder of this chapter I will refer to the randomized, permanent, national, electoral constituency as the "random constituency." We should not forget that the constituency is also permanent and national.

I will develop this thought experiment as it applies to electing members of the U.S. House of Representatives, considering first how moving from its territorial system to random constituencies would change some features of national politics and, second, taking up some normative problems that would be raised by such a move. In what follows, I hold as much of the institutional landscape unchanged as possible so that the effects of the random constituency may come more clearly into view. This means that electoral constituencies would still elect a single member by plurality vote every two years and that the Senate

---

[4] See Chapter 2.

[5] This assumption could be relaxed; perhaps very large random constituencies would return more than one representative to the legislature, though I will not pursue this option here.

and all other national (and local) political arrangements would function as they do now. Leaving all other institutions intact, we will be able to observe more clearly the dynamic effects of this one change. The need to hold everything else constant is thus a reflection of the complexity of doing fanciful counterfactual analysis, but should not be taken as a judgment pro or con about these other arrangements.

Although the random constituency is developed in the context of the U.S. system, the argument may more generally be applied to any large system of representative government. In cases of often entrenched national party or group conflict, including that of India, Israel, and Iraq,[6] the ideas of this chapter would serve as a provocative and useful way of thinking about the creation of a national legislature that forces subgroups to deal with each other in productive ways. Like the United States, each of these nations exhibits persistent group conflict (though of admittedly different kinds) and designing institutions to reflect existing groups risks reifying group identities and strengths, instead of creating a legislature with built-in institutional incentives to deliberate about the common good. Even more promising would be using random constituencies for a global representative body, though this would be problematic and at present less advisable for a host of reasons that I will not address here.

Given the hoary use of terms like "common good" and "virtue," and given the utopian-sounding innovations discussed in this chapter, I repeat that this discussion is no more or less "idealistic" than any other argument for institutional design. The development of any set of rules to govern a group – whether a constitution for a nation or the bylaws to govern a local parent/teacher organization – can be legitimately justified only by an appeal that those rules (rather than some other rules) facilitate the common good. The argument that random constituencies are preferable because they would more reliably allow the common good to emerge is thus not a particularly distinctive feature of this plan.

The thought experiment that follows is theoretical in four senses of the word. First, sections 9.2 and 9.3 take the form of a set of empirically testable hypotheses that predict how political actors (citizens and representatives) would respond to the random constituency. As with any predictive theory, it will either correctly predict what would happen were random constituencies adopted or its predictions will be mistaken. Given the limits of my knowledge, I would not be surprised if some, perhaps many, of my predictions turned out to be wrong; if I knew which of these were mistaken in advance, I would have written a different account. Still, as a first cut, the discussion can be used as a point of departure for thinking about the implications of the random constituency.

This account is also theoretical in the normative sense. In sections 9.4 and 9.5, I argue that the outcomes I describe in sections 9.2 and 9.3 are endorsable

---

[6] For a discussion of how random constituencies might reshape the politics of Iraq, see David Ciepley, "Taking the Ethnic out of Multiethnic Democracy: Dispersed Constituency Democracy for Iraq," unpublished manuscript, 2003.

ones. This discussion depends less on the accuracy of the predictions I will make, and more on the general value of instituting principles of majority rule, robust democratic deliberation, and the creation of the right sorts of electoral incentives by paying attention to electoral constituency design.

The discussion here is theoretical in a third sense of being informed by the history of political thought. In particular, I self-consciously intend the account to be a contemporary way to institutionalize James Madison's thoughts on defeating factionalism and creating a way, in Jean-Jacques Rousseau's terms, that the will of all might get reliably transformed into the general will of a people. Thus, in my support for heterogeneous electoral districts, I attempt to adapt the argument of *Federalist 10* to contemporary practice. As with Madison, this plan does not assume that representatives will be virtuous, it assumes only that individual politicians want to be reelected and will respond to incentives that emerge out of different electoral arrangements.[7] Similarly, I am concerned with creating a legislature that more closely corresponds and represents the national will (properly conceived) as a way of transforming the will of all into a Rousseauian general will.[8] Of course, the present account is more Madisonian in that it views representation as beneficial to democratic self-rule rather than rejecting it, as Rousseau had.[9]

I won't develop these historical threads any further here. Whether or not I have read Madison or Rousseau correctly, and whether or not this account in fact conforms to their arguments does not matter to whether we think the proposal is endorsable. The historical connections do, however, illustrate how a concern with the history of political thought continues to be relevant to the study of contemporary politics.

The discussion here is theoretical in a final and more colloquial sense: The random constituency is unlikely to be adopted.[10] One reason is that a move to national constituencies of the kind I propose conflicts with calls for group representation, calls that may well be justified in a host of situations. The discussion here allows us to consider what representation of the whole might look like. Indeed, rather than assume that representation is always about the representation of subnational groups (be they territorial, racial, or ideological), I assume the presumption is instead that we can represent the whole, and indeed it is deviations from representation of the whole that must be justified. Thus, any argument in favor of group representation needs to do more than justify why these kinds of groups should receive representation over those kinds of groups; they need also to explain why representing their group's particularity

---

[7] See the discussion in section 7.2.1 for more on the incentive effects of electoral constituencies.

[8] For a superb treatment that explicates Rousseau's tension between the will of all and the general will, see Frank Lovett, "Can Justice Be Based on Consent," *Journal of Political Philosophy* (Oxford, UK: Blackwell Publishing), pp. 79–101, esp. 81–5.

[9] Jean-Jacques Rousseau, *On the Social Contract*, ed. Roger D. Masters, trans. Judith R. Masters (New York: St. Mary's, 1978 [1762]), Book 3, Chapter 15.

[10] Or as Yogi Berra is reported to have said, "In theory there is no difference between theory and practice. In practice there is."

is preferable to representing the whole. Further, in cases where protecting minority groups against the tyranny of the majority is a justification for group representation, we should worry whether the whole can reliably form a democratic society at all, an issue I will raise in more detail later in this chapter. In any case, while this chapter may be read as a policy proposal, it is more usefully treated as a thought experiment to question the prevailing wisdom of increasing electoral homogeneity through group representation of any kind, whether ethnic, racial, or ideological.

This chapter proceeds over four more sections. In section 9.2, I lay out the mechanics of the random constituency, and in section 9.3 I will try to anticipate what political life would look like under such a plan. In section 9.4, I take up issues related to the national interest and the increased majoritarianism that the random constituency would bring about. Issues of heterogeneity or diversity raised in the context of recent deliberative theory are taken up in section 9.5, and I will answer there the objection that, in the United States at least, the random constituency would likely result in a legislature of white males.

9.2 RANDOM CONSTITUENCIES: APPLICATIONS AND RESULTS

In this section, I describe how random constituencies could be established and maintained. Again, I assume we are creating 435 electoral constituencies for the House of Representatives, each one of which elects a single member whether by plurality, majority, or single transferable vote.

The most transparent way of randomizing electoral constituencies is to draw a random number between 1 and 435 (inclusive) for each voter, assigning that voter to the electoral constituency named by whatever number is drawn. The draw might easily take place at the time of voter registration. For example, a voter might register via the Internet and receive his randomly generated constituency assignment, along with detailed instructions for communicating with his representative and fellow constituents through a secured web page.

After the creation of random constituencies for the first time, new citizens (and those who come of age) would be randomly assigned in the same way. All registered voters would have to have "contact" information – whether an e-mail address or a street address – by which their representative could communicate with them. As we will see, in section 9.3, this contact information will play a key role in minimizing the difficulties of campaigning and communication that the random constituency would admittedly create.

Randomizing constituencies in this way will ensure that each district is almost exactly the same size[11]; we can be 95 percent certain that the population of each

---

[11] An alternative method that would secure exact population equality could be used instead, but it would be less transparent and less easily understood: Assign all voters a unique number between 1 and n (where n is the number of the total voting population) and then group voters in $n/435$ increments.

district will be within .1 percent of each other; with 200 million voters, each constituency would have 459,770 members, plus or minus 1327.[12] (As I argued in Chapter 8, even much larger differences in voting power should not worry us if they are created in a nonbiased manner.) Because death rates and emigration rates would be the same over time for each randomly defined constituency, there would be no need to adjust population size regularly, thus eliminating the problems of gerrymandering.

The almost half a million members of any one constituency would be demographically identical to every other, each an exact demographic representation of the nation, each reflecting all of the nation's salient demographic and ideological features. For example, if 10 percent of all Americans live in California, 15 percent are black, and 27 percent are Catholic, then all electoral constituencies would be 10 percent Californian, 15 percent black, and 27 percent Catholic. All groups larger than about five thousand individuals would be represented in every constituency to almost precisely their actual proportion of the population. (Note that the kinds of groups that most people think are relevant to national politics are at least the size of five thousand: African Americans, women, Hispanics, neoconservatives, liberals, Democrats, Republicans, Elks, Greens, Catholics, Reform Jews, and so on.)

Once formed, random constituencies would be permanent. As I argued in Chapter 8, permanent electoral constituencies make sense of what we mean by "democratic self-rule," ensuring temporal continuity between a constituency's authorization of a candidate at the time of first election, the candidate's deliberatively accounting for her actions while in office, and a constituency subsequently holding that candidate to account for her activity when she stands for reelection. To summarize the argument I made in section 8.3, the fact that authorization as a normative matter requires that a representative give reasons for her actions to those who elected her creates the need for a constituency to contain the same members from the moment of authorization (election) up until the moment of the next authorization. Elections, whether they authorize or sanction (or both), are not simply about the future or past. Rather, they ought to be designed to allow for either or both. So, once randomly placed in the seventy-fourth constituency, a voter would always be in the seventy-fourth.[13]

Finally, we will make one additional change and assume that a candidate need not be a member of the particular constituency for which she wishes to

---

[12] Assuming there are 200 million voters and 435 electoral constituencies, the expected value (size of the constituency) is: n * p = 200000000 * 1/435 = 459,770. Under repeated sampling, that will vary (with 95 percent confidence): +/− 1.96 * sqrt (n* p * (1−p)) = +/− 1.96 * sqrt (200000000 * 1/435 * 434/435) = 1327. I thank Andrew Martin for assistance with these equations.

[13] Regulations would have to allow for individuals who leave the country and then return and presumably other conditions – perhaps incarceration – in which voting rights are temporarily rescinded and then reinstated. It seems to me that the permanence of the district would apply to a particular person even under these unusual conditions; upon rejoining the community, the citizen would rejoin his former constituency.

run.[14] So, for example, a member of the 51st could run for a seat in the 286th. This represents less of a change than it might appear to because it simply applies the current logic of the residency requirement to the random constituency. In the United States today, most representatives have to be a member of the particular constituency from which they wish to run for office.[15] This reflects the sentiment that representatives will do a better job representing members of their own district if they are similar to their members along the dimension on which the constituency is defined.[16] The logic can be applied to other constituency definitions: Were constituents defined professionally, we would presumably (though not necessarily) want doctors to represent doctors, maintenance workers to represent maintenance workers, and so on. Since random districts are defined only in terms of being a member of the national whole, we assume that any citizen should be able to run for any seat available, as membership in the 45th constituency is in no substantive or symbolic way different from membership in the 345th constituency.[17] The importance of this change will become clear toward the end of this chapter.

Random constituencies would define a group in which citizens could repeatedly and permanently participate and deliberate about national issues with others who would also be part of that group for life. Place of residence would become only one of the citizen's many interests that would be salient for national political representation. Most importantly, random constituencies would be national, and permanent, each looking like the nation they collectively represented.

9.3 LOGISTICS OF PUBLIC DISCUSSIONS AND CAMPAIGNS: THE INTERNET AS POLITICAL TOOL

If the random constituency were adopted, political life would be transformed in two very basic ways. First, political campaigns would not be able to benefit from

---

[14] This allows the possibility of secure seats for particular groups without the problems that homogeneous constituencies bring about, a possibility taken up in section 9.5.

[15] Constitutionally, representatives need only be residents of the state they serve. State law establishes whether a representative must be a resident of her constituency or not.

[16] The residency requirement also has roots in logistical necessity: Candidates in American colonial government were more reliable representatives of their districts because they knew them firsthand. Or in Montesquieu's words:

One knows the needs of one's own town better than those of other towns and one judges the ability of one's neighbors better than that of one's other compatriots. Therefore members of the legislative body must not be drawn from the body of the nation at large; it is proper for the inhabitants of each principle town to choose a representative from it.

Baron de Charles de Secondat Montesquieu, *The Spirit of the Laws* (New York: Cambridge University Press, 1989 [1748]), P. Book 11, Chapter 4, p. 159. On the origins of the territorial constituency in the United States, see Chapters 3–6.

[17] This is admittedly a much too sketchy account of qualifications for office. See section 9.5, which addresses qualifications for office in greater detail.

the geographical proximity of constituents; similarly, the activity of constituents qua constituents would be hindered by their lack of physical proximity to one another. Second, the random constituency would radically alter the incentives of politicians once in office and therefore alter how they deliberate, vote, and serve their constituents while in office. In this section, I speculate about these changes. Section 9.3.1 considers how the random constituency would affect the activity of ordinary citizens. Next, in section 9.3.2, I consider how random constituencies might affect representative service, campaigns, and political parties. (The random constituency would also greatly increase the power of majorities to dominate in the House of Representatives, a discussion I defer for sections 9.4 and 9.5.)

I repeat again that the following discussion is impressionistic and necessarily partial; any complete account would take a book-length study and perhaps be beside the present point. The sketch here is meant instead to give a better feel for some of the contours of national politics under random constituencies, even if the particulars need much more theoretical clarity and empirical evidence to justify.

9.3.1 Voter Interaction and Deliberation

The costs of any electoral system change will be highest when the system is first adopted. If the costs are surmountable and justified by the long-term results, then these transition costs are not themselves a reason for resisting change. A transition to random constituencies might alienate members of the political community, but we must consider whether these immediate transition effects would be outweighed by long-term gains. In this section, I consider first the transition effects of adopting such a plan, and then consider how the change would affect some features of democratic politics, particularly citizen participation.

As proposed here, transitional costs would be minimized somewhat because only the electoral constituency for the House of Representatives would change. All the other familiar institutions of government in the United States would remain the same – single-member representation, state representation within the Senate, and so on. Still, upon adoption of the plan in the United States, the immediate effect of the random constituency would be jarring and corrosive of national attachment. The familiarity of being represented by where one lived would be lost, and it is likely that, at the moment of change, citizens would feel even less connected to Washington than they currently do. Some of these costs include the elimination of familiar modes of political organization and communication. If randomly assigned constituents wanted to organize their fellow constituent members for political action, it would no longer be useful to talk to their neighbors; probably all of their neighbors would be members of other electoral constituencies.

One reason we deliberate (and sign letters, petitions, and so on) with our neighbors is for strategic reasons: Because our neighbors (but not other people) are likely to be in the same electoral constituency as we are, they are what we might call "relevant deliberators." Thus, any plan that de-territorialized electoral constituencies would dramatically decrease incentives among neighbors to deliberate with each other at all. If, as a practical matter, physical proximity is necessary for between-constituent deliberation, then a critical feature of any democratic political order would unacceptably be lost. If constituents are unable to communicate with each other, we would lose the purported benefit of heterogeneous constituencies deliberating with each other about their collective interests. These are very serious problems since we value citizen participation, deliberation, and attachment to the national government.[18] The question is, would these features be permanent or transitional?

First, territorial proximity is necessary for constituent deliberation when there are no other ways to deliberate. But the Internet provides the potential for meaningful deliberation among nonterritorial constituencies, a potential that will only increase with time. Technology provides the opportunity for innovative thinking about political organization without giving up the value of deliberation within the polis.[19]

How would this work? Recall from section 9.2 that at the time of voter registration, constituents would receive secured access to a website dedicated to issues of national concern. I assume further that current text-based "chat-rooms" limited to written (typed) communication would form only one possible point of deliberation. Increasingly, we should assume that real-time audio and video will become available, thus forming more opportunities for individuals to choose media that best suit their talents and dispositions. For Web-based deliberations, biometrics – identifying a person by fingerprint or DNA analysis – would ensure that an individual is who she is claiming to be when speaking. And because it would be easier for nonconstituent members to participate in a debate "off-screen," we might imagine that individuals would be required to go to a public location, such as a public library, where they could be easily monitored to ensure that they were speaking for themselves.

Although this may sound draconian and overly "public," in fact it is no different than how territorial constituent meetings happen (or should happen). People publicly identify themselves when they speak, and write down their names and addresses when they write a letter to their representative or sign a petition. Indeed, if they lie about these things, we rightly call that fraud. And if a speaker at a constituent forum turned out to be a member of some other electoral constituency, we would properly discount his testimony as carpetbagging or at least as inappropriate. The use of technology does not

---

[18] See Chapters 6 and 7, and more generally, Nancy L. Schwartz, *The Blue Guitar: Political Representation and Community* (Chicago: University of Chicago Press, 1988).

[19] This may be overly optimistic given evidence that the Internet can shield individuals from other arguments that would help moderate their own positions. See, for example, the discussion in Cass Sunstein, *Republic.Com* (Princeton, NJ: Princeton University Press, 2002); idem, *Why Societies Need Dissent* (Cambridge, MA: Harvard University Press, 2005).

change the need for publicity in deliberation, but it does increase the opportunity to cheat and manipulate the system. We should thus think through how to create spaces in which "members only" could speak.

Chat-rooms could not accommodate all half-million members of an electoral constituency in a deliberative forum. Indeed, any particular deliberative space (a video chat-room, for example) might be limited to a few hundred participants at any one time. But again, this does not constitute a change from any deliberative forum now used in territorial systems. Deliberative bodies always need to be small enough for conversation – as I noted before, no one today deliberates with the entire membership of their territorial constituency at once.[20] Thus, the imperative is only to create possible and plausible deliberative spaces where the territorially proximate ones are eliminated. But consider the benefit of moving the deliberative space onto the Web: Constituents could more efficiently watch others deliberate about politics, whether these were fellow constituent members or their elected representative. The Web actually raises the possibility that all constituent members could observe a smaller group's deliberation.[21]

Finally, we must be concerned about equal access to technology, since the kind of technology I am envisioning – real-time audio and video chat-rooms, biometric identifiers next to every computer, and so on – is still expensive and out of reach for many members of the public. These are critically important because they could disempower the poor and less powerful in society. But given advances in technology, such a concern would be shortsighted, about as good of an argument as one might have made in 1938 that the television and the telephone should not be relied on for political organizing and deliberation because they were only available to the affluent. I am very explicitly thinking of a future when access to the Internet is as universal as these earlier technologies are now – a future that is probably no more than twenty years away, if that.

What, then, would happen to local deliberation between neighbors? No matter how electoral constituencies are defined, neighbors would still be able to talk to each other about issues that concern them, much as we currently might talk about these issues with family members, friends, or coworkers who do not live in our territorially defined constituencies. If every neighbor were a member of a different electoral constituency, each would have a different point of access into the national system. Today, if ten neighbors deliberate about an

---

[20] See Chapter 7. The fact of extremely large size formed the critique of Schwartz's panegyric to territorial constituencies in section 2.1. Schwartz, *The Blue Guitar*.

[21] For the importance of the "audience" to deliberative settings, see Gary Remer, "Two Models of Deliberation: Oratory and Conversation in Ratifying the Constitution," paper presented at the Political Theory Workshop, University of Chicago, Chicago, IL, 24 May 1999, available at http://www.spc.uchicago.edu/politicaltheory/remer99.pdf; Nadia Urbinati, *Mill on Democracy: From the Athenian Polis to Representative Government* (Chicago: University of Chicago Press, 2002). The Internet could, of course, be used to foster deliberation within existing territorial constituencies. The benefits that accrue from more open, accessible, and observable communication thus do not require national constituencies. Rather, new technology would allow these national groups to function in a deliberative way.

issue, they can write ten letters of support to their one common representative. But using random constituencies, their ten letters (or e-mails) would go to ten different members of Congress, and their voices would be heard (or ignored) in ten different electoral constituencies. The fact that most people you know locally would not be members of your constituency would thus transform your local political activity from a concentrated effort to influence one member of Congress into a broad-based effort to influence many members using new technologies. This might actually encourage deliberation between neighbors as a way to enhance their roles as citizens, because it would effectively transform local neighbors into citizen-representatives of their own neighborhood to each national constituency.

Choosing random constituencies over territorial ones thus constitutes a trade-off of depth of influence for breadth. The trade-off is critical, though, to achieving the benefits of argument framing in heterogeneous deliberative spaces, a benefit I will describe later in this chapter. Any argument we would make to our fellow constituents would have to be framed in terms of some generalized principle that would appeal to fellow citizens far removed from our particular neighborhood. The most successful arguments would have to be framed in terms of the national good, since we would be framing our arguments to a constituency that looks like the nation of which we were a part. The random constituency would thus provide local communities with many more points of contact into the legislative system and provide constituents themselves the opportunity and imperative to cast their needs in public, other-regarding ways. I emphasize again that these "public, other-regarding" arguments would not emerge because people were virtuous. Rather, given the electoral structure, these kinds of arguments would be more likely to attract broad support.[22]

Perhaps the clearest example of this comes in thinking about military base closings and national spending contracts. Currently, the best predictor of whether a particular member of Congress will vote for or against a particular base closing or spending contract is not on the merits of the case, but rather on whether her constituents stand to benefit from it. If they were beholden to national constituencies, individual members of Congress would stand to benefit no more or less from where money was spent, and could thus be free to make decisions based on where the base (or spending project) is most needed. Even local arguments – "bring the jobs to St. Louis," for example – would not have particular weight on a member of Congress, and so their own arguments would

---

[22] For a similar discussion, see also Thomas Pogge, "Self-Constituting Constituencies to Enhance Freedom, Equality, and Participation in Democratic Procedures," *Theoria*, June 2002: 45–6. Because electoral constituencies would be entirely voluntary under his plan, Pogge correctly notes that representatives would not know ahead of time whether a constituent would remain a constituent for the next election, and therefore be less likely (at the margins, I would add) to respond to a letter of concern. The permanence of the random constituency would thus answer Pogge's concern, of course at the expense of making electoral constituencies involuntary.

have to get at the merits of the case rather than the external benefits associated with it.

There would be other informal but beneficial consequences of such geo-graphically dispersed constituencies. As I said, under the current territorial system, it is very likely that geographical neighbors are members of the same electoral constituency. With national, randomized constituencies, the odds that any neighbor would be a member of a citizen's electoral constituency would be only .0023.[23] The flip side of this is that any United States citizen would have a .23 percent chance of being a member of the same constituency with any other citizen he met, no matter where each lived. Passengers on a bus, on vacation at the Grand Canyon, or at a baseball game or other sporting event would be equally likely to be members of the same random constituency. To the extent that most of our interactions are with people who live outside our current congressional district, this actually *increases* the likelihood that others we meet would be members of our own electoral district. I do not want to over-state the point: The odds are still 99.77 percent that any particular person with whom we interact would not be a member of our constituency. Citizens would only infrequently discover a fellow member of their national constituency, even as it is reasonably certain they will come to know some. However, because the random constituency would be permanent, the probability of knowing one's fellow constituents would rise dramatically over time.[24]

Would this system undermine national attachment in some fatal way? The ef-fects of the random constituency might well *strengthen* national attachment for a number of reasons. First, it would provide fresh opportunity for representa-tives themselves to earn their constituents' attachment, as Alexander Hamilton long ago recommended.[25] Second, because the constituency is permanent, a kind of transterritorial community could form in which one identified with being part of an explicitly national group, a type of group that is nowhere to be found among the current political institutions of the United States. For ex-ample, it seems plausible that every few years, perhaps once a decade or so, a group of the thirty-sixth constituency might convene for a conference of its members; perhaps there would be seminars and colloquia on issues of national governance now possible because a person would be a permanent member of a

[23] That is, $1/435 = .0022999$.

[24] To use a more familiar example, assuming birthdays are equally distributed (in fact, more people are born during August–October), there is a .27 percent chance that any other individual on the planet was born on the same day you were. With 435 possibilities, there would be slightly fewer matches (again, $p = .23$ percent rather than .27 percent). As with the birthday example, we would expect every person to know at least a few other members of their constituency just through informal contact alone. Indeed, we should expect to know even more people who share our constituency than we know people who share our birth date because the information is likely to be more publicly known than birthdays.

[25] See Chapter 5. The reference to Hamilton provides one historical point of contact, but should not be mistaken for a normative argument. The fact that Hamilton recommended such institutional designs is not a sufficient reason for us to accept them.

constituent group.[26] A sense of solidarity that each member is part of a national group might overtake the proceedings. The permanence that the randomized constituency offers should, over time, provide more deliberative opportunities and engagement in civic life, and more civic patriotism, than other forms of constituency definition precisely because it would allow its members to move within the nation without losing or changing their status as members of a national whole.

9.3.2 The Transformation of Political Life under Random Constituencies

How would the random constituency affect the relationship between constituents and their representatives? As with all of these details, we can only proceed in a sketchy, speculative manner, but we can ask three more specific questions. First, how will representatives serve their constituents in their role as advocates within government? Second, how will the random constituency affect campaign dynamics? Finally, how will political parties fare under this system? I will take each in turn.

Constituent Service. When a citizen has a problem with the national government, whether it concerns national benefits, navigation of the federal bureaucracy, or the delivery of a passport, representatives advocate for their constituents' personal interests.[27] And they act this way for at least two reasons. First, representatives are acting responsibly: Regardless of how a voter voted or will vote, representatives envision the obligations of their job to include constituent advocacy within the federal government. Second, representatives provide such service for self-interested reasons, to increase their odds of re-election. A representative assumes that a constituent whom she serves is more likely to vote for that representative. Further, this service will have effects beyond the individual as the constituent is expected to publicize to her friends and neighbors the fact that "Jones helped me."

All of these features would remain unchanged under random constituencies. First, representatives who acted responsibly would continue to act responsibly, serving their constituents because it was part of the obligations of their job; there is no reason to expect them to be more or less "responsible" in this way. Second, self-interested motives would produce the same response

[26] Ed Macias has suggested to me that, over time, each constituency might develop its own character for varying reasons, including the personality (or experience) of its particular representative. So, for example, if a former basketball player were elected as the representative of a constituency, members of that constituency might self-consciously take on an identity as being, for example, members of the Michael Jordan constituency. This seems quite likely, though it is unpredictable how such identities will arise.

[27] The definitive treatments of this are Bruce Cain, John Ferejohn, and Morris Fiorina, *The Personal Vote: Constituency Service and Electoral Independence* (Cambridge, MA: Harvard University Press, 1987); Richard Fenno, *Home Style: House Members and Their Districts* (Boston: Little, Brown, 1978).

under random constituencies: Representatives would continue to serve their particular constituents (members of the 133rd constituency, for example) because it would be a good way to increase the likelihood of future electoral support. The reputation effects of constituent service would, however, change under random constituencies because a constituent's friends and neighbors are less likely to be members of the same constituency. Thus, when a constituent tells her friends and family "Jones did a great job," it is less likely she will be spreading that news to Jones' own constituents. However, given the ease of e-mail communication, these indirect effects might be achieved electronically, as an individual could post her praise or critique of her representative's service for every constituent to view or hear. If e-mail had this kind of effect, we should expect representatives to be even more responsive to constituent service, although this is not a feature of the random constituency per se, but rather a result of using the Internet. Thus, under random constituencies, no change is likely in a representative's level of service to his constituents.

Campaign Dynamics. How would the random constituency affect political campaigns more generally? Who is likely to run for office and what are their campaign strategies likely to be? As I noted in section 9.3.1, I will separate transitional effects from long-term stable outcomes.

Recall from section 9.2 that any national citizen could run for any electoral constituency. Who, then, is likely to run for office and win? In the transition period, nationally known celebrities would have a decisive advantage and are likely to win numerous elections. Because of this, we should expect to see a surge of "celebrity" candidates[28] or at least political celebrities with truly national reputations. This is a troubling prospect for anyone who believes (with Plato) that competence in stage craft – to say nothing of begging for votes – is not a good proxy for competence in office.[29] But political parties would also be strengthened if for different reasons: In the face of little information, voters would use signals such as party membership to make candidate decisions.[30] In

---

[28] The 2003 California gubernatorial recall election won by movie actor Arnold Schwarzenegger provides corroborating evidence that open elections with few restrictions for running may favor celebrities with little prior experience in political life.

[29] I note Plato here only for historical continuity. The two most prominent actors turned politicians in recent United States history – U.S. President Ronald Reagan and California Governor Arnold Schwarzenegger – have recently received tremendously positive analysis in terms of their political leadership. Further, it is not clear that actors would be any more or less good as legislators than other representatives who enter office from similarly unrelated careers – doctors, pharmacists, football players, and so on. Measurement problems abound here (how do we define "good" for starters; what counts as an "unrelated career," and so on). But given the issue, it would be helpful to know empirically whether Plato's reasonable oft-repeated concerns are in fact borne out by empirical evidence.

[30] Edward G. Carmines and James H. Kuklinski, "Incentives, Opportunities, and the Logic of Public Opinion in American Political Representation," in *Information and Democratic Processes*, eds. John A. Ferejohn and James H. Kuklinski (Chicago: University of Illinois, 1990), pp. 240–68.

the short term, this is likely to create single-party legislatures because a small majority of support for one party within the nation as a whole would be reflected in every constituency, and thus all constituencies would elect someone from the same party. In the long run, however, both effects are likely to be moderated: Parties would very likely moderate and become less distinctive on policy issues, and candidates would more likely be those with interests in crafting efficient rather than ideological law.

To see why this might happen, I want first to describe how electoral campaigns would likely be run and then see how legislative behavior would respond to these dynamics.

What will electoral campaigns look like under random constituencies? Currently, territorial constituencies allow representatives to hold local "town hall" meetings to communicate with their constituents and generate publicity in the local media, whose reach overlaps a representative's electoral district. Thus, campaigns under single-member territorial systems involve direct contact with one's constituents – often physically meeting them in their neighborhood – and indirect contact through the various media.

Under random constituencies, direct physical meetings and indirect communication *through third-party media* would be far less productive and less likely to be used. Consider how difficult and counterproductive it would be for a candidate to physically meet her constituents or potential constituents. Informal practices of, say, trying to meet one's constituents on a street corner (or other public place) would be counterproductive: a candidate who stood on a corner with 2,000 passersby would be lucky if five or six of them were her own constituents (and even luckier if they identified themselves to her!).[31]

To increase her chances of meeting a constituent directly, a representative might consider organizing a meeting in a densely populated area, but even this would be inefficient, and for the same reasons so would advertisements on broadcast media. I will take each in turn.

Imagine a candidate sent mail (electronic or otherwise) announcing a campaign event to all of her electoral constituents in a metropolitan area of 3 million people. Doing so, she would reach about 6,900 constituent members, about 1 percent of the total constituency. In the unlikely event that she could draw 10 percent of this group to a meeting,[32] she would net 690 potential voters or roughly one-tenth of 1 percent of voters. If all candidates for a seat took this approach to campaigning, the total number would likely be somewhat less for each candidate (only a subset of the whole is likely to attend meetings of all candidates). In short, meetings arranged by direct mail would probably not be worth a try.

[31] That is, $2,000/435 = 4.6$.

[32] I suspect this is a very high estimate. Of all voters who received the invitation, a large number would not read it. Of those who did, a large number would not be interested. Of those who were, some number would not be able to make the date. Of those who could, some number would forget – and so on.

Yet currently, most campaign events for a congressional seat are unlikely to be attended by more than a few hundred voters anyway; sometimes only a few dozen show up. But in territorial systems, these meetings are still useful for their spill-over effects. They may generate word-of-mouth "buzz" that spreads from neighbor to neighbor about a candidacy. More importantly, if a local event generates local media coverage, the media will report a sparsely attended meeting into tens of thousands of homes via newspapers and television. Although the word of mouth via the Internet might be useful if verifiable, the use of local media under random constituencies would be less important. With random constituencies, the strategy would become terribly inefficient because any urban area dense enough to attract one candidate would be equally attractive to the hundreds of candidates who are running for all 435 seats. With such a vast field, and hundreds of events, it is unlikely the local media would cover these events at all.

To illustrate this, assume there were only two candidates for each House seat, and they all decided to hold a public event in Chicago because of its large media market. If each event were evenly spaced in time to reduce the number of events held on any given day, there would still be more than one event every day in Chicago alone during a two-year term of office.[33] More realistically, candidates would want to attract coverage during the three months prior to their election and that would result in almost ten meetings per day. This figure underestimates the frequency of meetings on a given day, since most candidates would want media coverage in the weeks, not months, prior to an election.

With such a large number of meetings happening, it is unlikely any local newspaper – let alone television news – would devote much coverage to them. In the face of these terrible prospects – low probability of being covered by the media and then only to be broadcast to a small percentage of one's voters – most candidates would simply not compete for this local coverage.[34] Of course, once most candidates decided not to compete for media attention in a densely populated local market, the value of holding a public event in that market would rise dramatically for each candidate. The same logic applies to local advertising. We should thus expect some equilibrium point to emerge in which some candidates, but not most, compete for local media coverage in densely populated areas. In a sea of faces, it would be hard to distinguish oneself, and again only to attract one of every 435 viewers. In both cases, an equilibrium of

---

[33] That is, 2 candidates × 435 seats = 870 candidates. Compare this to the 730 days in a two-year period.

[34] The downside of such a plan is that it would reduce the local media's close scrutiny of any particular member of Congress. In exchange, national media would now have to follow and scrutinize members of Congress more closely. There is a trade-off here, though: Members of Congress who currently come from areas without a vibrant local media (such as in Idaho) are likely to receive more scrutiny under the random constituency, while members of a vibrant media area (such as New York City) might likely receive less. Whether the total scrutiny would be lessened is an important question that I leave unaddressed.

some candidates competing in every market is likely to emerge, though I leave the precise details for others to calculate.

Attracting national media attention, either through purchased advertisements or generating news coverage, would probably exhibit the same general dynamics. Only one of every 435 people watching a national ad or reading the newspaper would be a constituent member. Again, were every candidate to take such a strategy, the result would be counterproductive to the candidates themselves; assuming every seat is contested by exactly two candidates, and every candidate bought a single thirty-second ad for national broadcast, any viewer would be exposed to 4.5 hours of campaign advertisements for every one minute that speaks about candidates for their particular electoral constituency. It is likely that voters would tune out whenever such an ad appeared. And again, an equilibrium of some but not all candidates running national ads is likely to emerge.

How then would candidates reach their potential voters if they could not rely on traditional electronic and print media? Most likely, candidates would use direct mail or e-mail to publicize their views, offering a more dynamic opportunity for using the Internet to engage citizens. To foster this engagement, I again assume that members of each constituency would have access to a secure Internet site restricted to members of one's own constituency. Thus, members of the forty-fifth constituency would be able to view a constituency website at www.45th.gov or some similar address. There they could follow a link (or otherwise receive by e-mail) campaign ads directly from their representative and opposing candidates. Similarly, constituent addresses could be legally used for campaign information from the representative and her opponents. Such direct contact would be the most efficient way for candidates to make their case known to their constituents.

The long-term consequence of relying on e-mail, list serves, or direct mail is that the costs of campaigning would plummet because these tools would eliminate the largest single expense of running a campaign for most candidates. Unable to use large media advertisements effectively, campaigns would have to speak directly to their electoral constituents through direct and low-cost e-mail and traditional mail sources. With the cost of campaigns reduced, we might expect, all things considered, money to have far less of an influence over the politics and policies of the House of Representatives.[35]

Political Parties and Partisanship. We can now begin to see how the moderate legislative dynamics I described previously would emerge, although as we will see, they will emerge only after a period of extreme partisanship.

---

[35] This is admittedly a utopian hypothesis. I say "might" only because these speculative comments have only taken up the impracticality of traditional campaign expenditures. I have not considered any original ways candidates would find to spend money to win votes, a project I leave to more enterprising readers.

Because individual campaign ads would likely be ineffective, the role and salience of political party affiliation would very likely rise in the short term, resulting in a far more partisan legislature. In the United States, affiliation with one of the two main political parities would likely be more important to voters than the qualities of the individual running. Further, party affiliation and endorsement would create a way around the inefficiencies of media advertising. Parties could efficiently purchase national ads promoting all of their candidates, and this would likely lead individual candidates to more strongly affiliate and run on a party label. The spill-over effect within the legislature would be to make legislators in the United States more distinctly identifiable as Democrats or Republicans. Furthermore, if party ID became the most salient feature, then each constituency would elect the same kind of candidate because each constituency would be demographically identical to every other constituency. After the very first election, the legislature would be comprised *entirely* of one political party (that is, 100 percent Democratic or 100 percent Republican), and it would not be surprising if the elected representatives were committed to promoting partisanship for perceived political gain.

The move to a single-party, highly partisan legislature would, however, be a short-lived, transitional effect. In the long run, following Anthony Downs, political parties would likely become substantively identical around the median voter for two reasons.[36] First, among randomly constituted voters, a more

---

[36] Anthony Downs, *An Economic Theory of Democracy* (New York: HarperCollins, 1957). In 1957, Anthony Downs argued that if political positions could be bundled together in a one-dimensional issue space, and if voters were forced to support a particular bundle (rather than pick and choose individual issues), the candidate or party that promised the bundle lying closest to the median voter would likely win. In the United States, the Republican and Democratic parties have been successful in bundling issues on security, welfare, moral positions, and so on into a one-dimensional issue space of "liberal" and "conservative." Parties, Downs predicted, would thus compete for the median voter because those to his or her ideological right or left would have nowhere else to go, a phenomenon that is regularly discussed in U.S. presidential elections. The "Downsian equilibrium" I thus refer to is the equilibrium that would emerge from this competition between parties over the median voter. Importantly, and as Downs had predicted, the median voter need not be "centrist" in ideological terms – if voters are not distributed in a normal, bell-curved shape, then the median may in fact be very far from the ideological poles. Further, under some conditions, voters converge on the mean bundle rather than the median, which has some important consequences for the kinds of positions that succeed. Whether voters converge on the mean or median bundle, the important point for the present discussion is that in a one-dimensional issue space, successful candidates are likely to converge on issue bundles lying either at the median or mean position of the electoral constituency. Thus, the mean or median of highly heterogeneous constituencies will be overall more moderate (by definition) than the mean or median of highly homogeneous constituencies. For more recent assessments of Downs' theory, see Randy Calvert, "Robustness of the Multidimensional Voting Model: Candidates, Motivations, Uncertainty and Convergence," *American Journal of Political Science*, 29, February 1985: 69–85; James Enelow and Melvin Hinich, *The Spatial Theory of Voting* (Cambridge, UK: Cambridge University Press, 1984); James Enelow and Melvin Hinich, "A General Probabilistic Spatial Theory of Elections," *Public Choice*, 61, May 1989: 101–14. I thank Gary Miller for a conversation about this issue.

efficient and pure Downsian equilibrium could emerge in which both parties took very similar positions on policy issues – positions located closely around the median voter rather than any extreme.[37] Second, party discipline within Congress would likely weaken. Since advertisements for national political parties operate as public goods for any candidate running as a member of that party, and since party membership is dependent only on a candidate's decision to join, an individual member of Congress would not have to worry about taking positions at odds with the national party leadership. In short, the party would only run national "Vote Republican" advertisements from which even "rotten" party members would benefit. This would again allow for less partisanship over time.

Let's imagine that randomization occurs tomorrow, and the next day voters elect their representatives on a straight, party-line vote. Every constituency being slightly more Democratic than Republican, the newly elected House of Representatives would be entirely Democratic. Let's imagine that this first class, enthused by their victory and total domination, passed extremely partisan bills to create a guaranteed minimum income, for example. Any aspiring Republican (and the party more generally) would realize that he (or it) had only to win a very small percentage of any centrist Democratic or independent voters within his district to defeat the incumbent Democrats. In the next election, all Democrats would be defeated and the Republican Party would take over the entire House of Representatives.

Of course, all the Democrats might predict this and temper their policies in the first place. Over a remarkably short period of time, we should expect that Democrats and Republicans would lose most of their distinctiveness within the House. The only useful characteristic of a candidate or party would be whether or not he was pursuing the aims of a solid majority of his constituents and here is where the deliberative and voting benefits of representing highly heterogeneous constituencies begin to be relized. In a case where the representative thought his constituents' preferences were bad – ill-informed, short-sighted, unjust, or such – he would have to convince his constituents (or the party would have to convince a majority of the nation) that his position was in fact a better one upon which to govern. Under current party makeup, a successful strategy would involve pursuing at least a moderate plan. The random national constituency would give incentives to prove one's self competent and account for one's actions in the broadest possible manner. Randomized electoral constituencies could give rise to the formation of a kind of non-partisan, professional legislator less electable under the current, highly partisan electoral system.

---

[37] Ibid. The fact that most territorial constituencies are highly homogeneous by party and non-competitive by party may in part explain why the U.S. Congress has become more partisan and non-centrist in its policies. The fact that U.S. senators represent far more heterogeneous populations may in part explain their moderation compared to the House. I thank Andy Sobel for this insight.

In the previous section, I speculated about how political life might unfold under random constituencies. The discussion was admittedly sketchy and would need far more empirical and theoretical development to confirm, let alone recommend for adoption. In this section, I address some normative and conceptual problems raised by the random constituency and in doing so explain why they capture some virtuous features for democratic institutional design.

Section 9.4.1 takes up the lingering concern that some substantive theory of the common good is being smuggled in by the continued reference to the "national interest." I will argue instead that it is no more or less conceptually coherent than any other kind of group interest and need not be specified to be useful. In section 9.4.2, I address the problem that a randomized constituency will increase the majority's power over legislative outcomes: Since all constituencies are identical, and each elects one representative, a simple majority of the nation will determine outcomes in the House of Representatives. To foreshadow, I argue that this is the way democratic institutions should be designed and would serve an important corrective to current American institutions that give a small minority within the nation an unjust influence over the whole.[38]

9.4.1 The National Interest and Interest Group Politics

I have argued that randomized constituencies will create incentives for representatives to pursue the national interest. This is so whether the "national interest" is defined in pluralist *or* republican terms, for reasons I discussed in Chapter 8. To review briefly, pluralism equates the "national interest" with the outcomes of a process of advocacy within the representative legislature. Good pluralist representatives are thus partisan advocates for their particular constituencies, and the national interest is said to be defined by the logrolling and bargaining that takes place between representatives within the legislature. Republicanism, on the other hand, assumes there is a national interest that emerges (or is discovered) through deliberation between representatives about the national good within the legislature. Republican representatives treat their own constituents' interests as points of information but do not give them priority over compelling arguments for the needs of all. These are conceptual distinctions: In practice, most representatives are pluralist some times, republican others, and most of the time perhaps a little of both.

As I argued in section 8.5, random constituencies essentially allow both pluralist and republican models of representation to operate simultaneously

---

[38] In the United States, this has meant a legislature dominated by right-leaning Republicans that produces legislation that is arguably far more conservative than the whole; in earlier decades, the same might have been said about left-leaning Democrats producing legislation far more liberal than the whole.

without conflict. If, with pluralists, a representative should pursue the particular interests of her constituents, those interests would be, by definition, the
nation's interest because random constituencies are demographically identical
to the nation they collectively represent. By contrast, if, with republicans, a representative ought to pursue the national interest directly, random constituencies
will provide her with the best kinds of electoral incentives to do so, since, again,
every representative will be most successful when her deliberations and votes
are, in fact, to the benefit of the nation as a whole.

Such talk, however, may appear to smuggle in some substantive concept
of the national interest.[39] I want to address the lingering concern that this
formulation of "national interest" is normatively "thick," containing some
hidden notion of what the national interest actually entails. In doing so, I will
also specify how the random constituency would contribute to the checks and
balances of the American system, and relate to non-electoral interest group
constituencies.

To begin, recall the definition of "interest" that I used in Chapter 7:

Interest = df. A set of future states of affairs that aim at a good to which a person or
group is related because of self-referential, duty, or rights-based reasons.[40]

The national interest of the United States, then, is simply that set of future
states of affairs that aim at a good to which the nation as a whole is related
for self-referential, duty, or rights-based reasons. This may strike many as un-
helpful because it dodges the fundamental and familiar problem of defining the
"national interest"; for any particular decision, how exactly does one measure
this good? Should one use "majority vote," a Rawlsian maximum-minimum
strategy, or restrict policy changes to Pareto optimal moves (and then again,
should these be Pareto optimal for all individuals or for groups)? Should we use
the pluralist model and define the interest of the whole by the outcome of advocacy and trade-offs of its subgroups? Or is the republican model of deliberation
under the proper conditions the right one to follow?

These are important questions, but ones that lie far beyond the scope of this
study. I have made no claim to know what the national interest is substantively;
I have only argued that institutions should be designed to best achieve it. This
is no more or less coherent than arguing that individuals ought to be raised and
nurtured to best determine their own self-interest without describing exactly
what an individual's self-interest would entail. As I argued in section 7.1.1,
the only thing I assume (and all the argument here need assume) is that there
exists a concept of "national interest," whatever its substantive content turns
out to be. Indeed, to repeat, the argument that electoral constituencies ought
to be defined by territory, party, race, or any other particularity must itself be
justified in terms that explain why advocacy for *that* particularity (but not some

[39] I am indebted to Sue Stokes, who has repeatedly raised this question.
[40] See section 7.2.

other) would be in the national interest.[41] So endorsing institutions because they will lead to the national interest does not assume any prior commitment to the substance of what that national interest will be.

What of the familiar argument that there is no such thing as a disembodied "national interest" independent of the particular groups or individuals that make it up? Or the similar claim that the "national interest" has no referent independent of the outcome of trade-offs between smaller interest groups? In short, this position is contradictory: If the "national interest" is conceptually empty, then so is any purported group interest because the "nation" is just a group of individuals. Or, framing this in the positive, if we can make sense of a group interest in the case of very large and diverse groups such as the NAACP, the Girl Scouts of America, the American Civil Liberties Union, and others, then we can conceptually make sense of a nation that has its own collective interest. If groups have "interests" that we can talk about without reference to the substance of their interest, we can accept and use the concept of "national interest" without any further specification.[42]

The discussion of the national interest and particular interests leads to a related and final reason to favor constituencies that look like the nation they represent: In political systems where citizens have the liberty to organize into voluntary associations (that is, non-electoral constituencies) to lobby and make their voice heard within Congress, electoral constituencies ought not to be defined to fulfill a similar function. There are obvious problems with this formulation because it assumes that all interests can be advocated, and clearly those of the poor and disadvantaged cannot be organized as well as those of the rich and powerful. But this is a problem of economic or other forms of justice. And defining electoral constituencies to represent the oppressed or the poor is unlikely to advance their cause; the interests of the powerless are more likely to be met if they are dispersed throughout many constituencies rather than being concentrated, for reasons we will pursue later. Indeed, rather than manipulating electoral constituencies to produce social change, we should instead address these very different (and, frankly, far more important) problems of justice. The influence of money on political outcomes and a more equitable welfare system seem to be a far more relevant and justifiable way of solving these problems, a far better way to meet these critical goals of ensuring fairness, decency, and basic justice, than does electoral constituency design.[43]

---

[41] Or to repeat the earlier formulation, if the national interest emerges from a process of logrolling between representatives, we need a separate argument to justify which logs should be rolled in the first place. See Chapters 1 and 7.

[42] I thank Jim Fishkin and Jeffery Tullis for clarifying this point.

[43] This argument in particular is admittedly incomplete. It requires far more defense of the claim that political representation is a weak public good, a defense that I cannot offer here. For a similar statement, see Russel Hardin, *Liberalism, Constitutionalism, and Democracy* (Oxford and New York: Oxford University Press, 1999).

9.4.2 Majority Influence over Decision Making

The random constituency magnifies the power of national majorities, translating a simple majority among the population into unanimity of party and perspective within the legislature. This presents two normative problems: First, it translates a slight majority within the nation into unanimity in legislative outcomes; and second, if related, it appears to stifle deliberation within the legislature, even when the nation is divided on a particular issue. I address the first of these problems here, leaving the more complex issue of deliberation within the legislature for section 9.5.

The concern that random constituencies would give enormous power to majorities is not unwarranted given the expectations described in section 9.3. If the nation were very closely split, for example, 51 percent Republican and 49 percent Democratic, the entire House of Representatives would become Republican after the first election under random constituencies. Yet I also predicted this would be a short-lived affair: Given the closeness of the split, parties and candidates would quickly converge on a median voter position as the only way to win seats reliably in Congress. The translation of a majority position into unanimous control is then better understood in spatial terms: The policies that are most likely to be supported in the legislature would be consistently those that are closest to the median voter within each constituency (and thus within the nation as a whole).

But why is this a problem? The fact that a majority of any group hold an opinion is a very good reason (if not the only reason) for it to be adopted as law. Similarly, the fact that a group's position is a minority view appears to be an excellent reason for it to be defeated. The concern, of course, is one of fairness. Perhaps we should let minority opinion prevail, or, following Lani Guinier, perhaps minorities – particularly ones that find themselves out of power more or less "permanently" – should have a turn now and then to rule.[44] How concerned should we be with these "Madisonian" permanent minorities?

This is an old question, of course, and I do not propose to answer it in any kind of comprehensive way. But I do think that a good deal of contemporary worrying about majority rule has led us to two conceptual mistakes about its use. First, in times of real minority harm, during times when minorities are oppressed by overbearing majorities, it is easy to forget the virtue and moral necessity of relying on majority rule. Second, and closely related, it is often easier to blame a decision rule rather than the underlying cause of bad decisions; in the case of overbearing majorities, the harm should be understood as that of underlying social justice. Together, these two conceptual mistakes threaten to replace a proper regard for majority rule with calls for what amounts to enlightened despotism. I will take each

---

[44] Lani Guinier, *The Tyranny of the Majority: Fundamental Fairness in Representative Democracy* (New York: Free Press, 1994).

in turn, although the treatment here is admittedly suggestive rather than complete.[45]

The fact that a group finds itself persistently in a minority position disagreeing with much or most of the law passed is not a good reason to give the group's views a turn, nor is it a good reason to worry that that group is oppressed. Quite the opposite: The fact that a group's position is consistently and permanently in the minority presents a very good prima facie reason for it to go down to defeat. It is a good thing, for example, that the Ku Klux Klan does not get a turn ruling simply by virtue of its minority status. Further, assuming all voices are heard (a matter to be taken up in section 9.5) and that there is robust deliberation, the persistent failure of a position to attract a majority of support is a very good indicator that it is a morally unacceptable position that should not be adopted. We hope, for example, that advocacy of slavery is persistently and permanently a minority position.[46]

But of course there are many minority positions that the majority does not prefer but should. The concern that majorities will run roughshod over minorities is tied to the historically familiar and very real cases of extreme injustice that unjust majorities impose upon just minorities. But far from illustrating that we should be wary of majoritarian influences, this concern illustrates a central limit of political representation, and more generally institutional design. Substantive limits on government are not endorsable by virtue of the fact that they protect minorities. Rather, if limits are endorsable, it is because they aim at some substantive concern of political justice. When we frame our substantive concerns with justice in terms of a procedural tension between majorities and minorities, we obfuscate this problem. It almost seems that the desire to correct injustice leads to a hope that changing the rules will change people's attitudes and norms.

Again this is not to deny the very real concerns about minority persecution and fairness. But while these cases are descriptively about "minorities," the violations that spark the concern are not about "minority status" per se, and thus should not be confused for an argument that minorities ought to be given power (or protections) simply by virtue of their minority status.

Consider a really heinous case of injustice, one in which some majority wants to slaughter or commit some other terrible act of injustice upon a small subgroup within a nation. The legislature, using simple majority rule, passes a law saying "The minority will be slaughtered on March 12." The group is then decimated on that date.

What terms should we use to describe, to make sense of, or otherwise to attribute cause in this terrible case? Would the tragedy in this case really be that

---

[45] For an excellent development of these issues that has helped frame the current discussion, see Jeremy Waldron, *The Dignity of Legislation* (Cambridge, UK: Cambridge University Press, 1999).

[46] This will depend on the underlying likelihood that the majority is right. See Robert E. Goodin and David Estlund, "The Persuasiveness of Democratic Majorities," *Politics, Philosophy and Economics*, 3, 2, June 2004: 131–42.

a majority dictated its will over a minority that disagreed? Descriptively that is exactly what happened: Majority rule allowed the tragedy to happen within the context of that legislature, and in this case, had the minority been given the power to veto the provision, the tragedy would have been avoided.

It seems far more apt, however, to describe this situation as one in which a group of people wanted to commit and then committed a horrible injustice upon another group of people. To frame this very clear case of injustice in terms of a failure of an overreaching of majority rule, or any other institutional design, is to mistake tragically a tool for the governing of stable society with a solution to injustice. Trying to solve deep problems of justice by crafting decision rules is like trying to fix a shattered windshield with masking tape and glue: It might be done, but it gravely misses the point of the problem.

So what of "turn taking" or concern for "power sharing" among groups that find themselves permanently excluded from power? Instead of claiming that justice is likely to be promoted by limiting majority rule, we should instead understand such "turn taking" in terms of majority rule itself. "Turn taking" is an appeal to the majority to change their mind about a particular issue (or for a particular candidate, and so on) based on an appeal to fairness and stability.

Imagine that a clear majority supported a tax bill that redistributed the nation's excess revenue to the richest 5 percent of the nation. Let's imagine that the majority's support is principled: The rich pay more taxes to begin with, so they, purportedly by right, should get more of the government's surplus. But the majority also notices that passing this bill would likely result in revolutionary instability among the poor. (Let us even assume the worst, that the majority thinks this revolutionary response is evidence of moral turpitude among the poor.) Despite the majority's support for the merits of the tax bill, it nonetheless decides to vote for the minority position out of a sense of fairness or concern for stability. As I described it, absent the consequences of passing that bill, the majority explicitly believes that the tax bill really is the best tax code for the country. The same logic applies to issues of candidate selection: Substitute "vote for a member of the demographic minority" for "pass the tax bill," and you have a paradigmatic case of Guinier's turn taking.

In such a case, the appeal to fairness and stability is thus attached to the consequences of a particular choice and provides an additional reason for some in the majority to support a minority view. If enough of the majority finds this argument from stability and justice to be a compelling reason for supporting a particular minority position (or candidate, or "turn-taking" provision) then, the minority *should* get its way. But if this happens, the "minority" position no longer *is* the minority position, and under these circumstances it is still by virtue of majority rule that the particular issue is legitimately accepted. And in any case, we should not describe these cases as ones in which the minority's preferences actually dominate majority preferences. Rather, as I have described, a majority now supports the "minority" position but for very different reasons. It is not by virtue of the fact that "minorities should rule now and then" that gives them the right to rule. Rather, as with anything else, it is necessary (but probably insufficient) that the majority agrees that "minorities should rule now and then" for the act to become law with legitimacy.[47]

The argument applies with equal force to constitutional provisions that protect minority rights (such as the freedoms of speech, assembly, and religion in the U.S. Constitution's First Amendment). They may have the effect of allowing minorities to do what the majority does not want them to do in some particular case, but the overall provision is justified as law in part because a very large majority thinks it's a good (just or stable) rule to allow minorities these rights; or, in the negative, there is not a sufficient majority to change the rule. And this endorsement of the whole plan is not simply a convenient arrangement; it is presumably a necessary condition for the law to be legitimate.[48]

9.5 DELIBERATIVE IMPLICATIONS OF THE RANDOM CONSTITUENCY WITHIN THE LEGISLATURE

As previously stated, the random constituency poses a serious problem for deliberation within the legislature because, in the case of the United States, it increases the likelihood that all elected representatives would be white males. As many others have argued, this denies perspectival differences within legislative deliberation, and leads to the suspicion that the legislative outcomes of this deliberation would be insensitive to the interests of nonwhite males.[49] This was the problem I claimed that deliberative theorists had not adequately addressed, the problem with which this book began.[50] To be sure, deliberative democrats have been very interested in maximizing the locations for citizen participation qua citizen. But in addition to turning out for a school board meeting and petitioning one's representative, how should we think about between-constituent

---

[47] This is an admittedly incomplete account. See section 1.2 for the description of legitimacy I am using in this book.

[48] I am ignoring here the enormous literature tracking the Ronald Dworkin, H. L. A. Hart, and Lon Fuller debates as to whether law can be binding if it is unjust. Engaging that debate would take us far from the random constituency, though would be required to argue these points to a sufficient conclusion. Instead, we assume that majority approval in some form (either direct or through representatives) is a necessary but insufficient condition for legitimate law. Whether the law, following Dworkin, might also have to be just to be binding is a critical, but separate, matter. Ronald Dworkin, *Taking Rights Seriously* (Cambridge, MA: Harvard University Press, 1979); Lon Fuller, *The Morality of Law*, revised edition (New Haven, CT: Yale University Press, 1969); H. L. A. Hart, *The Concept of Law*, 2nd ed. (Oxford, UK: Oxford University Press, 1997).

[49] There are other reasons to favor (or consider favoring) diversity within the legislature, not the least of which are role model effects for citizens and basic issues of fairness and equality. The discussion here illustrates how the problems of diversity raised by the random constituency might be fruitfully solved and thus does not form a reason to reject the random constituency outright. The discussion is necessarily abbreviated and thus not meant to be exhaustive of the issue of deliberative democracy or the value and problems of diversity. For a superb treatment of these issues, see Michael Rabinder James, *Deliberative Democracy and the Plural Polity* (Lawrence, KS: University Press of Kansas, 2004).

[50] See section 1.4.

deliberation about their representative and the quality of that representation? "Between-constituent" deliberation forms another horizontal sphere.

It is surprising how little progress has been made in describing and developing a theory of deliberation that applies to "between-constituent" (qua constituent) interaction within representative governments. Deliberation theorists have developed theories that apply to the deliberative conditions between a representative and her constituents, and between representatives within the formal institutions of government; or what Jane Mansbridge has described as the vertical and horizontal deliberative spheres of representative government. Amy Gutmann and Dennis Thompson see the similar dimensions in terms of how representatives justify their positions *to* their constituencies or *between* themselves within the legislature, but not in terms of how the electoral constituency might form a locus of deliberation for the purposes of representation.[51]

The failure of deliberative democrats to appreciate the value of diversity within the electoral constituency may be closely connected to their implicit acceptance of a model of "liberal representation" in which national political representation is defined as the representation of homogeneous group interests (the term is used as described by Melissa S. Williams[52]). In such a view, heterogeneous electoral constituencies undermine the very purposes of political representation. As I have argued throughout this book, it is entirely possible, even plausible, that some groups *should* receive representation *as* groups – whether ethic or racial groups, ideological groups, or territorially proximate communities. But, as I have also argued, particularly in Chapter 8, the burden of justification rests on those who would advocate subgroup representation to explain why we should move from a default position of representation of the whole.

Indeed, if deliberation requires a multiplicity of voices and perspectives, there is no a priori reason to exclude such perspectival diversity within the constituency itself. If this is a value worth achieving, the task then would be to design an electoral system that retained a multiplicity of voices simultaneously within the electoral constituency *and* within the legislature. This requires some innovation since, as I described in section 1.4, almost all reforms aimed at increasing voice within the legislature have come at the cost of homogenizing the electoral constituency either through gerrymandering around race or political party, or through the use of "voluntary constituencies" under proportional representation and group representation of various sorts.[53]

We may now answer the question of voice that the random constituency raises by reference to two arguments that I will briefly outline here. The first is

[51] Amy Gutmann and Dennis Thompson, *Democracy and Disagreement* (Cambridge, MA: Belknap Press, 1996), pp. 128, 144–64; Jane Mansbridge, "Should Blacks Represent Blacks and Women Represent Women? A Contingent 'Yes,'" *Journal of Politics*, 61, 3 August: 628–57.

[52] Melissa S. Williams, *Voice, Trust, and Memory* (Princeton, NJ: Princeton University Press, 1998).

[53] Gender quota laws in France and Latin America that require a certain percentage either of the legislature or of a party's candidate are exceptions to this trend. For a good overview, see Lisa Baldez, "Elected Bodies: The Gender Quota Law for Legislative Candidates in Mexico," *Legislative Studies Quarterly*, 29, May 2004: 231–58.

a practical concern: The usual practice of increasing legislative diversity through the creation of homogeneous electoral constituencies may be counterproductive because it leads legislatures to adopt policies that are, as David Lublin has put it, "paradoxically" worse for the very groups for whom the electoral constituency was created.[54] Instead – and this is the second response – deliberative diversity within the legislature can be achieved without these costs by shifting our attention away from the electoral constituency toward another ignored institution: qualifications for office. I will take each in turn.

Recent empirical evidence has shown that defining constituencies to ensure electoral outcomes of minorities may actually be counterproductive to their own goals because while it does help secure the election of minorities, it also marginalizes their elected representative once elected to the legislature.[55] This is because in order to create minority-majority districts (extremely homogeneous constituencies), minorities must be "moved out" of districts that become more homogeneous around the majority population. For example, to elect more African Americans to the U.S. Congress, African Americans have been concentrated into "majority-minority" districts, leaving other districts that much "whiter" for the change. Once in the legislature, representatives elected from these, "super-white" districts form a majority in the legislature and because they have fewer black constituents, now have much less to gain from a compromise with minority representatives. Minority representatives are thus more easily marginalized and ignored by other members of the legislature because those other members will not face much electoral penalty for ignoring these issues. Indeed, if the job of representatives is to advocate for the interests of their members, there is good reason for them to ignore the voice of nonconstituent members.[56]

By relying solely on the homogenization of electoral constituencies to achieve legislative diversity, reformers make the legislature look more like the nation it represents only by making its underlying electoral constituencies whiter, blacker, and altogether less diverse. The cost of getting a minority voice into the legislature is thus to decrease the incentives of majority legislators to pay attention to that voice. Conversely, representatives elected from diverse constituencies have more incentives to pay attention to the wide variety of interests of their

---

[54] "Paradoxically" refers to David Lublin, *The Paradox of Representation* (Princeton, NJ: Princeton University Press, 1997).

[55] Lublin, *The Paradox of Representation*. Lublin surveyed the effects on legislative debate and outcomes resulting from twenty years of redistricting intended to elect more African and Hispanic members of state legislatures.

[56] The marginalization of minority representatives from homogeneous constituencies is thus arguably endorsable based on democratic values, legitimacy, and procedural justice. This is not to deny that racial or other bad motives increase minority group marginalization beyond its legitimate place. It is, however, to say that the outcome of marginalization is likely the result of a moral collective action problem in which individual representatives are representing the interests of their constituents responsibly. The extreme results are then brought about by the use of homogeneous electoral constituencies rather than because of moral impropriety (such as racism or other discrimination). The solution will rest in diversifying electoral constituencies.

constituents – no one can predominate, but a majority coalition on a particular issue is less likely to form or be particularly stable.[57] Minority "voice" is thus attained within the legislature only by giving the other representatives ear plugs.

If every legislator were elected from a constituency that looked like the nation, every legislator would have demographically identical-looking electoral constituencies, and thus identical incentive structures. In cases where majorities of the population clearly supported a particular policy, there would be little deliberation on that issue within the legislature. But in most cases where a majority position was not decisive, legislators would have strong incentives to work collectively toward figuring out the common good; given the disagreement within the nation (and thus within each of their own constituencies), they would have to justify whatever position they took in terms of the greater good.

Still, even if white male representatives have incentives to act as if they cared about the public good, they cannot deliberate as if they were black women. If diversity within a deliberative setting is important because of the range of voices that it brings with it as well as the range of interactions and experiences that it forces upon the deliberators, then we still have to address the fact that under random constituencies, members of privileged groups will more likely be elected and serve as representatives denying this voice.[58] So the problem is to somehow achieve "voice without ear plugs." One solution may be to shift our attention to qualifications for office.

Recall that in section 9.2 I assumed that current residency requirements for office would be unnecessary under random constituencies because all electoral constituencies are identically construed. Put differently, there was no good reason one would have to limit candidates for the forty-second seat in Congress to be members of the forty-second electoral constituency. Rather than looking to electoral manipulations in order to create legislatures that look a certain way, we could achieve the same goal through clearly stated qualifications for office without any of the other negative political implications.

Imagine that under random constituencies the qualifications for holding a congressional seat were changed. Perhaps in 40 percent of all constituencies a candidate would be required to be a woman to be eligible to run; in 20 percent, only African Americans could serve. (If definitional issues appear to loom

---

[57] This is a rough description of the phenomenon; the particulars are more complicated. A minority may be ignored if it is too small. Lublin's argument is that minorities would fare better if their presence within an electoral constituency was substantial but less than a majority.

[58] For a sample of the more prominent accounts of the importance of deliberative diversity, see James Bohman and William Rehg, eds., *Deliberative Democracy: Essays on Reason and Politics* (Cambridge, MA: MIT Press, 1997); Bernard Manin, *The Principles of Representative Government* (New York: Cambridge University Press, 1997); Joshua Cohen, "Deliberation and Democratic Legitimacy," in *The Good Polity: Normative Analysis of the State*, eds. Alan Hamlin and Philip Pettit (Oxford, UK: Basil Blackwell, 1990), pp. 17–34; Gutmann and Thompson, *Democracy and Disagreement*; James, *Deliberative Democracy*; Mansbridge, "Should Blacks Represent Blacks..."; Williams, *Voice, Trust, and Memory*; Iris Marion Young, *Justice and the Politics of Difference* (Princeton, NJ: Princeton University Press, 1990); Phillips, *The Politics of Presence*.

large – as in, "who decides what counts as "African American?" – they are no more insurmountable than they would be in any other case in which these categories are used to define districts, benefits, and so on.) Just as Article I, Section 2 of the U.S. Constitution forbids a resident of Florida to be elected for a district in the state of New York,[59] this proposed law would require that only African Americans could run in electoral constituencies 1–87, and that only women could compete for office in constituencies 88–261. Were these two rules alone followed, the House of Representatives would become at least 20 percent black and 40 percent female, even as each representative was accountable to demographically identical, if different, national constituencies. And the underlying heterogeneity of each district would prevent the kind of marginalization of minority perspective that now happens with the U.S. House of Representatives.

As I said in section 1.4, these ideas show how the arguments of Anne Phillips might be institutionalized in a way that does not require the further homogenization of the electoral constituency.[60] And to repeat an earlier point, in recent years, institutions around the world have been experimenting with gender quota provisions as a way to achieve voice within a legislature without manipulations of the underlying constituencies.[61] The principle of restricting candidates to look like or be like a particular kind is not new. But the ability to use them to achieve legislative diversity without corresponding homogenization of the electoral constituency offers a preferable alternative.[62]

Altering qualifications for office directly rather than indirectly through homogenizing the electoral constituency through gerrymandering (or proportional representation) has three benefits. First, it is more transparent and open to collective debate; the question "should we have this many or that many 'democratic,' 'black,' 'Hispanic,' seats in the legislature?" would then get the appropriate public debate that kind of question deserves. Second, focusing on qualifications for office allows the underlying electoral constituencies to retain the virtue of "voice" that deliberative theorists have persuasively argued is necessary for robust and legitimate political debate. Finally, even though the "voice" that was brought to the legislature might be a minority voice, her actual voting and activity would have to be justified in terms of the heterogeneous, diverse electoral constituency to whom she would be accountable rather than

---

[59] "No person shall be a Representative...who shall not, when elected, be an inhabitant of that state in which he shall be chosen."

[60] Phillips, *The Politics of Presence*.

[61] The practice varies, but generally, the law requires political parties to put up a more diverse set of candidates, thus generally resulting in a more heterogeneous legislature. For early results on how effective these laws have been, see Baldez, "Elected Bodies"; Phillips, *The Politics of Presence*.

[62] It would thus "adequately integrate" the ideals of mirror representation and democratic accountability in a way that did not presume interest representation, as Will Kymlicka was taking up when he used that term. Will Kymlicka, *Multicultural Citizenship* (New York: Oxford University Press, 1996), p. 149.

upon the partial interests of her group. The partiality of her voice would be tempered by the generality of her electoral incentives.

These last points concerning qualifications for office lead to a host of other theoretical problems and questions. Is "standing for office" a presumed right of citizenship? If so, under what conditions does the government have the authority to impinge upon this right? Why on this issue does almost every constitution bind its citizens, keeping them from electing, for example, an eighteen-year-old as a member of its legislature? Despite their presence in virtually every constitution, the question of what makes some qualifications for office legitimate, just, or even democratic is a surprisingly neglected area of political theory and institutional design. These issues are now well beyond the scope of this book.

The discussion in this chapter was meant to suggest institutional arrangements not yet tried. It is an incomplete account and needs far more theoretical and empirical development before we should endorse it. But the goals of this chapter were to set out an option to a familiar political institution in a manner that I argued in the last chapter is more consistent with basic notions of political legitimacy. I don't imagine the arguments contain a complete answer, nor are they likely to sway many readers. But in some ways they don't have to. The importance of this account is as much conceptual as it is substantive.

I return to the point that began Chapter 1: Political representation excludes virtually all of the population from the nation it purportedly represents. By looking at the electoral constituency as an institution worthy of its own analysis, we can imagine new, innovative solutions to solve this very basic problem of modern democratic government. This is what a complete solution to the problem of democratic exclusion would entail.

Epilogue

The Random Constituency Fifty Years from Now

The arguments of this book have brought conceptual, historical, and normative analysis to bear on the concept of constituency in large, democratic nations
generally, and the case of the United States of America particularly. Territorial
constituencies may be judged more reasonable and justifiable than I have portrayed them in this book. Proportional representation, whether used in large
territorial constituencies or within the nation as a whole, may be viewed with
even more charity than I have presented it here, particularly because of the
deliberative benefits associated with various electoral systems.[1] And it may be
that our thought experiment of Chapter 9 – the random constituency – is too
radical an idea ever to be adopted. In this book, I have sought to demonstrate
what can be done with the concept of constituency when it is treated on its own
terms. None of many options – territorial, racial, ethnic, gender, or ideology –
is an unreasonable justification for an electoral constituency, as long as it is
publicly justified and well known to the citizens of the polity it purportedly
represents. Additionally, I have argued that the default position of permanent,
electoral constituencies that look like the nation they collectively represent is
stronger than some might have otherwise thought.

I conclude this book in an unconventional manner by taking the discussion
of Chapter 9, in which I proposed using random constituencies for political
representation in the United States, and asking, "What would an observer of
the American system observe were he to visit the nation fifty years after the
random constituency was adopted?" These observations serve as an epilogue
for and a summary of some of the key arguments of this book. They do not, I
hasten to add, form an argument themselves.

On September 19, 2085, Emma Hoben turned eighteen years old. As a con-
scientious citizen of the United States, she registered to vote by pointing her

---

[1] Michael Robinder James, *Deliberative Democracy and the Plural Polity* (Lawrence, KS: University
Press of Kansas, 2004).

web browser to the official citizen registration web page and completing its registration form. After clicking the Submit button on the last page, a confirmation appeared informing her that she was now a member of the forty-first constituency of the House of Representatives. Hoben would now, and for the rest of her life, cast a vote for the candidate running for the forty-first seat of the U.S. House of Representatives.

The assignment into the forty-first was made randomly by computer among the 435 possible electoral constituencies, each of which elected a member of Congress, a process that every citizen went through the first time he or she registered to vote. Emma's mother was a member of the 264th, her father a member of the 412th, and her grandfather, who had been alive when the new system was adopted in 2035, was an original member of the 239th. Today there are 300 million eligible voters in the United States, so each constituency has almost seven hundred thousand members. Because membership in an electoral constituency is randomly determined, members of each "district" (the now anachronistic term for the electoral constituency) are randomly distributed across the country. Most of Emma Hoben's neighbors are assigned to different electoral constituencies. In fact, of the ten thousand adults in her neighborhood, only twenty-three are in Emma's electoral constituency. Of course, no one is ever required to live anywhere they choose not to. Rather, membership in a constituency is nonterritorial, just as membership in most professional associations has been for centuries.

The fact that voters are randomly assigned into a constituency for life means that the membership of each electoral constituency remains extremely stable, and always reflects the demographic diversity of the U.S. adult population. Whites are thus the largest group within every constituency, but since losing their majority status in the middle of this century, they now make up about 45 percent of each constituency. Nonwhite minorities comprise the other 55 percent of each constituency, reflecting the diversity of the country. Because no single racial, cultural, or political group dominates the electoral constituency, a representative now has to make the case that the policies she pursues are good for the whole. And, perhaps most importantly, because each representative is authorized by and held accountable to an exact microcosm of the whole nation, what is good for any one constituency corresponds exactly to what is good for the nation as a whole. The electoral incentives of all representatives to serve their own particular electoral constituencies thus correspond exactly with the national good.

This new system of randomly assigned, permanent electoral constituencies replaced the older one of territorial districts. Territorial districts had their origins in Western democracies at least as far back as thirteenth century England, where local towns were given "representation" in order to affirm the King's request for taxes. The size and stability of the local groups of that time made the logic of territorial, residential representation clear: Small towns and counties had definable local interests that could be coherently represented in what later became a national representative body (parliament). As both

England and its colonies in America grew, however, the use of territorial districts was never challenged or questioned even as electoral constituencies became much larger than the small size that had justified their original use. Where, for example, colonial and state electoral districts in America averaged about three thousand people each (and closely conformed to local town, county, and parish boundaries), electoral constituencies even by the 1790s numbered above thirty thousand people each. The size of the electoral constituency quickly grew so that by the late twentieth century, "local" districts were hardly local, some spanning thousands of square miles and each containing over half a million potential voters.

In 2035 the people of the United States rejected territorial constituencies in favor of random constituencies for two reasons. First, because of their very large size, it was clear that territorial constituencies no longer defined any coherent "local" interests, but instead created perverse incentives for national legislation. Some argued that territorial districts still allowed "regional" interests – urban and rural districts, for example – to be represented. This argument failed, however, because of the multiple ways in which these regional districts were already represented through state and local governments and the U.S. Senate. After extensive public debate, the American people realized that the only reason "all politics was local" was that districts were territorially defined: Territorial districts were the proximate cause of "local pork," the term used for a representative's advocacy of national legislation that favors her own local interests in order to generate support for the member's reelection. There was wide support for eliminating these institutional incentives that encouraged political representatives to increase local spending simply because it facilitated their reelection rather than because a particular local project was good on its own merits relative to the other varied needs of the country.

The second reason territorial districts were rejected was that even if some interests could be represented through territorial districts, no one was able to argue successfully that territorially bound interests were more important than other kinds of interests, whether professional, cultural, or economic ones that could not be so defined. The point was dramatically made when a surprising coalition of social radicals and conservatives marched on Washington in the summer of 2026 demanding separate representation for men and women. Gender representation, unlike racial or party representation, was not possible under a territorial system as long as men and women lived in close proximity to one another. Neither could one argue that these and other nonterritorial interests were less deserving of their own electoral constituencies.

Having rejected territorial constituencies, advocacy groups began promoting various forms of representation for different reasons. Some argued that historically oppressed groups should elect their own representatives to give them voice in the legislature, foster trust toward the national government, and provide them reparations for past harms. Civic participation advocates argued that electoral constituencies should be defined to maximize citizen engagement and participation. And advocates for proportional representation and voluntary constituencies urged everyone to endorse their systems because they would maximize consent and political equality. No one wanted territorial constituencies, but neither could they agree on any form to replace them, or even on a standard by which to judge a preferred form. A national crisis of confidence emerged.

The crises began to subside with that now mythical discovery by a bison farmer in the desert outside of the University of Phoenix of a seldom read (and very expensive), twenty-five-year-old text. The book suggested that the path to reform began with three widely shared principles of democratic legitimacy. First, everyone agreed that representatives ought to be held accountable by the same group who elected them – it would not be "self-rule" if the representative from San Francisco had to stand for reelection by the people of Cleveland. From this they agreed that once formed, membership in electoral constituencies should remain as stable as possible. Second, everyone agreed that legitimate representatives (those who had the right to make laws) should not act "improperly" by legislating to maximize their own personal good. And while there was widespread disagreement about what "proper" activity meant, both sides agreed there were really only two options: Either representatives could advocate for the particular interests of their own constituents, or they could be free to deliberate impartially about the national good. From this, a consensus emerged in favor of individual constituencies that looked like the nation they collectively represented. Under such a plan, when representatives acted as advocates they would promote the nation's good, and when acting as deliberators they would be held to account by voters who represented the nation as a whole.

Finally, although everyone agreed that institutions should always be more consensual and voluntary, they rejected proportional representation and voluntary plans because these would create unstable and homogeneous constituencies, thus undermining the first two goals. Further, they understood that consent would be more meaningful if expressed at the constitutional level. Thus did the constitutional amendment emerge in favor of permanent, involuntary electoral constituencies, each of which looked like the nation the constituencies collectively represented. Five years later, randomized constituencies were adopted, and the first elections under this system took place in November 2036.

In the decades following the adoption of randomized electoral constituencies, constituent interaction, political campaigns, and legislation all changed dramatically. Because members of each constituency were distributed randomly across the nation and each constituency still elected only one member, communication between constituents, and between constituents and their representatives, occurred primarily over the Internet. (Secure biometric security devices restricted access to constituent members only; they also guaranteed that debate would be public, just as local meetings had been under territorial systems.) This deliberation was crucial as advocates for the random constituency had successfully argued that deliberative democracy required robust deliberation *among* constituents, which in turn required extremely diverse constituencies that looked like the nation they collectively represented. Further, fears that a reliance on technology would create even greater divides between economic classes proved unfounded as 98 percent of the nation had regular and easy access to technology by the end 2021 (much as the telephone and television had become virtually universal in the twentieth century). And thanks to the tremendous advances in video and audio technology in the early part of the century, public deliberations could happen both in written, audio, and real-time video forms.

Because voters were scattered across the country, political campaigns began to rely more on Internet contact also, and spending on other forms of ads became so ineffective that they are now pointless. Since every electoral constituency is now randomly distributed across the nation, any candidate who wants to purchase TV or radio advertisements has to buy time on national programs. But even when extremely well-financed candidates could spend money on a national advertising campaign, they chose not to because of the decreased effectiveness of competing with the hundreds of other congressional candidates. Lacking the ability to target their constituents through the broadcast and print media, and facing an overcrowded market that would confuse and further obscure their particular appeal, television ads – the single most costly expenditure in political campaigns – long ago became ineffective. Instead, again, the Internet developed as the central place for political campaigns, as targeted e-mail to members could be sent for free.

Today, legislation that emerges from the House is described derisively as "maddeningly moderate" thanks to the electoral dynamics that emerged. But in the decade of transition immediately after the shift to random districts, politics and policy were anything but moderate. In the first election under the random system, Republicans took over every seat in the House of Representatives, turning a 51 percent vote share among the U.S. population into victories in every electoral constituency (a result of every constituency being demographically the same as the nation as a whole). The most conservative legislation in U.S. history was passed in that year, despite the moderating influence of a closely split Senate and the election of the centrist President Kerri N. Bush. Yet precisely because the nation had been so evenly split, the extreme Republican agenda allowed Democrats in the next election easily to win the support of more centrist voters. The result of the second election was a complete turnover of every seat in the U.S. House, as Democrats now used their slim majority to their advantage. This went on, back and forth, through the first decade until the now famous "moderate politics" emerged in midcentury, as successful representatives learned that random districts provided them with electoral incentives to work for policies and programs that promoted a compromise position rather than favor any particular base. This relied not on virtuous representatives, but on electoral facts: Those who did not get the message and pursued partisan legislation instead were promptly defeated at the next election.

Index